The Way I Remember It ...

By Jim Spencer and Larry Dablemont

The Way
I Remember It ...

Short stories from the outdoors, by two of the best-known outdoor writers in the Midwest

Copyright 2022
Treble Hook Unlimited

ISBN: 978-1-7356117-1-6

Library of Congress Control Number: 2021922552

Table of Contents

Chapter   **Page**

  1.   Blackwater Reflections   6
  2.   Two Dollar Bass   11
  3.   The Calls in the Closet   16
  4.   The Green Tradition   19
  5.   The Camp   25
  6.   Christmas Fur   33
  7.   The Turkey Hunt   40
  8.   The Intruder   46
  9.   A Bird the Color of Autumn   53
10.   The Buck that Killed Widow Flaherty   59
11.   The Old Red Oak   66
12.   Legend of the Flying Raccoon   73
13.   The Loaner Gun   77
14.   The Church in the Deer Woods   81
15.   First Trophy   87
16.   A Bicycle for Christmas   89
17.   This is Why You're a Duck Hunter   97
18.   Grandpa's Knife   101
19.   The Gift Bird   105
20.   The First One I Ever Heard   112
21.   The Cattle Boat Chronicles   118
22.   Joe's Visitor   126
23.   A Day in the Life of a Marsh Dog   129
24.   The Legend of the Dutchman Brothers   136
25.   The Old Mallard   141
26.   Old Lures and a Christmas Memory   147
27.   Why I am a Trapper   153
28.   The Buck that got Away   159
29.   The Last Trophy   164
30.   The Kid Who Went to War   169

31.	Meditations on Squirrel Hunting	173
32.	Firewood for Christmas	177
33.	Bobble Your Stopper and Wiggle Your Piminnow	184
34.	The Christmas Hunt	187
35.	A Curmudgeon's Take on Fishing	195
36.	Conversations with a Coyote	198
37.	Hunting on the Shady Side of 70	204
38.	Showdown in a Country Ditch	210
39.	Legacy	213
40.	The Angel and Zeke Jones	222
41.	The Great Turkey Conspiracy	226
42.	Two Gobblers	230
43.	An Aging Schoolboy Trapper's Dream	232
44.	Armour and the Panther	236
45.	A Turkey Runs Through It	242
46.	Grandpa and the Ghoul	247
47.	The Romance of the Road	251
48.	An Engine Ain't an Injun	254
49.	Maybe They'll be There in the Morning	256
50.	Norman and the Noon Flight	261
51.	C.A.R.P. – An Idea Whose Time May Never Come	267
52.	A Two Dollar Gift	271
53.	Red-Tailed Cats of the Amazon	273
54.	The Value of a Quarter	276
55.	The Benchwarmer	280
56.	The Legend of Hobart Johnson	285
57.	Dues	292
58.	Old Joe	299
59.	Epitaph for a Turkey Hunter	302
60.	Just Another Passing	310

Chapter 1

Blackwater Reflections

By Jim Spencer

It is peaceful here in the swamp, if you understand that by "peaceful" I mean there are no telephones ringing and no horns honking. You can stay here until the crack of doom and you will never hear the blare of a television. There are no salesmen, clerks or bill collectors. There is no yard to mow. You won't even hear the ping of an incoming email; there's no coverage here.

There is only the swamp, and I won't tell you where it is. You see, this swamp is mine, not by deed but by heart, and if it's all the same to you I'd rather you found your own. I would probably like you if I met you – I like most of the people I meet – but I don't want to meet you in my swamp. Truth be told, I don't want you there at all. Swamps are for solitude.

I will tell you this much, because I want you to know how the place is laid out: my swamp nestles in a wide, sweeping bend of a pretty good- sized river in the southeastern United States. It is easily accessible by parachute or by helicopter, but if you want to get there by more ordinary means, you'll have to expend some extraordinary effort.

First you must take a boat ride on the river, either nine miles downstream from a poorly-maintained dirt boat ramp or seven miles upstream from a slightly better one made of broken asphalt chunks and gravel. Then, after the boat ride, you must grab your fishing tackle, somehow climb a slick red-clay bank that varies in height from five to 15 feet (depending on river level) and take a long, boot-sucking hike through steaming, mosquito-infested woods. This is not a place you visit casually.

There are alligators in my swamp, and swamps are better with alligators in them. There is an egret rookery, too, and the sight of 500 snowys and great egrets in the sun on the limbs of a dozen pale green cypresses is a vision not easily forgotten. There are coons and possums, turkeys and mink, otters and deer, and where the ground is drier you may see bobcat and bear sign. In the winter there are ducks to beat all hell.

In the backwater are several beaver lodges, rising improbably out of the tea-colored water like giant rootwads. But beavers are a minority in this swamp, for here the nutria is king. Toward nightfall you can hear these

South American invaders calling back and forth. They sound vaguely like calves or lambs, and the noise reminds me of the civilized world I've left behind. Every time I hear it I smile; somehow it is good to be reminded of civilization when you are knee-deep in a primordial swamp at sundown.

Sundown: a time for various awakenings in the swamp. One of the loudest of these awakenings is the bullfrog chorus. One old settler far back in the brush will tune up, hesitantly at first, as if his vocal cords were sore. But gradually he picks up in both volume and tempo until the very leaves tremble with his noise. The another will join in, and another and another and another, and you know without a doubt why they call them bullfrogs.

This is when I like my swamp best, when the shadows lengthen and the gloom deepens and the bullfrog chorus starts.

There is a little blackwater lake in the swamp, and I reach it this day just as I hear that first sore-throated frog. There's an old cypress boat there on the bank, pulled up and tied to a tupelo sapling. I have no idea who owns the boat; I assume it belongs to the swamp. At any rate, it's always been here. Of late it's been a little the worse for wear, but it still serves.

In the more than 20 years I've been visiting the swamp, I've never seen another human here. Nor, save for my wife Jill on one single trip, have I ever brought anyone here. Sometimes I see signs of other people – a busted spinnerbait left in the boat, perhaps, or a muddy footprint on the seat. But no people. Maybe this is because I'm a little out of step with the rest of the world. I haunt the swamp at night, when other, saner folk are home in bed.

Whatever the reasons, I'm thankful for them. I wade through the mud to the little boat and stow my tackle box and two rods amidships. Then I slide the boat off the mud and into the dark water, standing clear of the gunwale and watching carefully for the snakes that like to hide underneath.

Sure enough, one is there. He's a big one, black as death, thick as a dirt bike tire, and he coils menacingly five feet from my thin tennis shoe. I feint at him, and he opens his mouth in that **come on, get you some** defensive posture that earned his species the name cottonmouth. The white of his gaping mouth is startling in the gloom, as evolution intended. I watch quietly, and the snake wavers. Presently he closes his mouth, uncoils and slithers into the lake, a thick, stubby hawser weaving away through the bushes.

I let him go unharmed, returning the favor.

The brush is thick around the shoreline, and it is strictly a matter of opinion where the swamp ends and the lake begins. A narrow, hacked-out trail leads through the flooded ironwood, and I scull the boat along the familiar corridor. It breaks hard to the left, then back starboard, and suddenly I'm in open water. The 10-acre lake stretches before me, oval-shaped; the only sign that anyone has ever been here is the white plastic Purex jug tied to a buttonwillow behind me. The jug marks the way out, and it's the only concession to civilization I will tolerate on my lake. After searching for the trail for three hours in the dark on my first trip to the swamp, I decided a compromise was in order.

The small private sea lies calm under me. For a while, at least, I am in control of my destiny. I am the master of my soul and the captain of my ship, and the fact that my ship is 12 feet long and leaks at the seams bothers me not at all.

Jill, at home 60 miles away, cannot understand why I love this place so much. She's as outdoor-oriented as I am, but she's of the do-it-in-daylight school and doesn't want any part of a nighttime odyssey to this place. Truth be told, she doesn't even like it much in daylight. It's dangerous, she says. It's muddy, she says, and icky (her word, not mine) and full of things that go screech in the night.

She's right on all counts. But I have never felt real fear here, not even the ink-black night I somehow turned the boat over in the middle of the lake and lost all my gear. Instead, what I feel here is a sort of calm excitement, a low-key adrenaline rush of utter contentment that recharges my batteries and leaves me cautious yet confident, tense yet relaxed. It's a complex mix of emotions I have found nowhere but in the swamp.

I think about Jill now, reading a book or working on her next magazine article, enjoying her own particular brand of contentment within the secure walls of our house. I know she'll be snug in bed when I get back, with Hotshot the Wonder Dog hogging my side, and somehow that knowledge makes me feel even more at peace. One of the nicest things about a swamp is that eventually you must leave it and go home.

Fishing is my excuse for coming here, but as you probably know by now, the real reason is the swamp itself. Sometimes the fishing is good, but usually it's not, and even when they're biting the fish run small. Still, I always make the attempt – more from habit than anything else – and tonight's pilgrimage is no exception.

Typically, the bass are not hungry this evening. The shadows lengthen and merge as I move along the brushline, laying cast after cast into likely-looking places.

Eventually I do catch a fish, and the fight is lively but one-sided. A one-pound bass is no match for a 200-pound man with greed in his heart. I hold the bass at arm's length, admiring him in the fading light. I like swamp bass. They're healthy and scrappy, and their markings are so black they look like holes, shading off into the deepest green you can imagine. Even the belly of a swamp bass has a greenish tint.

He flips in my hand, still fighting me, and I smile and turn him loose. I've been known to kiss swamp bass before releasing them, but this one is too small to rate such treatment. He'll be bigger next year, though. Maybe I'll smooch him then.

Daylight is leaving fast now, and at the other end of the lake a barred owl shatters the dusk. At midnight in the swamp when this bird cuts loose directly overhead, he can make you wish you were somewhere else. But at sundown and at a distance, the sound is soothing, the raucous ***hoo-hoo-ho-hoo, hoo-hoo-ho-hooooooo-awwwww!*** providing perfect countermelody to the bullfrogs and nutrias.

By now it is too dark to see the edge of the brush, so I move out into the lake to wait for moonrise. I cast a small white grub randomly in the open water, catching a few sub-keeper crappies to pass the time. But after a while something big and ugly takes my little lure away from me, and after this happens I just sit and wait and listen.

Nutrias swim back and forth nearby, apparently ignoring me. It's hard to tell what a nutria is thinking. Somewhere back in the brush a beaver slaps its tail. Owls and chuck-will's-widows call intermittently, walking on each other's music, and the frogs fill the night with an almost visible noise. There are mosquitoes, of course, but they're bearable out here on the open water. I choose to ignore them rather than stink of deet for the rest of the night.

It's 9:30 now, and finally the full moon breaks over the trees to the east. It bathes the tiny lake in a wash of blue-gold light that looks cold even in summer. I shiver involuntarily as I east the ancient johnboat closer to the brushline.

A bull alligator bellows somewhere between me and the landing, and I shiver again, as close to afraid as I ever get in the swamp. I tell myself the feeling is justified: a 'gator's roar is a scary thing, even in the daylight. I've spent a lot of time in south Louisiana's coastal marshes where the calls of alligators are as common as those of shorebirds, but it's a sound I've never gotten used to. Somehow, a dark row of moonlit cypresses makes the sound even more ominous. I glance involuntarily over my shoulder, but of course the 'gator is nowhere to be seen.

I begin fishing again, moving slowly along the vague brushline, listening to night sounds, catching absolutely nothing. I'm having the time of my life.

The night passes, and by three a.m. I've circled the lake twice and am almost back to the landing. The only thing I've caught is a bowfin as long as my arm, a prehistoric, living fossil too tough (or too stubborn) to vanish with the dinosaurs that were his contemporaries. We call him grinnel here in the South, and he is ferocious. This one waylaid my spinnerbait as it came by a cypress knee, hitting with the explosive violence characteristic of his kind and pretty much having his way with me until I managed to subdue him and – carefully, those teeth are sharp – turn him loose.

Many fishermen kill these primitive predators, but here again I am out of step. I don't, because a grinnel is the embodiment of my swamp-strength, permanence and efficient death in one compact, savagely beautiful package. When I release this fish, he lazes beside the boat and eyes me malevolently in the moonlight before swimming leisurely away. Is he unconcerned, or merely uncomprehending? I have never been sure, but many of the grinnel I've released have acted this way. It unnerves me a little; I'm glad they're not 10 feet long.

The new day isn't far off, and it's time to go. I cut off the grinnel-chewed spinnerbait and close my box. Just before the boat enters the brush, I hold my breath and spray myself everywhere I can reach with insect repellent. I can put up with the relatively few mosquitoes that venture onto open water, but I'm not tough enough for the multitudes in the woods.

It's nearly daylight when I pull into the driveway. No sense going to bed now. I make a pot of coffee, and while it perks I shower away the stink of the bug dope. Later, outside again, I set the porch swing in motion, lift my steaming mug and toast the dawn.

Miles to the east, I know the swamp is preparing for a new day. It will be beautiful under the sun, but I don't miss it much during the daytime. I'll take my swamp at night, with the moon breaking over the cypresses and the owls and nutrias calling and the bullfrogs and alligators vying for low note.

It's much better that way.

Chapter 2

Two Dollar Bass

By Larry Dablemont

H e was the fishingest kid you ever saw...just a kid with tousled blond hair that looked like it hadn't been cut in a long time, and maybe never combed. He wore raggedy flannel shirts, faded, patched blue jeans and tennis shoes that were always a little too big because his mother bought them knowing he'd grow some more before her salary did. Her husband, the boy's father, had been killed in Korea ten years before and she had never remarried.

At Keane's Hardware Store, Billy Johnson was a regular most Saturday mornings, needing a few hooks or a few sinkers, admiring the rods and reels and lures that he couldn't afford. The old men who sat around the stove, gathered at the domino tables, or just sat on a bench and had a cup of coffee as they discussed the local news, always got a kick out of kidding the Johnson boy about his fishing exploits. But Mr. Keane was his staunch supporter, and he never left without what he needed, even if the coins in his pocket didn't quite cover the cost of the bare essentials.

"Well, Billy," Mr. Keane said to him that late September morning, "who you rootin' for in the World Series, the Yankees or the Pirates?"

"I hate them dad-blamed Yankees," the boy answered, "I want the Pirates to win, but they won't I don't figger...nobody I want to win ever does."

"Sometimes I feel the same way," the storeowner said with a laugh. "I want the Pirates to win too. I use to play catch with Bill Virdon you know, when we were kids over at West Plains. He's a friend of mine."

One of the men looked up from the domino table and said he'd bet his money on the Yankees. Then he addressed the boy..."Billy, have you caught any good fish lately?"

"Yessir, I shore have Mr. Weston," he said, "I got a five-pounder just the other day, down at the big eddy below Potts Shoals. Caught 'im on a crawdad."

A couple of the men sitting on a nearby bench chuckled and elbowed each other. The boy was only 13, and he probably hadn't ever seen a five-pound fish, but he was known to tell some pretty big tales.

"I shore would like to have a good bass for supper," Elwood Smalley remarked. "Tell you what, boy, if you catch another one of those five-pounders today, an' you can get him in here before closin' time, I'll give you two dollars for 'im."

Everyone laughed about that, but Billy didn't. To Billy, two dollars was a lot of money. His old fishing rod was tied across the handlebars of his bicycle, and he was headed toward the river. He was back in only two hours, before the crowd of old-timers had left for lunch. Wet to the knees, Billy was as excited as he could be. He had caught a genuine five-pounder, as he saw it. He hauled it into the hardware store on a binding twine stringer, dried out just a little from the ride back to town, but still a respectable 17-inch largemouth bass.

"I brung you a five-pound bass, Mr. Smalley," the boy said excitedly. "I wasn't there hardly no time at all till he grabbed a night crawler and like to run off with my fishin' pole. I thought I never would get him cranked in and hauled up on the bank. But here he is an' I come for my two dollars."

There was an outburst of laughter around the hardware store's pot-bellied stove, where the men liked to gather on a Saturday morning while their wives went to the dress shops and grocery stores.

"There it is Elwood," somebody hollered, "a genuine five-pounder for supper. "

With a big grin on his face Elwood Smalley took off his hat and scratched his head, looking at a straggly bass that wouldn't go much more than two pounds.

"Now boy," he said, "if that's a five-pound bass, some of 'em I've caught out of my old farm pond would go ten or fifteen pounds."

With everyone laughing and kidding the youngster, he just wilted. His shoulders slumped, a frown replaced the big smile, and the bass he held so high only moments before dropped to the floor. It was then that Mr. Keane intervened.

"Why fellows," he shouted above the laughter, "if that isn't a five-pound bass, I've never seen one. Ain't none of you fellows been fishing lately, a bass that size on the river is a fine fish, they been getting shorter and heavier for years now."

He reached into his pocket and pulled out a handful of change. "Get your money out Elwood," he said with a nudge of his foot against the old farmers leg, "You're eatin' bass for supper tonight, and I'm givin' this youngster a bonus for bringin' that lunker in here for a good picture to put up on the picture board yonder."

The picture board had lots of hunting and fishing pictures on it, every time someone brought in a deer or a turkey or a big bass or catfish, Keane would haul out a camera and take a picture which went on the wall. This time he handed the camera to someone and knelt beside the boy, to help him hold the bass out before him so it would look bigger than it really was.

When Billy was gone, the hardware store owner took a lot of ribbing for what he had done. Elwood Smalley good-naturedly remarked that he had felt robbed before in Keane's Hardware store, but never quite as bad as that day.

"Two dollars," he said, shaking his head and laughing. "I just give two dollars for a bass that ain't gonna hardly smell up my skillet."

"Now fellers," Mr. Keane said as the laughter subsided, "I just ask you... can't you remember being a boy once?"

The Pirates beat the Yankees in the fall of 1960, and Billy Johnson moved away the next spring, as his mother remarried, and his new stepfather had a job in another state. At Keane's Hardware Store, the old men who had grown quite fond of that kid who loved to fish, got together and gave him a tackle-box for a going away present, with a half dozen new fishing lures inside. But Mr. Keane went a little farther, and gave the boy a brand new fishing rod with a Zebco reel. Billy just stared at it, as if he couldn't believe his good luck. With his eyes to the floor, he said 'thank you' to everyone, and said he was coming back someday to catch another big bass from the river. But when he left, they watched him walk slowly across Main Street and up the alley toward his home. Billy Johnson was never heard from again.

• • •

Main Street was bustling with traffic. Mr. Keane sat on the bench in front of the hardware store listening to the St. Louis Cardinals on his radio. A middle-aged man walked up and sat down beside him.

"Who's winning?" he asked.

"Nobody yet," the old white-haired man answered, moving his cane so the visitor could find room on the bench. "I don't think they have the team this year they've had in the past, but it's only May, who knows what they'll be like in September."

The newcomer pulled out a cigar and lit it. "You know," he said, "I was just a kid in this town when the Pirates whipped the Yankees in the World Series, forty years ago come October. Remember when Bill Mazeroski hit that home run?"

"Yeah, I sure do," Mr. Keane replied with a smile. "It's funny how good I

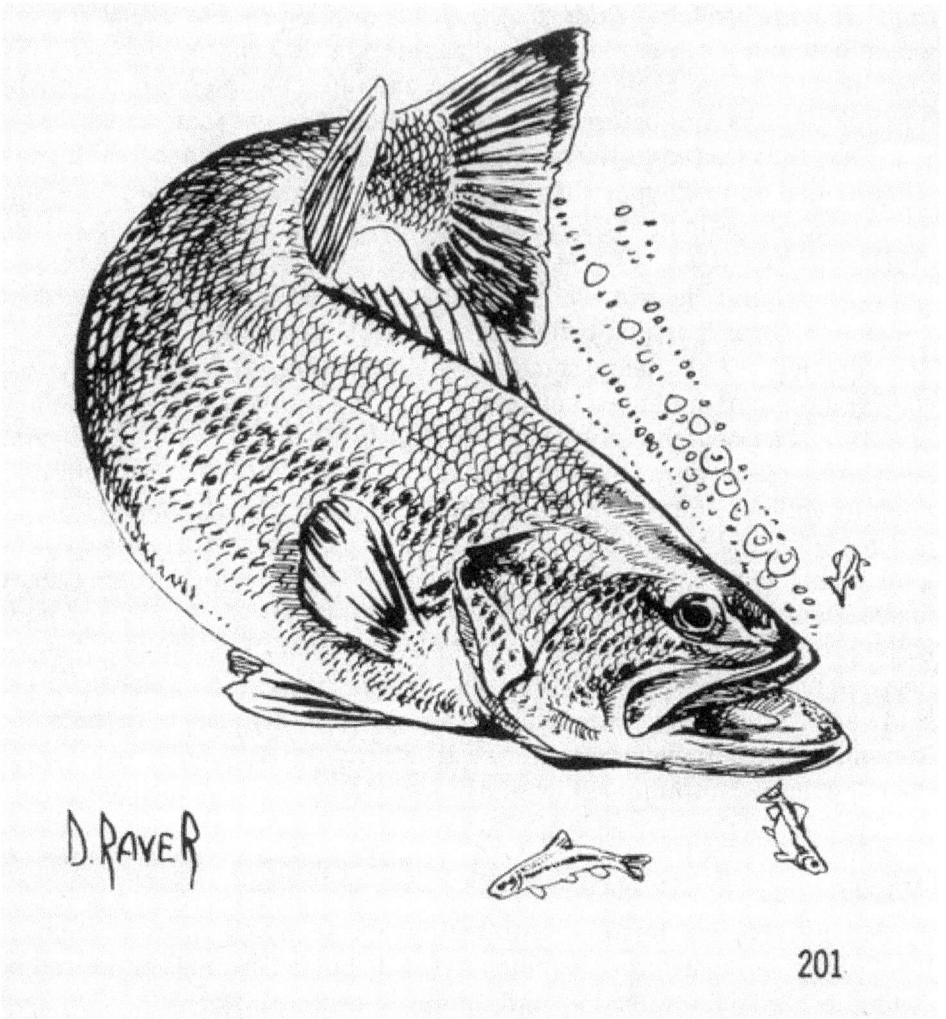

D. RAVER

201

remember that, and sometimes I can't remember what I had for breakfast."

The younger man laughed, and asked a question, "Do you remember how to get down to the Willingham hole on the river? I heard you liked to fish there once."

"I surely did, Mister," the white-haired man replied. "I loved that place... caught many a big bass there in years gone by."

"Bet you never saw a five-pounder come out of there," the man said. "Oh sure I have," Mr. Keane replied, "I saw a few quite a bit larger than that, back years ago. Course the river ain't what it was." He paused a minute, and then laughed. "Course I ain't what I once was neither."

"Well, Mr. Keane," the younger man said, "folks tell me you like to fish, and I need a guide. I've got a real nice big roomy cargo canoe, and I want to go fish the river again. When I was just a kid, I caught an awful big bass there, and I haven't seen it in forty years. I thought maybe you'd go fishing with me, down at the river, if I'd do the paddling. You can just sit there and throw some lures and tell me about the good old days."

"Well now Mister, I'd love to go fishing again, but I don't know you from Adam!" the older man said.

The newcomer laughed and pulled an old photo from his shirt pocket, "Sure you do, Mr. Keane, I'm the kid that caught this big old bass you kept on your wall for awhile way back there. And for a lot of years, all the fishing tackle I had came from your hardware store."

The old white haired man looked hard at the picture, and then a broad smile spread across his face. In a low voice he said, "Billy Johnson... danged if you ain't that little Johnson boy." Then he looked squarely at the stranger, and you could see him remembering.

"Well son, I wouldn't be much of a fishing partner, but it would be nice to go see the river again."

Two days later, the little Johnson boy, who had grown to become a man, spent much of the afternoon paddling the old man around a couple of holes on the river, paying a debt for some lures and a fishing rod, gained forty years before. Mr. Keane landed a few nice bass, and one of them weighed a little short of three pounds. Bill Johnson said it was a five-pounder, easy, and he said if he remembered right, Elwood Smalley would pay two dollars for a fish that size!

Chapter 3

The Calls in the Closet

By Jim Spencer

They hang by their lanyards from a nail in the corner of my closet. I see them twice a day: when I get dressed each morning, and again when I hang up my clothes at night.

For most of the year, they don't get much attention. They're just part of the closet. But sometime during that first string of crisp nights in October, when the leaves change from tired green to the hues of miracle, when the sound of snow geese fills the night, those two beat-up old duck calls start pulling at me.

The pull gains both in strength and in purpose, and by Halloween I've started carrying them with me in my truck, fooling with them, blowing them, practicing on them, re-familiarizing myself with the lingual intricacies involved in making a duck call do what it's supposed to do.

By the time duck season opens in late November, I'm as accomplished with these two old calls as I'm ever going to be. Which is to say, I'm good enough on those days when the ducks want to cooperate, but pretty much out of the ball game if they play hard to get.

Over my long career as an enthusiastic and relentless duck hunter, I've learned my natural ability as a caller has a fairly low ceiling. Good news: I can reach that ceiling with a minimum of practice, and thus re-acquire my personal level of calling expertise very quickly. Bad news: no amount of extra diligence, no amount of grueling repetition, will take me to a higher level of performance.

Over the decades I've come to accept this hard, cold fact, and, in truth, things are easier this way. Nowadays I just blow the calls in October because the activity and the noise help fight off the heebie-jeebies that descend during those last interminable weeks before the law goes off the duck.

One of the calls in my closet is an antique Chick Majors Dixie Mallard Call that was my father's. It's a beautiful piece; not so much duck call as musical instrument, not so much musical instrument as work of art. The grain of its curly walnut barrel is as intricate as any custom gunstock, and the barrel is set off by a rosewood insert, a piece of wood so hard and dense you couldn't cut it with a knife. Together, they create a drop-dead gorgeous duck call.

More than 60 years ago, Dad and I stood at Chick's shoulder in his tiny woodworking shop in Stuttgart, Arkansas and watched him lovingly turn the barrel of this call down on his wood lathe, the shavings coming off the hard walnut in a fine rain of powder. Dad carried that call on every duck hunt from that day until the end of his life. I've had it since, and it has yet to miss a hunt under my stewardship, either.

The other call in the closet isn't as old as the Dixie Mallard, but it's old enough. An original, all-cedar Duck Commander, it was made during the first

year or two of that company's existence. More than four decades ago now, I bought it in the parking lot of the Gibson's Discount Store in Winnsboro, Louisiana, from a wild-bearded man whose name you may know: Phil Robertson. The call is plain as mud and twice as ugly, with straight lines and hard angles and none of the graceful curves that characterize Chick Majors' work. But when I blow it, it sounds like a duck – or at least as much like a duck as I'm capable of making it sound – and thereby earns its place on the nail.

And also on the traveling team. That clunky old call hasn't missed a duck hunt, either, not since the day Phil laid it in my hand. I carry the Dixie Mallard for Dad and for me, but the Commander I carry for the ducks.

My grandfather, born in 1893, got in on the tail end of the great era of waterfowl hunting that started with the settlement of this country and ended with the Dust Bowl days of the 1930s. He quit hunting about the time I was born, but he used to tell me stories that made my mouth water – of skies literally black with ducks, of shooting legal limits of 35 mallards in an hour, of flights of a thousand ducks settling into the timber around him like oversized, drifting leaves.

We who hunt ducks today will never see such things. There are too many of us now to allow for the large bag limits Granddad enjoyed, and even when ducks "blacken the sky," it's just a figure of speech. They don't, not really.

But still we love this grand sport, and for the same reasons my grandfather loved it. We love the anticipation as dawn changes from promise to reality. We love watching a flight of ducks make that downwind swing and work back to the call. We love to see them cup and drop into the decoys, heads stretched forward over breasts, orange feet reaching for the water. It's not how many ducks we can shoot in a day that's important; it's that we can still get out there and hunt them.

And so, come Opening Day, I'll find myself leaning into the rough, muscular trunk of some gnarly willow oak deep in the backwater. I'll run my fingers over those two familiar old duck calls and think about Chick, and about Daddy, and about Phil, and about Granddad, and about a few old friends who are no longer around to share the magic.

Then the first flock of mallards of the new season will come by, and I'll start to call – haltingly at first, then with more confidence as instinct takes over from conscious thought. And when the time comes to raise the old pump gun and fire the season's first shot, I'll be awfully glad I lived to see it, just one more time.

Chapter 4

The Green Tradition

By Larry Dablemont

Buck has a new grandson, I hear. They named him Barkley, which is what Buck's real name is. He hated that name since he was a boy, said it was the only cruel thing he ever knew his mother to do. Buck and Sam and I have been friends since childhood. We've been going to Canada fishing each year now for about thirty years. But four years ago was one of the most memorable trips ever.

We were going to take Sam's oldest boy that year, but at the last minute he had to back out, so Buck was coerced into taking his daughter's 20-year-old boyfriend, Stewart. Buck was threatened, I think; had his arm twisted and household privileges like eating at the dining table withheld until he agreed to take the boy. Stewart wasn't Buck's choice for his daughter's boyfriend. You would have had to meet the kid, and since you didn't, I will try to describe him for you, but it isn't easy. He grew up in town, had no father, was going to the local community college, read lots of books, liked that modern country music, had skinny arms and no chest at all, hadn't worked a day in his life, and thought he was an intellectual. No doubt he was a smart kid, but he got it all out of books. He didn't know a stump from a Studebaker!

But there he was, fishing in Canada with us, and he had a book or two to tell him what kind of trees grew there and what the scientific name of a pine marten was. Tinker Helseth flew us out to the little cabin where we always stayed on Crooked Lake. We hadn't been there long enough to unroll the sleeping bags, and the kid was trying to clean it up like it was a dormitory room.

Sam picked out the bunk where he wanted to sleep, and in the windowsill next to it, he found a small bottle filled with some pine colored green gunk in it. Getting out my reading glasses, I could see it was a bottle of fingernail polish. Green fingernail polish! Can you beat that...some ninny had brought his wife up there! It caused Sam to smile and think of a way to put it to good use. The wheels were turning in his head and he told me and Buck to just go along with him.

That evening as we sat around getting our fishing gear ready, he mentioned that there was a tradition all old Canadian fishermen followed when they brought newcomers to a fishing cabin. Then he got up and went to rummaging around in the cabinet and hauled out that bottle of green fingernail polish.

"Here it is," he said, "There's always a bottle of this green polish in these Canadian fishing cabins. For many, many, years first-timers up here have been painting their toenails green for good luck."

Buck just sat there shaking his head, so I picked it up. "I remember when Jim Montgomery brought his boy up here for the first time," I lied. "Painted his toenails green and the next morning he hadn't fished an hour before he landed a six pound crappie and a thirty-two inch walleye. Never seen anything like it!"

I saw Buck put one hand over his face in amazement, but Sam kept it going. "It goes back to the very first white men who saw this country, Irish Vikings that sailed up the St. Francis Riverway through the Great Lakes. They painted their faces and their feet green for good luck."

"It's the St. Lawrence," Stewart said, "and the Vikings were of Norwegian ancestry. Actually the first white men to come here were French."

He was about to continue, but Josh cut him off. "I think the Irish may have made their trip over here a hundred years or so before there was any history. They taught the Indians how to make pizza." We all had to laugh at that.

"Anyway," Josh said, "it's something we all do up here as part of tradition, painting our toenails the first time we get here...but if you don't want to be a part of it, Stewart, you don't need to. You are quite a bit different than most of us, and I can't see no reason to want to continue the traditions that mean so much to ol' Buck and us."

I wouldn't have believed it, but I guess that last statement made the kid think he could make a good impression on his girlfriend's daddy, and he picked up that fingernail polish and dabbed it on all ten toes. Josh got out his camera and took a couple of pictures, to show that the young man was eager not to break Canadian fishing traditions. I had to go outside. It took me ten minutes to come back in acting serious.

That night, for the first time in his life, Stewart visited a country outhouse, and we heard him screaming his lungs out. We dashed out there with a lantern, and there was a porcupine in the outhouse. Stewart thought it was a young bear. We told him that porcupine was more dangerous in some ways than a bear, and when I drifted off to sleep he was up reading about it in one of the books he brought.

At daylight, we were all up making coffee and frying bacon...all of us except Stewart. He hated getting up that early, couldn't believe it was so light at 5:00 in the morning. Buck told him it had always been that way in Canada in the summer, and groggy-eyed he drank a cup of boiled coffee to wake up while explaining to us the science behind it...why the sun rose so much earlier in the summer in northern locations and set so much later in the winter. He knew more about it than we did, but I never did understand half of what he was talking about.

We had two of those V-bottom aluminum boats with 9.5 horse motors, and I knew Josh and Buck wanted to go back into one of their favorite spots to fish for bass with topwater lures, so I volunteered to take Stewart with me. We figured Josh could take him out on day two and Buck could take him on day three.

I'll say this for him...he had practiced enough with that spinning outfit Buck had given him to be pretty good with it. He said he and Buck's daughter had taken it down to the college fountain and practiced for hours with a lure with no hooks. I hadn't expected that. He pulled out an old Zara Spook that looked 20 years old and started giving me the history of it. Seems he had looked it all up on a computer.

I tried to tell him that the old Spook was a hard lure to work and he ought to put on a spinner bait or something simple which would catch a bass or two, but I thought to myself, 'what the heck, he probably ain't gonna catch nothing anyway, so he might as well catch nothing on that Spook, as he would on something else.' What a beautiful morning it was that day, the mist rising from the water, the surface back in that cove just so still and calm, and an otter playing among a raft of big green lily pads intermixed with tall reeds.

I laughed to myself when I saw Stewart yanking that old Spook back to the boat like he was trying to jerk a hot-dog away from a cat. In little time, my spinner bait had scored, three nice fat largemouth bass in thirty minutes, like footballs, maybe two pounds apiece. I offered to tie one on for Stewart, but he wouldn't have any of that. He said he had researched the Zara Spook and knew it was a lure deadly on bass and northern pike both.

I didn't say anything. I knew that since he didn't have on a steel leader he would hook some hammer-handle sized northern and it would bite his line in two and he'd lose it. Then I would give him a spinner bait and teach him how to use it.

About the time I was thinking that, he splashed that 8-inch lure out about four feet from a stand of reeds in five or six feet of water, and a gigantic swirl sucked it under. It must have been the dumbest northern pike in Canada, or else it was attracted to hot dogs flopping around on the water. But that northern was no hammer-handle, he was a monster, bigger than any I had ever caught in that lake. I knew it would be a short fight, and Stewart looked as if he was scared half to death. But he hung on, and as it sometimes, but not often, happens, the back treble had hooked that old pike so securely in the top of the mouth that the line wasn't even in his teeth.

Instead of boring back into the reeds, that dumb northern worked out

into open water, and he jumped a couple of times, seemed like four feet in the air. Stewart was trying to say something, but he couldn't get it out. His eyes were about the size of loon eggs and his jaw was dropped so low you could have stuck a beer can between his teeth.

If I were a real good writer, I could write a whole magazine article about that 20-minute fight out there on the little lake, with loons calling in the distance and that old northern pulling us around while Stewart kept muttering "Oh darn, oh darn, oh my gosh."

Maybe he would have never landed him if I hadn't pulled into a sandy spot and let him pull that tiring fish up onto it, where I pounced on it with a dip net that wasn't really big enough.

We put it in the boat and headed back to the cabin where we would tie it up to the dock. Stewart just couldn't believe it...he sat looking at the fish like he had been the one that had been landed, and the fish had caught him.

Well, it was quite a day. We caught bass right and left on topwater lures, and late in the evening we went out to an underwater reef and caught a bunch of nice walleye for supper. Buck and Josh admired that northern pike Stewart had caught, which we think might have weighed close to twenty pounds, and remarked that it was the biggest any of us had ever seen at that little wilderness lake.

That night after supper, we sat around the fire outside the cabin and relaxed. Stewart told all about catching that big northern again, and never left out a detail. When things got kind of quiet, we listened to loons wailing out on the lake, and the kid opened up to us.

"I'm awfully thankful you fellows let me come along," he said. "I never dreamed I would ever do something like this. I guess my dad never fished, but I never really knew him. I was awfully young when he was killed in that car wreck, and my Mom's family were city people. Out here, it seems like I have three dads."

Nobody said a word. I couldn't see Buck's face very well in the firelight, but he was as sober as I ever saw him.

"I can see I missed an awful lot." the young man went on, "seems kind of like God is trying to make it up to me all at once."

I heard Josh snoring a little when we turned in, but not Buck, I think he was lying there thinking for awhile. Maybe like me, he was wishing we hadn't had that kid paint his toenails with that green polish.

As dawn came, we got up to find Stewart out of bed and gone. He wasn't in the outhouse, he was down on the shore fishing. We heard him hollering and yelling a long time before the sun came up, but we couldn't see him very well because of the fog and the mist. He came running up to the cabin, holding a big old largemouth bass by the jaw, literally beside himself with excitement. Buck was pulling his shirt on as he came out the cabin behind me.

I heard a low whistle escape his lips, and Josh exclaimed, "Holy mackerel, what a bass!"

The boy had gone down there and started fishing an old Jitterbug I had given him the day before. It was about 5 inches long, and I thought we might use some of them after dark. I guess he woke up early and couldn't wait to try it, and the result was a huge bass, bigger than any we had ever caught in Canada, ever.

"He'll go darn near seven pounds," Josh said as he fumbled with his camera. "Never seen a seven-pound largemouth up here before...can't hardly believe my eyes."

We got plenty of pictures, and then we all went down to the water to release the big fish. You could tell Stewart didn't quite understand that, but he went along with it when we explained why you release bass of that size, out of respect for the old fish, knowing what he had gone through to get that big. Bass in those cold waters that reach five pounds are old, old fish.

Josh took Stewart out that day, and I guess in the late evening the young fellow hooked and landed a five-pound walleye. They got more photos, and released it. We had plenty of walleye fillets for supper.

Finally, he and Buck spent a day fishing, and that night around the campfire, when it got quiet, Stewart didn't talk about fishing. He stood up and told Buck that he never met too many men he respected more and he wanted to ask if he would give him permission to ask for his daughter's hand in marriage.

I thought Buck was gonna fall off his bench. He stammered around and finally said that Stewart needed to talk to his daughter about that, not him. But the young man made it plain he wanted to do what tradition required, just like those green toenails. He said it was obvious that the things we did worked. He felt like he had been the luckiest guy in the world on that fishing trip, with all those big fish.

I think we all headed back home with an entirely different opinion of that young boy...no, not boy...that young man. He and Buck's daughter were married in the fall, and Josh and I were there standing up for him, first time I wore a suit in the last ten years.

And like I said, Buck is a grandpa now. I saw the little boy crawling around on the floor at Buck's place not long ago, and he had green toenails!

Stewart is a man now, a far cry from the beginner we took fishing four years ago. He hunts ducks with ol' Buck, and killed his first deer last winter. Now I'm not saying he's one of us just yet, because he talks in a language we still don't always understand.

But we have quite a trip every summer, when a bunch of us go to Canada fishing. Stewart knows the joke we played on him, and he was a good sport. His wife Cynthia never did see those photos of Stewart and his green toenails. But the last time we went, Stewart brought the green fingernail polish, just to continue with tradition. Buck wouldn't have any part of it, but Josh always paints his, right alongside of me and Stewart. He says he's just wanting to do that in remembrance of those long ago Irish Vikings who sailed the St. Francis all the way into the middle of Canada.

Chapter 5

The Camp

By Jim Spencer

It is October, and I am where I've been every October for the past 60 years – moseying along the bottom of a draw in the lower reaches of the White River bottoms of southeast Arkansas. For the past 20 minutes I've been moving slowly along in my pitiful version of stealth, crunching limbs and leaves underfoot and trying without success to slip undetected within range of feeding squirrels. Behind me, the draw snakes southward a few hundred yards and merges with four similar draws to form a local landmark that on the topo map looks like the twisted fingers of an arthritic hand.

Unimaginatively enough, we call the place Five Forks. For the six decades I've been coming here and for many centuries before that, it has been a strategic, easy-to-find rendezvous point for hunters both red and white. This I know because I found an arrowhead here once, a sparkling chert wonder that glinted in the sunlight and set my imagination racing when I bent to pick it up. The point was broken, and I believed then, with the wonderful romanticism of youth, it broke when some buckskin-clad brave drove it through muscle and sinew and lodged it with precision against the spine of a buck deer. Six decades of worldly disillusion and disappointment have done nothing to alter my faith in this area.

The red hunters are gone now, of course. But as I wander along the draw, it isn't hard for me to imagine they're still around. I expect the timber looks much the same, although it's true the huge virgin stuff is gone. Still, the trees are plenty big enough, and it's still pretty wild country. Especially if you stay away from the infrequent logging roads and discount the occasional smooth-sawn, moldering stump. The terrain is adequately wild to sustain my illusion, anyway, and today I'm content to be a modern-day Dan'l Boone, padding in the footsteps of that long- dead trailblazer.

The sun sends its first rays into the new day and I lean against a red oak trunk to enjoy it. Only one thing is lacking from this near-perfect morning – a squirrel to go after.

As if on cue, a limb shakes farther down the ravine. Was it a bird? No, I think not; the movement was too slow, too deliberate, made by a creature

with no wings to fall back on in the event of a miscue among the branches. I strain my eyes, willing something to show itself.

And sure enough, there he is, big as a cat and red as a rooster. Even from a hundred yards away, I can tell this old settler will be tough. But squirrel mulligan is a tradition in our camp; I can taste it already, and toughness is of no importance in a bushytail when you're planning to boil him for half a day anyway. I watch for a few more seconds to make sure he's not going anywhere, and then I begin the stalk.

It's an easy job, even for me – a short stroll up the smooth-bottomed ravine, a solid rest against a handy tree trunk, a brief wait until he presents the proper target in the scope, and *crack*! Squirrel stew comin' up.

The megasquirrel hits the ground with a muffled whump and I relax to savor the moment. Then I walk over to pick up my first squirrel of the season.

I'm all bent over, picking him up, when I hear the rattle of limbs overhead and straighten hurriedly. But it's too late; all I see is a gray blur arrowing down a tree trunk to disappear into the thick ground cover. No chance for a shot.

Dang it! Daddy taught you better than that. You always wait, always, when you've just shot a squirrel, because often there will be another one nearby, and the noise will make him run for it. Stupid, rookie mistake.

At first I'm angry with myself, but before long the proper perspective reasserts itself. It was only a squirrel, after all, and this place is full of 'em. Not to worry, there will be other chances. Anyway, there are far worse places to be than in these woods.

And there are. Other chances, I mean. The squirrels are active this morning, and even with my tangle-footed technique I have my limit before nine o'clock. There's a black one in the bunch, no real rarity among southern fox squirrels, but unusual enough to make me proud.

• • •

Back to camp and the coffeepot. Two of our loosely-knit group have already had the same idea, and the coffee is ready when I arrive. I pour a steaming mug of it and fall into a folding chair at the edge of the shady bank overlooking the river. One by one other hunters come in, and by 10:30 everyone is in camp.

Already the camp has acquired a personality, which is not surprising when you consider the diversity of the individuals who have gathered here. Steve and John are partners in a grain brokerage company. James Lee has a Chevrolet dealership. Pete is an optometrist. Jerry fixes teeth for a living, W.D. drives a truck, and Peck and Gary grow rice and soybeans. Jimmy manages a cattle-feed mill. Malcolm is a lawyer, Jim is an insurance adjuster, and J.D., in his own words, is "sort of an architect." By the same token, I suppose I am "sort of a writer."

But this week, as has happened each fall for the past 30 years or so, we have set vocations aside and come together to become factors in the common denominator of The Camp.

Squirrel hunting was our original purpose for assembling here, but it's become much deeper than that. The means has become the end, and though the hunting is necessary, it is also incidental. Some years we do pretty good with the squirrels, but we could bring home just as much meat (and do it a lot cheaper) by hunting closer to home and sleeping in our own beds. Our wives remind us of this, but every year we pack up and go anyway.

The nearest maintained road ends four miles away, and normally the only way to get to camp is by boat. But this year has been hotter and drier than most, and we have taken advantage of the moderate drought by driving a 4x4 into camp, four miles as the wood duck flies, but more than eight over the serpentine, overgrown logging trails that eventually lead to the camp.

The truck is undeniably more convenient than boats for hauling in our mountainous pile of gear, but somehow things are not quite the same for our having used it. The sight of a battered red vehicle parked behind the tents adds a note of discord, eroding the subtle mood of solitude the river and the Big Woods create. The consensus is that in future years we will not drive to camp but will come in by boat as we always have, hoisting our gear to the top of the bank with the help of a jury-rigged block and tackle suspended from a sturdy overhanging limb.

Red truck notwithstanding, the camp is peaceful and remote. There are other squirrel camps scattered here and there along the river, but none are nearby and we have a big chunk of woods to call our own.

● ● ●

There are bears here. It's a pleasing thought, but there's a worry, too: we have a super-abundance of good-smelling foodstuffs in camp, and during the morning hunt each day, the camp stands empty for several hours. So far, though, we've been fortunate. No bear encounters, in camp or otherwise, although last year on a dark, drizzly day I came across a set of tracks so fresh water was still seeping into one of them. Overcivilized and overprotected soul that I am, it does not embarrass me to admit the hair stood up on the back of my neck as I stood over that track, looking around at what suddenly seemed a dark and ominous forest.

There are also feral hogs, though not so many now as before. Swine figure heavily in many of the war stories told around our magnum-sized campfire every night. "War stories" is a polite euphemism hunters use when what we really mean is "lies."

But some of the lies aren't lies, especially those concerning wild hogs. The tales are usually enjoyable and funny and everyone always laughs, but it is the nervous laughter of a night walker in the cemetery. Because each of us knows that one of these hogs can do you in, and they're so tough that if you killed one, all it would do is make him mad.

I got between a sow and her piglets not far behind the camp one day, and before it was all over I was wishing I was somewhere – anywhere – else. My dad came face to face with a 400-pounder while crawling through a canebrake on his hands and knees many years ago, following what he had assumed was a well-worn deer trail. "I thought that cane was too thick for a man to run through," Dad told me later. "I was wrong."

And then there was the time a buddy of mine came to camp and got chased up a honey-locust tree by an ill-tempered old boar with teeth out to here. Ned said he went up that tree like a starving possum after persimmons.

"Whyn'cha shoot him? I asked. "Couldn't. I ran away from my gun."

"Whyn'cha climb something besides a thorn tree?" "Nothin' else was close enough. I was in a hurry." "Didn't it hurt, going up through all those thorns?" "Nah. It wasn't a lot of fun coming back down, though."

But hogs are not the topic of conversation around the campfire at this moment. Right now, Jim the insurance adjuster is holding forth. From the snatches of conversation I have been catching, his tale seems to involve a somewhat less than sober weekend on R&R from Viet Nam, a weekend during which Jim and an accomplice drove a rented Subaru into a Japanese living room and got shot at by the gentleman of the house for their rudeness.

Stranger things have happened, I suppose. Maybe. But true or not, the story is entertaining, and none of the fire-worshippers is about to accuse Jim of bending the truth. For you see, each listener has his own whopper to tell, and he wants to be believed when his turn comes. He who is blameless must cast the first stone. No one in this camp qualifies.

The river flows peacefully along below me, and my eavesdropping shifts direction, focusing on a vociferous knot of camouflage-clad hooligans playing dealer's choice poker at one of our slap-dash camp tables. It's two bits a chip, color notwithstanding, and some of the pots have been colossal. Peck is dealing a hand of seven-card something-or-other, sitting on a two-foot section of wind-thrown hackberry and running the cards around the table with the dexterity of a shell-game huckster. His lower lip is bulging with Skoal, there's a toothpick in the corner of his mouth and he's wearing a tattered straw goat-roper hat with a turkey feather in the hatband. Pure class.

Malcolm, seated beside me and helping me watch the river, was in the game until a few minutes ago. He cashed in because he says a fellow needed to be a CPA to keep up with some of Peck's games, and he's just a lowly lawyer. Games such as seven card low-hole deucey, Jokers and one-eyed Jacks wild, roll your own all the way, last card up or down. That sort of thing. "He'll probably deal a hand of Dr Pepper before he's through," Malcolm grumbled, sipping on a longneck Bud.

In addition to lying and playing poker, there are plenty of other camp activities to keep a body out of mischief. Cooking, for example. Eating well is something we take seriously in The Camp. At the moment, Don, a visitor here from Tulsa, is busy dealing pieces of squirrel into a Dutch oven the size of a bassinet. This is the beginning of what will become our nonstop stew; it starts life as a squirrel mulligan, heavy on onions and carrots, but God knows what it'll be a week from now. As it starts getting low, somebody will chunk more stuff in – hamburger, half of a left-over ribeye, mac and cheese, who knows?

There is also a bubbling pot of venison chili that will make you reach for the water jug. (Its dregs will also be added to the stew pot, most likely.) There's 25 pounds of catfish fillets in a big cooler; that's for supper tonight. Another cooler holds about 20 steaks, each two fingers thick. That's tomorrow night. There is enough fruit to stock a produce stand: apples, oranges, cherries, pears, grapes, bananas. And three kinds of cheese. And sandwich stuff. And cookies, and chips, and candy bars. There is a gallon jar of pickled eggs, and another of pickled okra. As mentioned, we eat pretty well.

As also mentioned, it's catfish for supper tonight, supplemented with fresh bass and crappie fillets if Steve and I have any luck this afternoon. But between now and the fishing trip there's time for a nap, and I feel it coming on.

● ● ●

Now we're into the second full day of The Camp. It was straight catfish last night – the fishing was wonderful, but the catching wasn't so hot.

Still, there are fringe benefits to a river-bottom fishing trip which, while they have nothing to do with the fact that you are fishing, nevertheless add immeasurably to the quality of the experience. There will always be the memory of the doe stepping nervously to the edge of the water, listening with waving ears to the faint sound of voices from the quarter-mile distant camp as she quenched her late-afternoon thirst. Minutes later, six wood ducks banked sharply around a point of trees, lit practically in our laps, then fled in hurried confusion when they spied us, the hens shrieking in panic. We watched for 10 minutes, smiling, fishing forgotten, as a pair of young fox squirrels played tag up and down the trunk of an overcup oak 15 yards from the boat. We had a gun aboard, but it never occurred to either one of us to shoot them.

Earlier this morning, I was standing in the middle of a beautiful oak/hickory flat, daydreaming about those two young squirrels, wishing they'd show up now, when it suddenly came to me that I wasn't daydreaming. In what seemed to be a delayed replay, two young fox squirrels came out of a hole in a big oak 50 yards away and started harassing each other. As I watched, a third one squirted out and joined them.

My approach was slightly crunchy, but the leaves were still dew-damp and the young squirrels unwary, so I made it okay. I got the first two easy enough, but the third one streaked back to the hole.

I was still standing fast, mindful of the previous day's lesson, when the overcup oak tree above me blew up. Out of the explosion, amid a swirl of falling leaves and swishing branches, came a turkey gobbler as big as an ostrich. As he banked away, he presented me with what would have been a perfect shot at his head and neck.

Swift as thought, I raised my rifle crossways. It had magically morphed into a hand-made osage-orange bow, and the young buckskin-clad warrior holding it sent a hand-crafted wooden arrow skyward, tipped with a sparkling chert point. The arrow took the gobbler clean amidships, and in my mind's eye he crashed to the forest floor.

I stood there quietly, my heartbeat thundering in my ears, my mind's eye watching the gobbler do his death flop in the leaves while my other eyes watched him fly away through the trees. When my pulse rate had subsided to near normal, I picked up my two young fox squirrels and decided that was enough, for this morning anyway. After all, I'd still be here tomorrow to hunt, and the day after that and the day after that and so on for the next week. No sense pushing past what was certainly going to be the high point of the hunt.

I turned and started back the way I'd come, the satisfying weight of the warm gobbler pulling at my shoulder. My elk-hide moccasins slipped silently through the ground litter as I moved effortlessly and gracefully toward camp and the waiting coffeepot.

Indians love coffee.

Chapter 6

Christmas Fur

By Larry Dablemont

He walked slowly up the old wagon road toward the little farmhouse on the hill. With traps across his shoulder, Satch Harris stopped and looked out across the river bottoms before him. It was a bleak-looking winter landscape, now that the leaves had all fallen, and the bottomland cornfields were yellow with the stubble left from harvested corn. Through the sycamores you could see the distant river, nearly black as he looked down upon it, with white fringes of ice along the edge. For a while at least there would be no more trapping. Grey clouds threatened snow for Christmas, less than a week away, and the cold had already spread a thin layer of ice over the slough and quiet backwater pockets.

As the young war veteran neared the old barn, his father walked out to greet him. "That's a fine cache of furs you got there, son," he said. "Has ol' man Fredrickson looked at 'em yet?"

"Yesterday. Offered me 240 dollars for the lot!"

The older man shook his head and looked at the ground, kicking at a rock. "That old skinflint," he said with a smile. "The richest guy in the county, I reckon, and he just can't get enough."

Elmer Fredrickson owned a dry goods and mercantile store in the small town nearby. He bought furs and cattle, invested in anything he could get for very little and sell high. Most folks had little regard for him. Satch and his father walked into the barn and hung the traps from a nail in a side shed, alongside others. In an adjacent stall, an old car sat covered with a large tarp.

"The old s.o.b. knows what a hard time we're having right now," the younger man said. "He wants me to sell him Grandpa's old car for five hundred dollars. I tell you Pa, I think I'll have to do it if we're going to pay all the bills. I hate to!"

"Hell boy, your grandpa would be proud to see you get somethin' out of it. It ain't run for 20 years, and that is an awful lot of money."

"I ain't sellin' him the furs, Pa, I think I'll take the old truck and take Linda up to see her sister in St. Louis and sell 'em there, either to F.C. Taylor

Company or McCullough and Tumbach.

"I think I ought to get $350 for the lot. That should be enough more to pay the gas and allow a little left over for her to buy the kids a Christmas gift or two.

"Gas is 19 cents a gallon in town now, it's gonna run you ten dollars or so to get you there and back if only those old tires hold up." The older Harris said, "They's still a stretch of Highway 66 that's gravel for a ways, south of Rolla, but I guess it's all concrete now from Rolla to St. Louis. Modern times is on us, son, I can remember when that road to St. Louis was more mud than anything, back before you were born."

Older folks all agreed that times were so much better than they had ever known them. The war had been over for more than ten years, the town had a new school and a factory that had folks working for good wages. But for the young man who came home to his father's farm, and married his young sweetheart without finishing his high school education, times didn't seem so good. The corn hadn't brought much that fall, and the hogs and chickens and calves they had raised didn't bring what he had hoped they would.

And there were two children, with another one due early next summer. His little girl was ten years old, and the little boy was about to turn eight. He wanted a gun for Christmas so he could go with his daddy when he hunted in the fall. But even second-hand guns cost way too much. Little Josh would have to settle for a toy gun again, and his sister a doll, like it was every Christmas. But it WAS Christmas, with his brother and his family coming for dinner, Linda's folks and his folks coming too, everyone bringing food and home-made candy. How could a man who nearly died on a foreign battlefield complain about hard times, when there was so much happiness?

The cedar tree he had brought in from the woods needed to be decorated that night after supper, and his wife and kids were excited about that. He tried to see to it the anxiety he felt didn't show. There was popcorn to string, Christmas carols to sing.

They left for the big city the next morning, a six-hour drive before them in an old pick-up manufactured before Josh was born. The boy was so excited to be going along, his sister looking forward to staying with her grandmother for a few days.

They made it over the rough graveled roads that crossed the creeks and rivers and spanned the steep hills south of Rolla without any flat tires, and Satch breathed a sigh of relief as they gained the well known Highway 66 and flatter terrain. The boy wrapped up in a blanket and went to sleep with his head on his mother's lap, as she talked, unable to contain her excitement about seeing her sister, to spend a day or so with her in the big city with a few dollars to spend shopping.

"God has truly blessed us," she said. "1 have been praying that we get another boy for you."

Her husband grinned. "Could you pray for an increase in raccoons and mink and beaver populations too?" he asked. "I'd just be tickled pink to have a nice healthy little girl and plenty of raccoons come next trapping season. Somehow I don't think we'll ever see any raccoons in the Ozarks, so I will just settle for a healthy baby."

It was quiet for a moment, and he added with a smile, "Maybe you might say one more prayer for me, since I don't ever seem to find the time to ask the Lord for much."

His wife looked at him with a questioning gaze. "I'd just like to see ol' man Fredrickson go broke and maybe break a leg or something," he said. "Satch," she recoiled, "what an awful thing to say. You are too good a man to wish bad things on another human being."

"Well maybe," the young man said as he concentrated on a passing bus which took up too much of the highway, "but Fredrickson ain't a human bein' as I see it. I do not understand how God lets those who are so evil prosper, and lets someone like you have so little."

She scooted closer to him and squeezed his arm. "I think we are very, very blessed," she said. "I will ask no more of God than good health for our children and you, and thank Him always for bringing you home to me from that awful war all those years ago."

The young man thought about it as he drove. His wife had more faith than he did. She never heard him pray, never heard him thank God. But he did... often; there on the river when he was alone, seeing a world where there was so much peace and quiet, trying not to remember the hell he had witnessed overseas so many years before. He prayed for things which he just had no faith in seeing come about. He knew that times weren't going to get better. But a man who has fought in a horrible war and survived it gets to thinking he can handle whatever comes, on his own.

St. Louis was something to see. There were bright Christmas lights strung everywhere, and even with directions written down, it was difficult to maneuver through all the trucks and cars and buses to find the warehouses of the F.C. Taylor Fur Company. He found it finally, and waited in line, finally meeting with a big heavy-set fellow who was to grade his furs. He had greased-down hair and a big mustache and seemed choked by that bow-tie he had on. But he also seemed very intent on the furs. "You know what you are doing, sir," he said, "Your furs are excellently prepared. From the Ozarks I can tell, but in good prime. Trouble is, Ozark furs aren't worth what they are from north Missouri or Illinois."

Satch waited, and the man left with his list, returning to direct him to a desk where another man sat looking through papers, thick glasses setting on the end of his nose. He removed the glasses, and stood to shake the young trapper's hand.

"We like your furs, Mr. Harris," he said, "and it is obvious you are a good trapper and handler of pelts. I know you must be up here for the first time and I'm sure you're thinking of showing your furs to other companies. But we'll offer you a top price, which I am sure no one else can top, 'cause in the future, we'd like to have you come back to us. You can look at this list of each of your pelts and how we are grading them. There are two mink pelts we are marking grade one large. We don't often see mink that size."

The young Ozarker looked at the list, and at the bottom of the column, the price was totaled at four hundred and ten dollars! He gulped hard and nearly dropped the paper. The fur buyer before him was smiling at his reaction. There was another handshake as they finalized the agreement with the trapper's signature. "I WILL be back again," Satch told him, "and if we get a stretch of mild weather in January, I might be back in early March with more furs."

He and his wife slept on a folded-down couch that night in her sister and brother-in-law's home, and it was a great evening, with kids running through the house and the grownups playing cards. But in the middle of the night, he awakened to find his wife gone, holding his son Josh, who was crying in the next room. The boy had a fever, and complained of his throat hurting. By sun-up, his temperature was extremely high, and they took him to a nearby hospital.

Satch waited in a small room while a nurse took the boy and his mother down a hallway to another room. He tried to look at an old magazine or two, but he couldn't concentrate. Hours before he had been so elated at his good fortune, and now he was concerned about his son, and knowing that much of the money he had collected for his furs now might be lost before they ever left the city, just to pay doctor and medicine bills.

Finally, he could take it no longer, and he rushed down the hall to the room where the boy was lying on a white bed, and an elderly doctor and two nurses were bending over him. He waited quietly and watched, not caring who noticed him bowing his head to say a prayer. Soon another nurse entered, and they took him and his wife to a side room, and moved the boy on the rolling bed to another section. The old doctor came in to talk with them.

"You can go be with your boy shortly," he said with a smile. "He's going to have to get an injection, and he'll probably need to spend some of the day here, until we get that fever down, but he'll be fine in a day or so. It's just a bad throat infection, something kids get from time to time. And I think we need to get you all on some medicine for a time to keep anyone else from getting it."

With that he was gone, and the boy's mother, with tears of anxiety in her eyes, breathed a deep sigh of relief. All that her husband could think of at that time was something he would never voice to her...the cost of this doctor and the medicine and the hospital would be much more than he could pay out of pocket, considering that most of his trapping money was needed to pay bills back home. How was he going to manage it all, how could he determine what to let go, and what to pay?

At the front desk just after noon, he stood waiting to get that bill, his son and wife beside him. A lady came in and asked if he was Mr. Harris, and he nodded his head.

"Dr. Hiesell asked me to have you come to his office a minute if you have time." With that she motioned him to follow, and he turned to tell his family he would only be a minute. But it would be awhile longer than that.

The doctor shook his hand and said he had learned a little about where he was from while talking to his wife.

"Just last summer I was there on that very river, fishing with an old timer who I think must know your family. He said the wooden johnboats we were using were made by a man named Victor Harris."

"That was my grandfather," Satch told him, "Grandpa made dozens of them that are still around and being used today. But he passed away two years ago. He was an old riverman, he taught me an awful lot about fishing and trapping and hunting the river. I still use those boats he made, we have four or five in our barn along with old sassafras paddles he made too."

"You don't say!" the graying doctor seemed fascinated. "I wonder if maybe you would like to do some horse trading with us. Your wife told me you have had some financial difficulties, and I was thinking I could maybe take care of the bills for your son here if you might want to take a friend and I on a couple of float-fishing trips come vacation time this next summer... how does that sound to you?"

"You must be kidding, doctor," the young man said," I would love to do that...I'd rather be on that river than anywhere else in the world. I've done that kind of thing for my grandfather back before the war when I was just a teen-ager."

They talked for some time, and agreed to make arrangements in the spring. "Bills will be mailed to you from the hospital," the doctor said, "but you just hold on to them and we'll take care of them when I come down to fish with you. I have to come down next spring anyway to meet with an old coot there in your little town by the name of Frederickson, who is trying to sell me an old car. A group of doctors and I have an interest in putting together an old automobile museum here in the city, and he wants to sell us an old Oldsmobile made in 1918. If it is half the car he says it is, I can't wait to get it."

Satch was reaching for the door, and then he slowly stopped and turned to face the doctor, shaking his head as his eyes narrowed. "Did you say Fredrickson? Elmer Fredrickson?"

"Why yes, that's who it is...I take it you know him."

"I know him all right, he is a...well, that automobile he wants to sell you, a 1918 Oldsmobile, is covered with a big canvas in our barn, and belonged to that old grandfather of mine. Elmer has been trying to buy it for a year, and he wants me to sell it to him for 500 dollars."

The doctor grinned, "He is trying to sell it to us for fifteen hundred, and it might be worth more than that if it is in good condition."

"Well, Doc, you come down and take a look at it whenever you can, and have dinner with us and maybe we'll go hunting for awhile on our farm. My grandpa bought that old car secondhand when he was a young man, and it quit on him about 1935. He put in the barn intending to fix it, and it has been there ever since. And Elmer Fredrickson ain't even going to be allowed in that barn anymore. I think me and you can make a deal on that old car without him!"

Christmas came; and Josh was healthy again. There was three inches of snow on the ground on Christmas day, and the sun broke out just before noon. Cars and pick-up trucks gathered at the old Harris farmhouse and there was more food on two or three tables than the entire family could eat. It had been quite a scene around the Christmas tree that morning before the relatives arrived, with more packages to open than there ever had been in past years. Josh Harris had a new gun, a Stevens over-and-under .410 and .22 combination that was likely a little too big for him. But he'd grow into it.

Satch Harris slipped away from the noisy family to bring in more firewood, to fill the box behind the cookstove. His leg was hurting a little because of the old wound, and he couldn't help but think about that winter in France more than a decade before, when the roar of distant artillery made Christmas a hard thing to remember. He looked out across the river bottom in the distance and said a quiet prayer of thanks. As he gathered an armload of wood, his wife came out and put her arms around his waist. "Now do you see that my prayers have not been wasted? God has blessed us this Christmas like never before.'"

"Well, it has taken awhile," the young man tried to sound skeptical and unconvinced. He knew she'd have him going to church on a regular basis if he wasn't careful. "But I am a patient man. Who knows, maybe one of these days these hills will be full of coons again and there'll be beavers in the river...if you keep praying."

He looked at her and smiled over the armload of firewood. "You'll have to be a little patient," she said.

"Lady, like I said, I am a patient man," he replied as he looked toward the little farmhouse where he could hear kids singing a Christmas carol. Then suddenly he dropped the firewood at his feet and turned toward her. "But I want a Christmas kiss right now and Christmas dinner shortly after and I ain't in the mood for waitin'."

Chapter 7

The Turkey Hunt

By Jim Spencer

Sometimes the urge holds off till after New Year's Day. More often, though, it starts pulling at me around Thanksgiving, when our family feasts on the succulent flesh of a wild turkey gobbler, the bird having been saved against this meal from the previous spring's hunting efforts. So far, we haven't had to get our Thanksgiving bird from the supermarket...but once or twice the Christmas bird has come from there.

Regardless of their pedigree, these holiday birds are still turkeys. And wild or tame, they set the cognitive wheels turning. Before the bird is even digested, the familiar fever starts its insidious work. Before day's end, I've dug slate calls, diaphragms and the trusty Lohman box with all the notches in its side out of the drawers and closets where they've been since May, and the house and yard are once again filled with clucks, purrs, yelps, cackles and cutts – rusty at first, but then sweeter and surer as the old skills resurface.

By the time the last of the inevitable turkey salad is gone, everyone within earshot is tired of the discordant-to-them, lovely-to-me sounds of hen turkeys in love. This, mind, is still in November, with spring turkey season still four months away.

Non-turkey hunters just don't get it. They can no more understand our compulsion than they can understand Chinese hip-hop. But they're not alone in this; we who are afflicted don't understand, either.

And compulsion it is, as surely as it is compulsion that drives lemmings into the sea. Veteran Alabama turkey hunter Tom Kelly admits this in his landmark turkey hunting book *Tenth Legion*: "I do not hunt turkeys because I want to, I hunt them because I have to. I would really rather not do it, but I am helpless in the grip of my compulsion."

But those of us who are so compelled aren't really complaining. We make noises like it from time to time, especially when the turkey gods are against us and/or the season is four weeks old and we're well into sleep deprivation, but by and large we've come to accept our lot. We are turkey hunters, for better or worse...and either it gets better or it gets worse.

Where turkey hunters are concerned, there is no lukewarm. There is no halfway. Either you is or you ain't, and thus we is, beset with all the attendant joys and sorrows, highs and lows, that are part and parcel to this peculiar pastime.

Even among outdoor types, non-turkey hunters outnumber turkey hunters by a wide margin. This being the case, some of you who are reading these words have no clue what we're talking about here. If you've never personally experienced the rush of turkey hunting, there's no way you can understand it. I know this for a fact, since for the first three decades of my life I didn't have a clue, either.

So go with me on your first spring turkey hunt, the way I did with a friend in 1978, and learn firsthand what this business is all about:

• • •

Turkey hunters get up early. Three o'clock is about right, if you're going to meet me at the crossroads by half past four. I'm not trying to threaten you here, but know this: if you're late I'll leave without you. Gobbling turkeys don't wait for tardy turkey hunters. Neither do I.

Lock your car and ride with me. Yours looks too shiny and new to go where we're heading. Old Blue is used to the rough roads, and looks it. Another ding or two won't even be noticeable. Don't forget any of your gear – shotgun, shells, camouflage, calls, gloves, coffee thermos, small water bottle. Just throw it all except the coffee in the back of the truck, on top of my stuff, but hurry up. We're burning precious time, and there's still 20 miles of bumpy gravel between us and our bird.

I roosted him late yesterday evening. In turkey hunter's lingo, that means I heard him fly up to his roost and gobble a time or two after he got there. I already know exactly where he is, and that gives us a little edge on hunting him this morning. But it's only an edge if we get there early enough to take advantage of it. Come on. Let's roll.

Driving through the inky night over the rough roads, we review the morning's battle plan. A turkey hunt isn't so much a hunt as a military maneuver. If he's gobbling, or if you've roosted him the night before – as we have this one – you already know the bird's location so you're not actually hunting him, in the strictest sense of the word. Rather, you're trying to get in a good position and entice him to overcome his inbred reluctance to come to an unseen hen, instead of holding his ground and letting the hen come to him, as is the normal course of things. You're trying to outsmart him.

No, excuse me. I misspoke. You can't outsmart him, because he isn't smart. He's a bird, after all, with a brain that would rattle around in a ping pong ball. How smart can he be?

What you're trying to do is out-maneuver him, to bend his will to yours, to get him to do something his instincts are screaming at him not to do. You have to overcome his native caution in order to achieve success, and to do so, you must contend with a set of senses – hearing and eyesight only; thank God they can't smell – so incredibly sharp even veteran turkey hunters are continually amazed. It's been said that a turkey can see through a thin rock, but of course that's ridiculous. What they really do is see around them.

Philosophy and semantics aside, we're here to kill this turkey, and now it's time to leave the truck pinging in the cool morning air and hike through the dark woods to where he slept last night. It's a classic case of good news/bad news: it's not far as the crow flies, but we're not crows. We have two deep valleys and two steep ridges to negotiate, and not much time left to do it. So let's go.

What? You forgot your face mask? Hold still then, and let me put some of this face paint on you. It's better than a mask, anyway. A face mask restricts your peripheral vision and doesn't do your hearing any good, either. A turkey hunter needs every edge he can get.

We'll be able to use our flashlights for about half the trip, because the bird is roosted on the top of the second ridge and he won't be able to see us or hear us until we crest the first one. Before we start, though, put on this orange vest and hat. We'll take off the deer hunting garb when we sit down to work the bird, but it's best to wear it while we're moving, even though it's still dark right now. There'll be some daylight when we get where we're going, and we're not the only hunters in these woods. Not all of them are as careful about target identification as they ought to be.

Now, follow me, and watch for loose rocks. If you step on one and break an ankle, I'll have to leave you. It would be much too difficult to carry you out, and anyway, there's this turkey that needs to be hunted.

I'm joking, of course, but be careful anyway. No sense ruining a hunt by getting hurt before it starts.

What did you say? We're moving too fast? Hmmm. Listen: there's a turkey gobbler sleeping in a bull pine tree two ridges from here, and I intend to be over there with him when he wakes up. Whether you're there or not is entirely up to you.

Okay. We've climbed out of the first valley onto the middle ridge, and it's time to turn off the lights. Don't worry, your eyes will adjust to the dark in a few minutes, and there's an old logging trace that'll take us down this ridge and up the next one pretty close to the turkey.

Here's the road now. It slants up the ridge, following the easiest slopes, and it'll be fast going and not too hard. Not as hard as the last ridge, anyway. Load your gun now, but do it quietly and don't forget it's loaded. We don't want to make any unnecessary noise once we get in close.

We're getting close to the top now. Keep your voice to a whisper, and don't talk any more than necessary. Remember that sharp hearing.

When we sit down to this turkey, we'll sit against the same tree if we can find one big enough. You'll be on my left, because you shoot right-handed and I don't, and that way we'll each have our best swing radius to work with. We're getting pretty close to where we need to be now. Don't break any sticks underfoot or I'll twist your neck in a knot. I'm joking again. Sort of.

Here, this is close enough. Let's sit against this old red oak. It's big enough for both of us, and we'll be able to communicate in low whispers - which I've learned the hard way is highly desirable when you're hunting with a buddy.

The gobbler is roosted down the slope to the left – your direction – in a small group of big shortleaf pines on the edge of an old clearcut. The cut is too brushy for him to fly down into, so we've got a real good chance of him coming our way. He's 100 yards away and maybe 25 yards downhill, and there's nothing between us but mature, wide-open woods.

It's a perfect, text-book set-up. I just hope this old boy hasn't read the book.

Take a few seconds to rake back the leaves and smooth the ground where you're going to sit. Do it as quiet as you can. Then take off your orange vest and use it for a cushion. You need to be as comfortable as possible, because we might have to sit as still as this oak tree we're leaning against, and we might have to do it for a long time. That's hard enough to do even when your ass doesn't hurt.

After you're sitting down, get your knees up and rest the gun across them, to make sure that's going to be a comfortable position when the time comes. There's a rock under where your right foot wants to rest, you say? Okay, that's why you tried it now. You've got time to dig it up and move it out of the way. Quietly.

Okay, we can relax and enjoy the coming of the day...and we didn't get here a minute too soon. There's already a strong reddish glow in the east. The cardinals haven't started yet, but I expect they're clearing their throats. The turkeys start gobbling not long after the cardinals start singing. That is, if they gobble at all.

There's the first cardinal. Their song even sounds red, have you ever noticed? He ought to gobble any minute. Maybe I ought to hoot like a barred owl...

Hooooo-awwwww!

Ah, good. My owling's not all that great, but that real owl did the honors for me.

Hooooo-awwwww!

Gobble, will you? What's the matter with him, anyway? Please gobble. There he is! Did you hear it? He's right where I left him last night, and that's never a sure thing. I've had lots of roosted birds move on me during the night, and I don't know why. But I know they sometimes do it, so I'm always a little nervous at first.

We'll let him sound off a few more times, if he will, and then we'll give him a tree cluck or two. We want to make him think there's a sleepy hen over here who's just waking up.

He's gobbling pretty good now, isn't he? I could sit here and listen to him all day, but he's not going to sit there all day himself, and there's work to be done. I like the slate best for this real soft stuff. Here goes. Cross your fingers, I'm not very good at tree clucks...

Good. That sounded good. The turkey seemed to think so, too. Did you hear how he walked all over me as soon as I made the first cluck? We'll let him gobble once more on his own, and I'll tree cluck to him one more time, and then we'll shut up until he flies down. He knows where we are, and there's no sense in overplaying our hand. Calling too much tends to make a gobbler stay in the tree, I guess waiting for the eager hen to come walking underneath him. We want him to think a hen is here, but leave him with the impression she's not too interested.

There he is again. Now, two or three more soft clucks and we're set.

Boy, he gobbled back fast at that series, even though that first cluck was a little sour. We've got his attention, so now we wait him out...

There! Did you hear him fly down? That was a long 15 minutes, wasn't it? I bet he gobbled 50 times, and it was a strain to keep from answering him. But now he's down here with us, and it's time to call to him a little more. I'm gonna yelp at him a little and see what happens. You be ready. He might come running, or it might take him two hours to cover this 100 yards. And then again, he might go the other way. With a turkey, you just never know.

Ah, that's what I was hoping for. He gobbled back before I even finished the yelp. In turkey hunting parlance, that's known as "cutting your call," and it's a very good sign. We might get a look at this bird.

Oooooh, boy, I can hear him drumming. Listen close; it sounds like a log truck a long way off, right out at the limit of hearing, pulling a hill in granny low. When I can hear that, the turkey is just about shootable. Keep your eyes...

Oops, there he is! Don't move. He's about 75 yards out, just to the left of that double-trunk dogwood about 45 degrees to the right of your gun barrel. He's strutting, and he's getting a little closer, but he's not in any hurry. Don't move.

All right. Fifty yards now. Do you see him yet? Good. Getting to watch the show is the best part of the hunt. Look at him, blown up as big as a Russian boar and just as black. Wait until he goes behind that white oak, then shift your gun around.

Good. He didn't see the movement. If we don't screw it up, you're about to kill this turkey. Let him come on at least until he's even with that stump. It's about 40 yards, and that'll put him in range. If he wants to come closer, though, let him. Thirty yards would be better. If he gobbles, try not to flinch. It'll be pretty loud at this range.

He's even with the stump now, but he's still coming so let him. Lordy, isn't he something! Look at that beard, thick as a bell rope. I bet he weighs 22 pounds. You've done everything right so far, so just stay as calm as you can and think things through. Don't blow it by making a mistake at this late stage of the game, the way I've done so many times.

Let him come. Let him come...

Thirty yards now, more or less. Don't shoot him while he's strutting; his brain stem is all pulled down into his chest and it's a smaller target now. Also, you're liable to shoot most of his beard off. Be ready, though. I'm gonna let him come another yard or so, and then I'll cluck at him pretty loud. That ought to make him break strut and stretch his neck to take a look, and that's when you need to shoot him. Aim at the base of his wattle, where it's biggest and reddest. That'll put the upper part of your pattern in his neck and head.

Here we go. Show time.

Cluck!

Chapter 8

The Intruder

By Larry Darblemont

It was the first morning of the turkey season, the north Arkansas Ozarks, April of 1991.

Well up the timbered hillside, just below the crest of the ridge, a turkey gobbled in the very first hint of morning light. A minute or so later a barred owl hooted well down the valley and he gobbled again. There was another gobbler answering down toward the river, and then another between the two.

Leather boots stepped cautiously over the boulders in the low area between the ridges where the cedar thicket grew. The boy didn't want to stumble in the darkness before the dawn, carrying the loaded shotgun and all. His mom had worried about that, but she worried about everything. His dad had said he was big enough, getting close to fifteen years old and taught well. He said the boy could try turkey hunting on his own this year, in the woods behind their home.

Never had he experienced such excitement, never such an urge to hurry. And yet he knew that if he didn't go slowly, his chances for success would be lessened. His dad had taught him that...locate the gobbler, go slowly and don't get too close. Set up and be ready before he leaves the roost. Hide well and call sparingly. Don't cock the hammer until you are ready to shoot and don't pull the trigger 'til there's no doubt. If you aren't looking at the beard and the head and the neck of a wild gobbler within 40 yards, don't shoot.

He skirted the cedars, and moved up along the flat bench where oaks and hickories grew and he found the big dogwood tree he knew so well, with just a little white beginning to show from the green buds. He stood beside it to listen, and all was still. He wondered if he had been too noisy, if he had worked too close. He waited and worried for what seemed like such a long time. Then the gobbler down toward the river sounded off, and in answer, the tom up the slope sent forth a loud and lusty gobble that shook the dew from the buds. He seemed mightily close. The boy trembled as he selected a good-sized tree trunk to sit against, hoping the rustling leaves which seemed so loud, and the sound of his own pounding heart, would not spook the gobbler.

Light was coming fast, the landscape was taking shape, and the boy heard several hens along that timbered break just below the high ground. Had he known more about turkey hunting, that might have worried him a little, but he had no misgivings about it. With or without hens, the gobbler would be no pushover. Right then, he was almost afraid to use the box call he had bought weeks before.

It seemed that all at once, it was morning. There was light, and birds flitting about and the sound of heavy wings leaving the roosts in the branches 150 yards away. He brought forth the call, and weakly stroked the lid against the box. It sounded awful. Moments later he heard the gobbler, not as loud and clear as before, but still a thunderous gobble, and another and another. He tried the call again, stronger and clearer, with hands calmed by a hint of confidence.

For an hour, the gobbler gobbled and the boy called and his hopes rose and fell and rose again. It seemed the old tom was coming to the call, then it seemed he wasn't. It seemed he was closer, then farther. The boy strained his eyes to see something, anything, moving before him. His eyes watered, and his neck began to hurt. And then, there was no more gobbling.

Finally it was just another morning in the woods. Squirrels were hustling along the forest floor, a blue-jay warning the world of a skunk ambling through the boulders at the bottom of the hillside. The sun was rising, it was becoming warm and the boy was getting sleepy. He put down the call, convinced he had used it too much and spooked the gobbler. A crow called, and the old tom hurled an insult toward the black nuisance, a short, loud gobble from about where he had been earlier in the morning.

The boy picked up the call and created four or five yelps, and wondered if he hadn't heard something similar from up on the ridge. Apparently the hens were moving up into the timber at the top, and the gobbler was following. He gobbled twice, and there was no doubt about it, he was moving higher, and away from the boy.

He called again and again, but it grew quiet. He waited. Fifteen minutes passed and he heard one more gobble, on the ridgetop, well above him. It was followed by the most awful sound in the world, a shotgun blast.

The youngster rose to his feet, and uttered a few words which might have surprised his mother. It surprised him too, a little. But that was his land, at least land his father owned, and it was posted. No one should have been there.

In his anger, he went up the hillside faster than he should have, and once on top of the ridge, he moved toward the sound of the blast. When he reached the old logging trail, he began to run. One hundred yards along it, he ran smack into the hunter who had ruined his morning. It was old Argie Roush, limping along with the big gobbler over his shoulder.

The two of them just stood there looking at each other, the boy nearly out of breath, the old man surprised to have been caught where he was not supposed to be.

"That was my turkey," the boy blurted out, "I was calling him. This is my dad's land and nobody is suppose to be here!"

The old man slumped his shoulders and looked back up the road behind him, pointing as the gobbler dropped at his feet.

"I was way back up yonder boy, this here gobbler wa'nt anywhere's close to where you was down there!"

"How did you know where I was then?" the boy asked, "He was the gobbler I was after and you just ruined my chance. Why can't you find your own place to hunt?"

The old man became defensive, "Aw hell boy, I ain't a quarter mile from my own danged house, an I ain't kilt 'em all. Go on out there an' hunt another'n an' quit jawin' at me. This ain't the only damn gobbler in the woods."

There was no use saying more, the boy's lip began to quiver and he turned and headed the other way, back toward his home. He knew his father would do something about this.

Old Argie watched him go. He knew he was going to be in trouble. These were new folks, outsiders moved in to build and post the land, with little use for those who had always been there. And the old man knew that whatever trouble there would be, he'd be the loser. He had always been the loser... always would be. He picked up the gobbler and limped down the old road toward the little shack he called home.

Early in the afternoon, the pick-up was parked in front of the sheriff's office, and inside, the boy and his dad waited to meet with a deputy to fill out the papers against the old trespasser. He was mad, this father who cringed at the thought of that meeting in the woods, his young son confronting an old reprobate that everyone said didn't amount to anything, and might be capable of anything. He meant to see to it that Argie Roush never set foot on his land again.

This deputy wasn't a youngster, and he wasn't new to his job. He had seen many such situations, and the boy and his father were surprised when he asked if the three of them could go across the street and have some pie and coffee before they got down to the business of legal retribution.

They found an out-of-the-way table in the little small town cafe, and the deputy made small talk. He asked if the family liked it better there in the Ozarks than they had in the big city they had moved from; said he used to go to that little country church they now attended out on Crumley's Ridge. He asked the man if he liked his job at the new hospital, and talked about how nice it was to have it, so that folks didn't have to go all the way to Springfield, Missouri when they came down bad sick.

And finally, when the waitress brought three pieces of chocolate pie, he got down to business. "Old Argie ain't got a cent I don't reckon, but we'll go out there and get him and let him spend a night in jail on a trespassin' charge. I know him, and he'll have his turkey tag, so there won't be no way to get him on wildlife violations. But spending a night in jail won't faze him, he spent quite a spell in a worse lock-up than ours, by far."

He paused for a moment to slurp his coffee, and the father was quick to ask..."He's been in prison? I might have figured that."

He couldn't have seen the slight smile on the deputy's face. "Oh yeah, when he was just a few years older than that boy of yours, he was a prisoner of war in Germany. Wounded pretty bad I guess and almost didn't make it, that's why he limps, took shrapnel in his leg. He's got a lot of medals, did some heroic stuff I've heard. Who would have thought it, looking at him now?"

Father and son both looked up at each other, but no one spoke.

The deputy went on. "Argie came back, but he wasn't ever the same. His older brother was killed over there on Omaha Beach at Normandy. And he had a little sister die of the fever just a few months after he come home. Up to that time his family were hard-working people, had a nice old two-story home not far from that little shack he lives in now. It got sort of rundown after the war, Argie's dad got to where he couldn't do much, never recovered from losing his oldest boy.

"His wife died and the county took a couple of the younger kids. If that wasn't enough, the old house burned in the 1950s. You probably never knew this, but all that land of yours and some of what the Wilsons own was once owned by Argie's folks. In the late 50s, the old man had to sell it all. You wouldn't want to guess what it brought. Land sold for peanuts back then. Finally there was just Argie, and he built a little place and married a woman who already had a couple of kids. Back in the 60's he straightened up pretty good, worked as a mechanic for the Ford garage in town, and went to that same church you folks go to. He loved those two kids like they was his own... well, eventually, most folks didn't know they weren't."

A couple of farmers came in and passed by, and they stopped to talk and joke with the deputy, and you could see the boy and his father solemnly thinking of what he had said. When the farmers went on, devoting their attention to the waitress, the lawman seemed concerned only with finishing his pie. The father propped his elbows on the table, folded his hands before him, and asked what had happened to the family.

The deputy polished off the pie and held up his coffee cup to attract the attention of the waitress, who headed his way with the coffee pot. "You know I don't know exactly what did happen. I know Argie moved off aways, maybe to Mt. Home or Harrison. Somewhere to make that woman happy. And when he moved back, about fifteen years ago, 1975 or '76 1 guess it was, he was alone, and nobody ever knew what had become of them. My guess is, she run off with another man. But I don't know."

"Thank you sweetheart," the deputy told the waitress as she filled his cup, and topped off the cup of the father, whose interest seemed to be in anything but the coffee and the unfinished pie before him. "You may be the best waitress this place ever had," he said with a grin..."for your age anyway."

The waitress answered that poor tippers shouldn't get such good service and the deputy laughed at that. But the father wasn't laughing. He sat in deep thought, disturbed by what he had heard.

The deputy sensed it was time to finish the story..."Argie came back an alcoholic, and couldn't hold a job. I wouldn't have give a nickel for his chances back then, but I didn't know how much he had in him. He reached down deep inside hisself and found the Lord for awhile and whipped his drinking problem. Now he may look like an old drunk, but he is as cold stone sober as the day he quit it, and I don't think he's had a drink in ten years. But now, it's a problem getting him to quit wandering around in those woods he grew up on. There's been a call or two about that. He just can't seem to stay on that little acre of his. He wanders here and there along the creeks with his old fishing pole, and hunts deer and turkey wherever he can find them...wherever he can get to with that bum leg. I guess it's time to crack down on him all right."

"You haven't just told us this to pass the time," the father said. "You know it changes everything to know all this. My father was a World War II vet. I can't go up there and charge that old man with trespassing now."

"I've heard well of you in the two years you've been here," the deputy said solemnly. "I was of a mind that you'd be slow to come down hard on the old timer once you knew it all."

"So what do you suggest?" the newcomer asked.

The deputy thought about that as he stood, and dug into his pocket to find a quarter or two for the waitress. And then he chose his words carefully. "I'll talk to him first, and I think the old man will listen to you, after that. Wait 'til after church Sunday," he said, "then go out there in the old graveyard and look at those headstones with the name Roush on them. Argie's whole family, and one stone for his brother, whose body was buried overseas. Then go talk with him, and tell him you want to keep those woods open for your boy to hunt. An' maybe you might see if you can get him to go back to church with you now and again."

Then the deputy looked at the boy and smiled, directing his words to him. "I know how mad you must be at that old man, son," he said, "But remember that when he was your age, he was climbing around those hills and ridges too. It was all his playground then, and he loved it like you do. Now he can't hardly get off the logging roads. And remember that it was him and men like him who went off to fight in the war and see to it that our land remained free. To old Argie, it seems like everybody around here has some of that freedom but him."

They walked outside the cafe, and stood there for a moment and the deputy had one more thing to say, as an afterthought. "There'll be lots of wild turkeys in your future, son, lot's of spring mornings! But old Argie... well, he's probably down to his last few of each."

• • •

It was the second Saturday of the turkey season, and the boy sat cross-legged at the edge of the old logging road, admiring his first wild gobbler. He was so proud of that 16-pound jake he could hardly take his eyes off of it. Behind him, old Argie Roush sat on a fallen log, smoking his pipe, his face beaming with delight. "Your pop ain't gonna believe it boy, first try and we got one."

"I never would have got him by myself, Mr. Roush," the boy said. "I never heard such good calling as you was doing."

"It's just this old cedar call here," the old man said, "It's prob'ly as old as I am, an' I'm gonna give it to you if it's alright with your pa. We'll teach him about this turkey huntin' so's he can get in on it." It was quiet for awhile, and then the old man spoke again. "I'd druther be out here like this without a gun, callin' up a turkey an' teachin' a young'in like you how I use to could do it, when I was younger. I reckon you'll have to forgive me boy for what I said last week, I'm plum ashamed of the cuss words I used. I want you to know I ain't a man to talk like that."

It was quiet for a long time, and a gobbler sounded off in the distance, just once. The boy realized the old man couldn't hear it.

"Mr. Roush, I know you was in the war, the same one my grandpa was in. I know that our country is free today because of what you and my grandpa did. Sometime...could you tell me about it, and how it was back when you was my age?"

The old man didn't say anything, he just stood up, and limped over to the edge of the logging road to look down into the valley below.

"I can't hardly wait 'til May gets here boy," he said, "when the suckers start to shoal. An' wait 'til you see the size of the catfish in that bluff hole down there in the river. Spring shore is a wonderful time...an' I had pert near forgot that. Maybe this summer when it gets hot an the fishin' slows down we'll sit on the front porch, turn on the fan an' eat us a watermelon. Then I'll see if I can remember how it was.

"Back then boy," he said, shaking his head, "we didn't have any turkeys! None a' tall.

"It's better today than it was back then!" he said as he turned to face the boy, his eyes set moist and bright within the leather mask of wrinkles and whiskers. "A sight better."

For Argie, it was, that day in April...better than it had been for a long, long time.

Chapter 9

A Bird the Color of Autumn

By Jim Spencer

The first wood duck I ever saw was actually a pair of them. I'm guessing here, but 1958 would be close.

These wondrous creatures came whooshing through a break in the forest canopy, just as the sun was sending its first slanting rays through the flooded timber. Dad and I were wading through the opening, headed for some hotspot duck hole he knew about. They came streaking through the timber like only woodies can, afterburners lit and the hen's *woo-e-ee-eeeek!* siren going full blast.

Dad saw them first, punched me on the arm and pointed skyward. I looked up just in time to watch open-mouthed as they flashed through a patch of golden, early-morning sunlight. They spied our upturned white faces and flared out through the treetops, framed for a last instant against a sky so blue it made your eyes hurt.

I'm sure Dad had time to shoot; green-timber duck hunters are often forced to shoot by instinct, and my father was an experienced green-timber hunter as well as an athlete with lightning reflexes and excellent hand-eye coordination. But he just stood and watched them with me, his shotgun still held comfortably over his shoulder. I don't know if his mouth was open or not, but I suspect it was.

"Why didn't you shoot?" I asked, after they were gone.

"Wood ducks," he said. "There aren't many of them around, and the season's closed on 'em. They're almost too pretty to shoot, anyway."

I don't remember how many mallards we shot that day. Some. But more than six decades on this Third Rock have failed to dull my memory of that wood duck moment. Those two birds are a long time dead, but in my mind's eye they'll last as long as I do, framed against that cobalt sky and flashing their colors like the flag team in a high-school homecoming parade.

• • •

By the time Dad and I crossed paths with that pair of wood ducks, their tribe had already experienced some serious ups and downs. Those two birds were survivors of a holocaust.

Before the Migratory Bird Treaty Act in 1918, duck seasons were liberal and long – usually from September to April, with either nonexistent bag limits or limits so large it took two men to carry one hunter's birds.

Game law enforcement was practically nonexistent as well, and market hunting was common. In my home state of Arkansas, for example, which has 52,000 square miles within its borders, there were only nine game wardens. The fledgling Arkansas Game & Fish Commission, established in 1915, had almost no operating capital, and these wardens were poorly equipped and even more poorly financed. They even had to use their own vehicles, with no plan for reimbursement. Wildlife agencies in other states were in no better shape.

Since wood ducks are more southerly oriented than most ducks, they took a harder hit from those long, liberal, poorly enforced hunting seasons. They were hunted all summer in the Midwest and the North, and the rest of the year in the South.

By 1900, it was plainly evident the species was in trouble. Many early conservationists believed woodies were headed for extinction. Noted ornithologist George Bird Grinnell wrote of wood ducks in 1901, "Being shot at all seasons of the year they are becoming very scarce and are likely to be exterminated before long."

Wood duck populations continued to dwindle, but somehow they hung around until that previously-mentioned 1918 Migratory Bird Act.

And then, under the full protection of the law and helped along by the beginnings of the conservation movement and the birth of scientific wildlife management, wood ducks began their long, slow recovery. The species took another downturn during the severe, prolonged drought of the 1950s – as did all duck species – but quickly recovered when conditions improved. Since the mid-1960s, wood ducks have ranked second or third in annual harvest totals in both the Atlantic and Mississippi flyways.

• • •

Wood ducks, as their name implies, are birds of the forest. They seldom leave the shelter of the woods, and this explains why they're primarily found in the eastern half of the nation. There's a West Coast population, but it's very small compared to the population in the East.

These Technicolor ducks nest in hollow trees, but readily accept man-made nest boxes when they're properly built and properly located. Although they prefer to be closer, wood ducks will nest up to a mile from water if they can't find a suitable nest cavity any closer.

Another peculiarity of wood duck nesting behavior is the common practice of "dump" nesting – two or more hens depositing their eggs in the same nest. One researcher recorded five different hens contributing eggs to a single nest. This sometimes results in a ridiculous clutch size, 40 or more eggs. On rare occasions, two hens will share incubation duties of these oversized clutches, but usually the work is done by a single hen. In up to 10 percent of dump nests, there is no incubation at all. At least one Mississippi study found that dump nesting increased when – take a wild guess – when wood duck numbers increased within the study area. Duh.

No one knows the reason for this odd behavior. Some biologists think dump nesting results from a shortage of suitable nest cavities, although dump nests are sometimes located in artificial nest boxes in woods that are loaded with them. Maybe, other researchers suggest, dump nesting is an aberrant behavior triggered by growing population pressures as wood duck densities increase. Then again, maybe not. Other studies have shown that most hens contributing eggs to dump nests also lay their own clutches in other nest cavities and incubate them. It's hard to find a straight answer, but then, maybe there isn't one.

Wood ducks nest earlier than most other ducks – again, not an eye-popping revelation, considering the more southerly nesting range of woodies compared to mallard, pintails, teal and their other puddle-duck cousins.

However, we're talking really early here. Sticking with the Arkansas example, wood duck nesting activity begins in early February and continues into late June, with the peak nest initiation period in the second half of March. Adult birds tend to nest earlier than yearlings entering their first breeding season.

As is the case with ground-nesting ducks, predation is a big factor in wood duck nesting, but the culprits wear different faces. Raccoons are serious wood duck predators just as they are for ground-nesting ducks, but the foxes, skunks, coyotes and opossums that prey on mallard and pintail nests are replaced in the wood duck's case by fox and gray squirrels, rat snakes, blue jays, crows and other birds. Starlings are a problem in some areas, not so much because they destroy the eggs, but because they take over the nesting cavity or box and harass the hen wood duck until she abandons ship.

The long nesting season (120 to 130 days in Arkansas and other southern states) allows wood ducks to renest after one clutch is destroyed – and they almost always do. Thus, wood ducks are able to maintain a high percentage of productivity in most years. A woodie hen usually begins laying a second clutch of eggs within two weeks of losing the first. Some hens even nest again after bringing off a successful first clutch, thus contributing two broods to a single year's production. During a two- year study on Big Lake National Wildlife Refuge in northeast Arkansas, researchers found that at least 27 wood duck hens brought off two clutches during the study period, and ducklings from at least 16 of the 27 first clutches survived to flight stage.

Although the drake wood duck doesn't share incubation duty, some pairs stay together until the end of the 28- to 37-day incubation period. The male then leaves, and the hen rears the brood solo. Drakes spend the summer months alone or in small bachelor groups.

During the eclipse, or summer molt, adults are flightless. This happens to both drakes and hens, of course, but being ground-bound makes little difference in the life of a nesting or brood-rearing hen wood duck; she's not going to be doing a lot of flying, anyway. The temporarily drab and flightless drakes seek dense cover during this three-week period of vulnerability, and it's during this brief time of summer when the wood duck population seems to evaporate.

• • •

When autumn comes and the annual migration begins, wood ducks join in. But while the rest of the puddle ducks have a long flight ahead of them, many wood ducks are already in the southern states. Wood ducks tend to migrate in hop-scotch fashion. Birds that summered in Louisiana and Arkansas pretty much stay where they are. Birds from Missouri drop down to Arkansas and Louisiana. Birds from Iowa drift south to Missouri, and birds from Michigan, Wisconsin and Minnesota drop down to Iowa. As winter progresses, the northernmost ducks continue moving south, until by January more than 90 percent of the continental population of wood ducks is south of a line drawn through Little Rock, Memphis and Nashville. Therefore, to hunt wood ducks where populations are highest, you must wait until the tag end of duck season and head for the Deep South.

Fortunately, hunters don't have to do that to enjoy good wood duck hunting. In fact, the best time to hunt woodies is in the early part of the season in your home state, going after resident birds or transient migrants.

The mallards may still be a state or two north of you when duck season opens, but the woodies will be there. Some states have special September wood duck seasons, to give hunters a crack at the resident birds before migration gets under way.

Although there are dozens of brands of wood duck calls on the market, they're mostly made to lure hunters rather than ducks. Woodies seldom respond to a call when they're on the wing. And decoys aren't all that effective either because woodies fly so fast and through such heavy forest cover that they rarely see decoys in time to react to them.

Pass shooting is the best way to hunt wood ducks, and for this, you need a partner. First, get there early. Woodies fly best at first light, and the legal 30 minutes of shooting time before sunrise is going to provide you with 90 percent of your opportunity for the day.

In flooded woods, find an opening where a tree has fallen and left a hole in the canopy. Stand in the middle of it with your hunting partner, facing in opposite directions. Be ready; they come fast. Sometimes the hens will give you a heads-up with that squeaky call of theirs, but don't hang your hat on it. Depend on your eyes, not your ears.

If you don't have flooded woods handy or for some reason don't want to hunt there, wooded creeks, bayous, sloughs and small rivers serve as flyways for wood ducks. Hunt with a buddy, set up where you have a good view both upstream and down, and you can have that same hot 30 minutes of pre-sunrise action. It's not a bad idea, if you don't have a good retriever, to hunt from a boat tied off to a tree or bush away from the bank, both to provide better visibility and to help you retrieve downed birds easier. Wear camo clothing and cover any bright objects in the boat (outboard motor, gas can) with camo cloth, burlap or vegetation, and sit still until it's time to shoot.

Floating a stream in a canoe and jump-shooting wood ducks is also an effective wood duck technique on small, brushy streams, and unlike pass shooting, jump-shooting can provide action at any time of day. Unlike pass shooting from a boat, with jump-shooting, you don't necessarily need a camouflaged canoe – although having one certainly doesn't hurt your chances.

One person paddles while the other sits in the bow with shotgun ready for action. Wood ducks almost invariably shriek their warning call when they flush, giving the shooter time to at least raise his gun before they're out of range. It's illegal to shoot from a boat that's being propelled by a motor, though, either electric or gasoline, so you must paddle while actually hunting. That's why a canoe is better suited for this activity.

One final productive technique is waiting near a roosting area and taking wood ducks as they funnel in for the night. Wood ducks often congregate in staggering numbers in some wooded sloughs in the South, and a hunt here can provide fast action without causing any harm to the roost. The problem is, unless it's cloudy, most of the birds won't come in until after legal shooting hours end at sunset.

However you do it, hunting wood ducks is worth the effort. It's a celebration of sorts to be able to take legal birds from a population that was once thought to be headed the way of the passenger pigeon, especially birds as beautiful as a fully-feathered drake wood duck. And beyond their beauty on the hand and in the hand, they're one of the best-tasting ducks on the dinner plate.

• • •

Between the day Dad and I saw that first pair of woodies and the end of his hunting career, a span of more than three decades, we shared many flooded-timber duck hunts. We bagged more than a few wood ducks after they once again became legal game. And every single time my Dad killed a wood duck in my presence, he'd smooth its feathers and hold it up for my inspection in such a way that the sunlight would catch it just right.

"Remember that day?" he'd ask, stroking the feathers of a bird the color of autumn.

I did. I still do.

Chapter 10

The Buck That Killed Widow Flaherty

By Larry Dablemont

It's a wonder the widow would even speak to me, the way I loved to hunt. She hated hunters. But I was only 19 years old, and she had been around me since I was just a little boy. My mom was like a daughter she never had and the widow Flaherty was always welcome at our little country home, only a couple of miles down the road. Mom said she was married when she was very young, and had a son who was gone off at a young age, something like her husband.

She had been alone since then, and maybe she couldn't be blamed for disliking men so much. She was Scotch-Irish and took her maiden name back after her husband ran out on her. She dropped the "O" in O'Flaherty and no one seemed to remember her first name. Everyone called her "Widow Flaherty" even though no one knew for sure her husband was dead. She had always made it plain that if he ever came back, he would be!

The widow Flaherty was about 84 years old back then, but she still had some red mixed in with her gray hair and fire in her eyes. She was quick to tell you what she thought. She didn't think much of Claude Lawry, her neighbor, who was a quail hunter. The widow owned 80 acres that had plenty of quail because it hadn't been farmed much. Half of it was big timber and half of it had grown up in weeds and sumac and cedar and sassafras saplings.

Claude Lawry had 200 acres and four or five bird dogs and he'd walk the property line that divided them with a hungry look on his face. The widow had been known to sit on that fence line with her old shotgun on a November Saturday morning daring one of those valuable English setters to stray over on her place.

It all went back to the time when Lawry killed a couple of stray cats, which he always called "quail killers". The widow Flaherty had an old barn where she had some chickens and old mouse-chasing cats and she never did figure that her cats could be a threat to quail and songbirds. After all, they didn't eat chickens.

She loved birds and rabbits and had plenty of them around her place. She also had lots of deer and that's where I came in that November day.

On the widow Flaherty's place was a thicket next to the big timber where a huge buck lived, a buck with antlers like the television antennae on one of those houses in town, soaring high into the sky and branching out in all directions.

I wasn't the only man in the world that the widow would tolerate. There was also old Kemp Anderson, who had saved the widow's life once by pulling her 1959 Chevy out of the ditch in a snowstorm, and giving her a good milk cow. Rumor had it that old Kemp and the widow Flaherty were awful, awful, good friends if you know what I mean.

He stayed on her good side over the years by promising her he'd whale the stuffing out of Claude Lawry if he ever shot one her cats or one of her quail. Kemp swore to the widow that the evil quail-shootin', cat-hatin' Claude Lawry was his mortal enemy. But when I'd see Kemp and Mr. Lawry in the pool hall, they'd always seem to be the best of friends.

Thankfully, old Kemp was my friend too, on account of when I was a little boy he and my grandpa would take me fishing and squirrel hunting and the like. He made it known to me that I should never let the widow know he was a hunter, and he always told her when he brought her a fresh-caught batch of catfish or perch, that I had helped.

I couldn't ask the widow Flaherty to let me hunt deer on her place, but old Kemp Anderson could, and he told me I could figure on being in a tree stand at daylight on opening day right next to that thicket, using his old "thutty-thutty" Winchester, with the widow's blessing.

It wasn't an easy thing to do, but Kemp brought the widow a load of kindlin' wood for her cook stove and ate a batch of her apple cobbler, claiming it was the best he'd ever had. And while they were sitting there at her kitchen table drinking coffee, Kemp got to talking about what a rough time November was for female deer and fawns.

He told her about the big buck on the back reaches of her 80 acres and how he had seen him chasing does, and what his intentions were. He said the thing that bothered him was seeing a young doe running from that buck, maybe half his size, and struggling to stay out ahead, most likely forced in time to go over onto Claude Lawry's place just to get away. He shook his head and said he hated to see that because does and fawns weren't safe there when deer season opened. Kemp said he knew there would be a bunch of Lawry's town buddies out there, bankers and lawyers and such, who would shoot a doe or a yearling at the drop of a hat and tie them over the hood of their cars and drive up and down Main Street, smoking cigars and braggin' about their kills.

He had the widow mad enough to chew the bark off a locust tree, and yet he coaxed a tear or two from her eyes with the plight of those poor does, not wanting to leave the safety of the widow's 80 acres, but left to face the raging hormones of that monstrous, adulterous buck if they didn't.

And that's where I came in. Kemp said that I was the kind of young hunter who could be counted on never to kill a pretty, graceful, little doe and the answer to the problem might be letting me hunt, under his guidance of course, hoping I could rid the land of that testosterone-laced, fourteen-point antlered menace.

He went on too, about how much some of the poor neighbors in the community could use the meat, ground up into hamburger, and doled out by one of the finest young men he ever knew...me. It was when he compared that big buck to Claude Lawry himself, that the widow Flaherty agreed to let me go out and hunt him down and shoot him like the lecherous woman-chasing ogre he was.

I had never been deer hunting before. There was a lot of preparation involved. Kemp and I went out two weeks before the season opened and put up a little platform about eight feet off the ground in the forks of a pair of limbs in a big white oak, not 40 yards from a heavily used trail next to a persimmon grove. There were trees along that trail six inches in diameter with all the bark rubbed off and Kemp said that was where that big buck had been rubbing the velvet off his antlers a month and a half ago.

But what really got him excited was a place he called a "scrape," underneath the overhanging limbs of a pin oak tree at the edge of the little clearing. The ends of the limbs were broken here and there, and underneath it was a big scraped out area of bare earth, where the buck would leave his scent. The old man told me how the deer would urinate down the glands on the inside of their back legs to leave that powerful scent.

Kemp taught me a lot about deer that day, and what to expect from that buck. He didn't do any work on the stand, he just told me how to do it. I nailed some heavy boards across three big oak limbs seven or eight feet off the ground, and hung a rope down to hoist up my rifle and pack, then leaned an old wooden ladder Kemp had brought along up against the tree.

The old hunter told me that deer might notice something different for a while, but they'd get used to it. He said it was important to always set up your stand away from trails and scrapes, so it wasn't too obtrusive, and he said it was also important to consider normal wind direction. But he said that by getting up off the ground in a tree stand, you keep your scent from being as easy to detect.

That old man knew what he was doing. He'd already taught me a lot about fishing and hunting, so I wasn't exactly a stranger to the woods. His rifle, the ".30-30" Winchester, was easy to shoot and I could hit a coffee can at 40 yards every time, even with the wallop it gave me when I fired it. Kemp said I would learn there was a big difference in shooting deer and shooting coffee cans.

I went to her house to thank her, and the widow gave me a big hug. "You shoot that darned bully if you see him," she told me, "but don't you dare shoot one of those little females. They've had a rough time of it, running from that one with the big horns. I don't know why it is that from some cute little fawn, there grows a big old horny animal like they turn into."

I told her that I would never let something like that happen to me, knowing she was remembering those years when I, as a little boy, ate cookies with milk at her kitchen table. But I don't know if I convinced her as I stood nearly a head higher than she. Then she looked at me and squinted her eyes scrunched up her face, to let me know the seriousness of what she was about to say. "Boy, if you was to see that no-good Claude Lawry out there or any of his worthless runnin' buddies, I'd hate to see you shoot 'em, but I'd shore be tickled if you at least would shoot at 'em!"

I couldn't wait to go deer hunting for the very first time. Some of the friends my age I knew, who were farm boys, had already killed two or three deer. Kemp said it was surely my good luck, having a place like widow Flaherty's place to hunt. It was Kemp's good fortune to get to go along, but he intended to hunt on the other corner of her place with a shotgun and slugs, since I was using his .30-30 Winchester.

• • •

It was cold and cloudy before daylight that opening morning of the deer season in 1968. I sat there in that little treestand platform waiting for the dawn, making out shapes around me in the earliest gray light.

Some little birds flitted around in the branches close to me and I thought I made out the dark shadows of three raccoons passing only a few yards beneath me.

And then it was fully light and the sun shined through the clouds for an hour or so. I strained my eyes and ears and shook with anticipation and cold. There were a couple of rifle shots early, off in the distance, but I must have been there two hours without any hint of a deer to excite me further. Then all of a sudden, there were two does out before me, leisurely walking along the trail leading out of the persimmon and sumac thickets into the woods. And as my heartbeat quickened just looking at those beautiful creatures, I knew that if I shot one, the widow Flaherty would surely shoot me.

My heartbeat went from 90 miles an hour to a 120, as I caught a glimpse of ivory-colored antlers about 50 yards behind the does. It was a big buck, stepping out a lot like Marshal Dillon did when he entered the Long Branch, head high, looking all around, suspecting trouble. He was headed for that scrape, and I just knew it was him, that giant buck that we had been seeing, the monster patriarch of the forest.

I couldn't really count points on his antlers, they were just big and broad, and his ears were up around them. He heard me cock the hammer on the rifle. He stopped in his tracks, and I tried to aim at his heart, as Kemp had told me to do. But, aiming a rifle is hard to do when violently shaking.

I think I jerked the trigger rather than squeezing it the way I had been taught. The roar of the Winchester broke the peaceful morning silence, and the recoil I had felt while practicing wasn't even there.

I saw the buck leap high and disappear into the woods and I knew I must have missed. In all my life, I never felt worse that I did right then. I felt worse than I did that time when on my very first date with Donna McKinney I let the car door swing back and hit her and broke the zipper on her skirt.

Well, you get the picture. I felt awful. I had had my chance and blown it. I was a failure as a hunter, an all around disappointment for the widow Flaherty and old man Anderson.

Kemp wasn't long getting there. He steadied the old ladder whilst I climbed down and I told him I had bungled the whole thing because of buck fever.

We went over to the scrape and I saw him smile, pointing his old shotgun at the trail. "Might as well learn to follow a blood trail, boy," he told me. I looked and I couldn't believe my eyes. There were bright splotches of red amongst the leaves.

We followed that trail and there the buck lay, dead as a hammer. His antlers spread high above the ground, and looked massive. It was an eight-pointer and definitely not the big fourteen-point boss buck that Kemp had been seeing. To me he was the biggest buck in the world and the widow Flaherty was pleased because Kemp told her my buck was chasing two does when I shot him.

I've killed a lot of deer since then and to tell the truth I'd rather hunt ducks or pheasants or quail. If the widow Flaherty heard me say that, she'd be awful disappointed in me. She went on to her eternal reward only a month or so after my first deer hunt in a tragic accident that I always sort of thought was my fault.

Kemp came to me that December morning with tears streaming down his face and told me she had been found out on her place. Apparently, she had been driving her old tractor, the one with really poor brakes, holding her old shotgun across her lap, when she hit a big tree going full blast.

There was a lot of head shaking about that. An 84-year-old widow out on a tractor, clutching a shotgun. Kemp figured she had seen that big old buck chasing a doe and was trying to run him down and shoot him, but I hope not. It eases my conscience to think maybe she was just out looking for Claude Lawry and his bird dogs.

I was a pall-bearer at her funeral, and it was a week later when a town lawyer came to our place and told me the widow had left everything to me via her legally drawn-up will. No one seemed to know where her son was anyway, so I guess he didn't mind. I still live on the old place and keep it much like it was, with a few cattle. But still, the oaks and hickories on the back of the place stand tall and the persimmons are sweet by deer season every year.

Claude Lawry turned out to be an awfully fine neighbor and on occasion I hunted quail with him until they got to be where there wasn't hardly any to be found. He and Kemp are both gone now and I tell my grandsons about them, and the widow Flaherty. I make her out to be a little sweeter than she was perhaps, but what the heck, my memory isn't as good anymore.

I'm going to set up one of those funny store-bought deer stands along a deer trail near where I killed my first buck, and take my oldest grandson deer hunting there this year. He's already been practicing with the "thutty-

thutty" Winchester that old Kemp left me! I've told him we're after that big old buck that's been out there chasing does and scaring fawns the same one that killed the widow Flaherty back in the winter of '68.

Chapter 11

The Old Red Oak

By Jim Spencer

It wasn't a particularly good day for squirrel hunting, but that didn't make much difference to the boy. When you are 13 and have in your possession a nearly full box of .22 bullets, with a whole weekend stretching out in front of you to hunt and mess around in the woods...well.

Things like a little wind and rain don't bother you too much.

On second thought, it wasn't a particularly bad day for squirrel hunting, either. It had rained hard the night before, and the heavy ground cover of oak and hickory leaves was soggy and quiet. There would be little problem sneaking up on squirrels.

If he could find them. The wind was moving the treetops quite a bit, which is always problematic for hunting squirrels, and the sky was still heavily overcast so visibility wasn't at its best. Rain showers were still breaking out in fits and starts, and every passing shower got the boy a little wetter, a little colder.

The squirrels were out, though, apparently resigned to the weather, and between rain showers the boy had managed to bag three, rib-caging every one of them because his grandfather liked squirrel brains and didn't want them shot in the head. Now, waiting out yet another shower underneath the leaning trunk of a massive old sycamore, the boy watched two young gray squirrels playing on the trunk of an equally large red oak 50 yards away.

The rain ended, finally, but by then the squirrels had vanished. The boy eased in the direction of the red oak anyway, reasoning that was as good a direction as any.

It was a good choice. He hadn't covered half the distance to the tree when the two squirrels ringed the tree again, chasing each other with the careless, youthful abandon which often prevents young squirrels from becoming old squirrels.

That was how it worked out for these two unfortunates. The boy slipped within 50 feet of the red oak before stopping beside another tree, braced the bolt-action .22 rifle against its trunk, and waited patiently for the chance to shoot. Meanwhile, the two squirrels continued to chase one another around in the old red oak.

The opportunity came, as the boy knew it would. One of the squirrels darted into a hole and turned around to stick his head back out, blocking his litter-mate's entrance. The littermate stopped, nose to nose with his brother, stretching out full length against the wet, almost-black bark of the tree.

The little 41-grain bullet took the bushytail squarely between the shoulder blades, breaking his spine and dead-centering his tiny heart. He peeled backwards off the tree and, dead in the air, dropped to the ground. The other squirrel pulled back into the hole while the boy reloaded the single-shot rifle. Within seconds he was back, peering down to see what had become of his sibling. He eased out of the hole onto the tree trunk, and when he was all the way out the boy squeezed off another shot. Now there were two dead squirrels at the base of the tree.

The boy reloaded again and held his ground, having learned from past experience this tactic often results in additional quick kills. But he saw nothing else, and when he heard a squirrel begin to bark 100 yards away through the woods, he decided to move that way.

Again, it was a wise decision. There were three more squirrels in the same cluster of trees with the one that was barking, and through devious sneaking and waiting out two hide-and-seek squirrels that didn't have enough patience to stay hidden, the boy killed three of the four. When the third one hit the ground, the boy, who had for the past three hours made absolutely no unnecessary sound or movement, let out a yip of excitement and ran to pick up the squirrel. This particular limb-gripper was just like any other, but special nonetheless; it was the final one of a limit of eight, and this rainy morning was the first day the boy had ever reached that milestone.

The final three squirrels, when added to the forked-stick game carrier the boy was stringing his kill on, had a satisfying heft. Carrying the squirrels like a stringer of fish, the boy shouldered his rifle and started through the dripping woods toward the camp.

His grandfather was already there, trying to encourage the reluctant flames in the soggy fire pit, and that made the boy's triumphant arrival all the better. No hunter ever brought in his morning's kill with more pride – or with more studied casualness – than did the boy as he sauntered into camp.

The grandfather, leaning over the smoking fire to reach for the blackened old coffee percolator, assessed the situation quickly. Seeing the hefty bundle of squirrels and the desperately nonchalant look on his grandson's face, he put two and two together.

"How many?" the old man asked. He already knew the answer, but he also knew the boy needed him to ask.

The boy tossed his squirrels onto the ground beside his grandfather's well-worn canvas hunting coat, a coat from which several squirrel tails were protruding.

"Oh, I think I got a limit," he answered, struggling to sound slightly bored by it all. "How about you?"

"Same as you," said the grandfather, carefully avoiding mention of the fact that he'd been back in camp for an hour and a half. He poured steaming black coffee in two heavy white mugs, then held one of them out to the boy.

Grandfather and grandson locked eyes over their raised coffee mugs, and before either took a drink, they both smiled.

• • •

The morning was clear and crisp. The boy, now grown, led his son through the woods and stopped by the familiar leaning sycamore to wait for daylight. The weight of 26 additional winters and the storms of 26 additional springs had broken a few more limbs out of the top of the old hulk, but it was still easily recognizable, and it would still provide shelter in the event of a rainstorm. The man hadn't been to the spot in more than 10 years, but he'd have known the tree anywhere.

He and the boy spoke in whispers as they waited for the light to come. "Used to be lots of squirrels in this area," the man said. "We ought to be able to kill one or two here. This is where I got my first limit, when I was the same age you are now."

The boy, holding the same single-shot .22 with which the man had done the deed so many years ago, seemed slightly bored. He respected his father and loved him very much, but athletics was his area of interest and he simply couldn't generate much enthusiasm for outdoor activities like hunting and fishing. He had come on this weekend squirrel hunting/camping trip only because he knew how badly his father wanted him to.

The father knew this, too, but hoped against hope he'd somehow be able to light that spark. He tried hard not to show his disappointment that his son had little interest in the outdoors, but he wasn't always successful. And every time he let his feelings show, both he and the boy felt guilty about it afterwards.

Daylight came, finally, and the squirrels woke up. The man saw the first one as it poked its head out of the same hole in the old red oak that had been blocked a quarter-century earlier by one of a pair of young squirrels.

How many squirrels, the man wondered idly, have stuck their heads out of that hole between that day and this one?

"There he is, Son," the man whispered as the squirrel came out of the hole and ran up into the crown of the red oak. "Let's get a little closer."

They moved ahead cautiously, stopping occasionally to relocate the squirrel, and when they reached the same tree the man had used for a rifle rest on that long-ago rainy morning they stopped again. The boy leaned against the tree and waited.

Maybe he wasn't very interested in hunting, but the boy was an excellent shot. The same athletic ability which allowed him to excel in sports gave him hand-eye coordination that far exceeded his years. The squirrel was moving rapidly down a limb when the boy aimed and fired before his father could tell him to wait for a better chance. But a better chance wasn't needed. The squirrel pitched out of the tree, drilled through the head.

Fifteen minutes later, without moving from that spot, they boy had shot four more times and killed four more squirrels. After dropping the last one, he turned and whispered to his father, "Want to go back to camp? I'm getting a little hungry."

• • •

Funny how different people have different ideas about what's enjoyable and what's not, thought the old man, standing beside his grandson underneath the leaning sycamore snag. His dad still doesn't care anything about hunting and not much about fishing, but this boy took to it like a squirrel takes to a hole in an old red oak.

The old man kept sneaking glances at the boy, who was eagerly and impatiently waiting for the rain shower to end so he and Grandpa could get on with the hunt. The boy was 10 now, and though he had been on several squirrel hunting trips with his grandfather, he had never been allowed to carry a gun. Until today.

And truly, it was strange. Two generations, 50 years, separated the old man from his grandson, but it was as though there was no age difference at all. The old man and the boy were great friends, fishing or hunting together nearly every weekend and working on various outdoor projects – building wood duck and squirrel boxes, planting food plots for deer and turkeys – between outings.

Nature over nurture for sure, thought the old man. At least in this case.

This boy was a hunter the minute he was born.

It had been a half-century almost to the day since the old man had huddled underneath this same sycamore, waiting for the rain to stop with the same eagerness his grandson now displayed. The old tree had lost nearly all its limbs now and was nothing more than a hollow shell, stubbornly holding its ground and resisting the elements to the end. But it was still standing, and it was still a good place to get out of the rain.

The red oak den tree was still there, too, although it too was showing definite signs of wear and tear. Lightning and wind had destroyed its topmost branches, and the heart-rot which had caused the loggers to leave it standing a century ago had now advanced to the point the old man was surprised the tree was still alive. Yet there it still was, home for squirrels, coons and other woodland dwellers. Even the old hole where the two young squirrels had played was still there, although woodpeckers or something had enlarged the opening.

The old man hunched his shoulders to ward off the chill and pulled farther into his grandfather's old canvas hunting coat, like a terrapin retreating into its shell. It was the same coat that had been laying by the campfire 50 years ago, when the old man had brought in his first limit of squirrels. He'd rescued the bloodstained, smelly old relic many years ago, digging it out of the throw-away pile his grandmother was making the week after the funeral. She'd fussed at him for wanting to keep such a disreputable garment, but he'd held firm.

It would be too much to hope for to see a squirrel stick his head out of that hole, the old man thought. Still, he gazed steadily at the dark opening, as if willing a squirrel to appear there.

When one actually did, the old man thought he was imagining it. But no, there he was, sticking his head out and, like the old man and the boy, waiting for the rain to end so he could get about his squirrelly business.

"There he is, Son," the old man said. "He's got his head stuck out of a hole in that big tree."

"I see him, Grandpa!" whispered the boy. "Can I shoot him now?" The boy started raising the little bolt-action .22 toward his shoulder.

"Not yet. He'll fall back in the hole if you do. When he comes all the way out we'll get a little closer."

The rain stopped and the squirrel came out of the hole, disappearing into the ragged crown of the old red oak. The two hunters, young and not-so-young, slipped closer. They stopped beside the faithful rest tree where the old man had stopped so long ago. It too was a red oak, and was a much

bigger tree now, tall and straight, a beautiful specimen. The old man sadly noticed it was marked with a slash of orange spray paint, showing it had been selected for cutting.

It was still here for today, though, and for that the old man was thankful. He and the boy stood beside the clean, straight trunk, and the old man whispered instructions. "Brace your rifle against this tree. When he stops moving around, shoot him."

The squirrel was rummaging around in the thick leaves in the top of the tree, searching for an acorn. Soon he found one, gathered it in and ran out onto a big bare limb to gnaw it open and breakfast on its bitter orange meat. As the sat on his haunches to cut the acorn, the boy took careful aim and squeezed the trigger of the scarred old rifle.

The old man heard the hollow *plock!* of the slow-moving bullet hitting its target just before he saw the squirrel wilt and topple off the limb. He didn't realize he'd been holding his breath until it left his lungs with an audible *whoosh!*

"I got him, Pawpaw, I got him!" yelled the boy. He was off and running even before the squirrel had hit the ground. The old man leaned against the orange-fouled bark and watched his grandson retrieve his first squirrel, thinking back to a long-ago day when another boy had run to pick up another squirrel in the same scope of woods. Somehow, that day didn't seem so far away. Who knows where the years go?

The loggers would be coming soon, the old man knew, and for a few years this section of forest was going to look a little ragged. But they wouldn't be cutting the old sycamore snag or the old red oak den tree. The first would continue to provide a place for hunters to get out of the rain while the second kept on serving as home base for succeeding generations of squirrels. And some day, maybe the boy who was now proudly carrying a dead squirrel to show it to his grandfather would bring his own son or grandson to this very spot and watch history repeat itself.

It's a nice thing to think about, anyway, the old man thought, fingering the worn canvas of his grandfather's coat. Maybe it's really true that some things never change.

Chapter 12

Legend of the Flying Raccoon

By Larry Dablemont

Coon hunters lamented the fact that there weren't many raccoons in my part of the country, back home in the hills of the Big Piney when I was just a boy. In my dad's pool hall where I worked after school, they talked about the time when a good coon hunter could darn near make a year's wages during a couple of winter months with a fair coon hound or two. In fact, I guess there was a time back there when a top-notch coonhound was worth a week's wages, 20 dollars or close to it. And that's why it hurt when you lost a coon-dog like Lumas Moore did that fall. I had never seen one of the front bench regulars come right out and cry, but that Saturday night after they had the funeral, they were all sittin' there on the front bench in the pool hall talking about his deceased hound, Old Rudd, and Lumas was reduced to tears.

What had happened was, Lumas was hunting over on the headwaters of the Big Piney, where the railroad ran through that section of the Ozarks, and a big old boar coon ran up on the tracks where a long trestle crossed the creek and decided to put up a stand there with a locomotive bearin' down on 'em. Old Rudd, out in front and leading the pack, caught up to that big old wise coon and they said you could hear 'em both, carryin' on with a tremendous fight, the old hound bawlin' and that coon squealin' and that train engine a-howlin'. And at the last minute the darned coon jumped off that trestle into the creek below and the old hound was just too slow to get out of the way.

Lumas said he wasn't so much tore up from losin' his old dog as he was knowin' that hound died thinkin' it was the coon that done it. That was of course, the worst thing that could happen to a coonhound.

About that time, as I remember it, there was talk of a legendary coon which lived on the west side of the Piney not far from the Cantrell Eddy Bluff just above Boiling Springs, which Bill Stalder reckoned would have had a hide big enough to cover a car hood, maybe worth 15 dollars. Maybe it was the same one that kilt Lumas Moore's hound and maybe it wasn't, but he was a smart old coon.

Jim Splechter said he knowed of him from a cousin who had trapped him once, well up the little creek that runs in at the head of the Blue Hole, and that the old coon had chewed through the trap chain, swum the river with the trap and pried it loose on an iron fence post. Jim swears he saw the trap, and one of the steel jaws was bent.

In time, word got around that there was a special raccoon on the lower Big Piney, and if your hounds met up with him, you might lose a hound. Farley Stogsdill did in fact, lose a hound in the early winter when that monster coon lured his whole pack into the stretch of deep shoal above the Boiling Springs crossing, and took 'em all on. Eventually the old boar coon swam to his safety, but he left a drowned hound behind him.

So several hunters got together and went after him, and that's when it got way past the responsible reporting stage that us modern day journalists insist on.

It was said that seven hounds treed the big old outlaw coon in a huge sycamore growing up at the base of a bluff, and when the hunters arrived they saw him leave the high branches and set sail for the other side of the river as if he had wings. Both Mort Thrasher and Charlie Suggs were there that night, and both of 'em swore, when they got back to the front bench in the pool hall, that the coon was at least ten pounds bigger than any they had ever seen, and he could fly! That's right, they swore he flew across that river just like he was half eagle. Bill Stalder never bought the story. He said Charlie and Mort both took a nip of the same moonshine that Charlie made on occasion in the old Sweet 'Tater Cave, and that night they had nipped a great deal of it. He figured that the dogs had treed a coon along that bluff, and a wild turkey had been roosting in it and flew out across the river in the dim light of their carbide lights and was mistook for an airborne coon. Whatever happened, it gave rise to the story of the Big Piney's flying coon, and soon it was took up and spread by normally regular kinds of folks who went to church and told the truth 90 percent of the time. The Lurton brothers, gigging one night in January, came in the pool hall wild- eyed and excited and swore that the huge coon had flown down off of the bluff, landed in their boat, growled at 'em and flew off with a great flapping of wings.

A week later, some backwoods preacher tried to get his insurance company to pay for a new-born calf that he claimed was picked up and carried away in the moonlight by a flying furred creature that he said appeared to have a long ringed tail and a mask.

So by spring, the word was out, and the flying coon was so well known that folks in our little town were expecting an increase in summer tourism just because of his notoriety. But such was not to be.

Before daylight one Saturday morning in May, the old raccoon tried to cross the highway in front of Ransom Odle's barn just west of Bucyrus, and he was squashed flatter than a soft-shelled turtle by a humongous log truck with dual wheels.

I had opened the pool hall that morning with Grandpa McNew, and I suppose that by eight o'clock three or four different members of the front bench regulars had reported it, that big old flat raccoon there on the highway with two black wings sticking up, one flapping back and forth in the wind created by the wake of passing motorists. Sure enough, it was a raccoon with wings!

So I could let it go at that, and it would make a heckuva story. Must have been 30 or 40 coon hunters and hound men from the Big Piney country drove out there when they got the word, and they'd get out and gawk at that smeared-all-over-the-highway raccoon with those two black wings, holding their noses and watching for any more logging trucks which might be coming along. It was a fairly hot day for May, and I don't have to describe what happens when something is right smack in the east-bound lane of Hwy 17 when there's been a lot of Saturday morning traffic. He wasn't much fit for taxidermy.

The deputy sheriff, receiving the word of the potential for an accident, went out there with a big old scoop shovel and got rid of the evidence by noon. There were some who said his actions alone cost the county sheriff some votes by next election. What became of that splattered, flattened raccoon left-over I do not know, but you couldn't doubt so many witnesses. It was a great big one, they all said, and it had black wings in the middle of its back.

But I reckon it is time to tell it all, and so here I am, 40 years later, breaking the silence to ruin the legend. And so here is the rest of the story:

It was the next fall, when I rode my bicycle up to Ransom Odle's place to get a kitten for one of my little sisters, and remarked about the flying coon that had brought fame to his region.

Ransom uttered an expletive and pointed to all those chickens out in his lot behind the house. "I plucked and cleaned four or five last May, and sold some of 'em and et another one. There was a big old rooster that had got sort of belligerent and flogged one of my grandkids, so I chopped off his onery head and just skinned him too, knowin' he'd be too tough for anything but stew." Ransom paused to cut loose a string of tobacco juice, and I waited, somewhat puzzled in my youthful and confused state.

"I threw his hide out there behind the barn, the old farmer continued, and that old coon snuck in there in the night and was draggin' that rooster skin back to the woods across the road. Reckon he had it sort of slung across his back when that big old truck came along, and that's the way folks found 'im,"

I kind of was stunned, the way you feel when you find out the Easter bunny doesn't really lay all those eggs. But I kept it to myself all these years, and finally it has just got to where it is more than I can bear, holdin' in a secret of that caliber.

So now you know, and if you pass through Texas County some day and stop to have a soda pop at some little country store, and some old timer there is talkin' about rememberin' the time he seen a monstrous coon fly across the road in front of him on a cold moonlit night, you don't have to wonder. Just don't argue about it, smile and go on and remember that it isn't so much an outright lie as it is a situation created by odd circumstance. Nope, there really never was a raccoon that flew...but as to the story of that flying saucer that lit in the alley behind the pool hall in the summer of 1963, I was there that night. I saw that with my own eyes!

Chapter 13

The Loaner Gun

By Jim Spencer

April 23, 1993, hot, clear, muggy. It's my first Rio Grande turkey hunt. I'm doing it in style, as a guest of Realtree on a 40,000-acre ranch near Alice, Texas. I'm 46, have been chasing turkeys – always Easterns until now – for nearly 20 years, and I'm beginning to think I've learned a few things. Subsequent years will prove me wrong, but those are other stories.

Bill Jordan, Realtree founder and host of the hunt, has sent me into a 2,000-acre section that, as it turns out, is stiff with uneducated, unsophisticated gobblers. In the first 90 minutes I've called seven longbeards into range. So far I've let them all walk; hunts like this are beyond my ken, and I'm in no hurry for it to end.

After Number Seven walks away puzzled but unscathed, I move toward a bird I've been hearing for a while now. He's not far away, but he's on the far side of a mesquite thicket and I'm not eager to fight my way through it. But I discover as I get closer I can get within 100 yards without entering the thick stuff. I take advantage of the situation, carefully choose a set-up, get everything ready, and hit him hard with a box call. He cuts my yelps with an equally hard double gobble. Thirty seconds later he gobbles again, much closer.

It's fortunate I got ready before calling, because mere seconds later I see his feet rapidly approaching along a deer trail through the thicket. I have barely enough time to shift my gun barrel when he steps into the open at 15 yards and comes to an erect stop. He looks five feet tall as I watch him over the gun barrel.

The gobbler is in full sunlight, I am in deep shadow. Nothing separates us but air. He is mine whenever I want him, but as mentioned, I'm in no hurry for it to end. I look him over, snood to toenails. His head and neck display the fiery red and almost startling white all turkey hunters long to see, his bluish caruncles all but swallowed by the pale surrounding skin. The flat place below each eye is a strange but beautiful amalgam of iridescent red and maroon I've never seen before on a gobbler. His beard is thick, full, odd-looking; I suspect a double. His breast feathers are dark as a cave, but they cast a metallic sheen like oil on still water. His spurs make me gasp; at 15 yards, in full sunlight, they stand out against the white dirt path like tapered ice picks.

He is, in short, magnificent.

It flashes through my brain that he is almost too fine a bird to kill, but the thought leaves as quick as it came. Pass this one up? Fat chance. There is no denying Longbeard Number Eight.

I must have snickered or snorted or emitted some other dismissive sound when I was having that ridiculous catch-and-release thought, because just then the gobbler did the trademark wing-shuffle, turned and took the first step back along the deer trail that would take him quickly out of sight. I didn't let him take the second.

My double-beard suspicion had been wrong. He had three. Back at camp, he weighed 22 pounds, impressive for a south Texas Rio. His beards measured 10-1/2, 8-1/2 and 6-1/2 inches; his spurs were twin 1-3/8-inch daggers.

This was before Realtree's partnership with Remington, and the gun *du jour* was a Mossberg 835. This was the first commercially available shotgun chambered for 3-1/2-inch loads, and the Realtree folks had several 835s on loan that spring, all in original Realtree camo. The next day I killed a second good longbeard with that gun, this one at more than three times the range of the first, and I fell in love with that ugly, stubby, mule-kicking, turkey-stomping 835.

At the end of the hunt I asked Bill if I could buy the gun. He said okay, but he needed it for several other hunts that spring and told me to remind him after the season and he'd sell it to me. I did, but Bill didn't sell it to me. He sent it to me as a gift, and for more than a decade afterwards it was my turkey gun. It accounted for an impressive number of turkeys as I used it in multiple states each spring.

• • •

Fast forward a quarter-century. The 835 has been retired for close to 15 years. The thing kicks like a howitzer, and eventually I laid it down in favor of other shot launchers that didn't give me a headache with every trigger pull.

It was a week before the 2018 turkey season. We were standing in the road in front of my rural home comparing scouting notes: neighbor Patrick, his teenaged son Clayton, me. I asked Clayton what gun he hunted with.

"This year I'll be using my trap gun," said Clayton, who competed on his high school shooting team. "It's an H&R trap model. But I'm saving up to buy a Mossberg 835. I won't have it this season, but next year I will."

"Wait a minute," I said, and went into the house, returned with the well-used Bill Jordan 835 and a box of 3-1/2-inch turkey loads. "Why don't you shoot this one this spring? Make sure it's really what you want." I told him how I'd come to own the gun, and his eyes widened at Bill Jordan's name. Bill was one of his heroes. Clayton took the gun in both hands, holding it as if it was some precious artifact. Which, of course, it was.

• • •

After the season ended Clayton brought the 835 back, along with seven shells from the 10-pack box. He'd wisely burned one shell checking pattern and point of impact. With the other two, he'd taken two big gobblers at 40-plus yards. Both were no-flop, dead-right-there kills.

"I sure appreciate it," he said, reluctantly handing me the 835. "I'm absolutely sure I want one now."

"Well, Clayton," I said, "if someone was to give you a gun like this, do you think you could use it for a few years and then give it to somebody else who was young and just getting started in turkey hunting?"

"Well, yeah," Clayton said, a little puzzled. "I guess I could."

I handed the gun back. "Then do it. This old gun is yours. It doesn't have to be anytime soon, but you have to promise me you'll give it to some young hunter you think is worthy and who'll also agree to pass it on to someone else when the right time comes."

There are moments you remember. We all have them, freeze-frame, clear as crystal, on instant recall. One of mine, now, is the expression on that young man's face as he looked first at the gun, then at his dad, then at me. I don't remember his words, but I'll not forget that look.

• • •

Not long after, I was talking to my old friend David Blanton, Bill Jordan's right-hand man at Realtree.

"I love it!" David said. "What's Clayton's address? I'll get Bill to write him a letter about the gun and how he came to give it to you."

And Bill did, even though he got the date wrong by a few years. So now my young friend Clayton has not only a fine turkey buster in his custody, but also a letter of provenance, on Realtree stationery, to support it.

He also bears a solemn and important responsibility. Granted, it's only important to a tiny universe: himself, Bill Jordan, David Blanton and me. But it's no less important because of its narrow scope. As Bill said in his letter: "It's nice to know that after Jim and I are both long gone, that old gun is still going to be killing turkeys, and that we were both links in the chain of its history."

Enjoy your shotgun, Clayton. Use it well and long. But be sure, be very damn sure, that someday you pay it forward.

We need to keep this thing going.

Chapter 14

The Church in the Deer Woods

By Larry Dablemont

C harlie Foyt, Ev Davison, and Alzie Robarts, all staunch members of the pool hall's front bench regulars, went to the same church as I did. In the fall of 1959, I think it was, they had a big meeting with the new preacher to get some things straightened out in our little country church. It was a little church that sat not far from the headwaters of one of the creeks that fed the Big Piney River, nestled in a beautiful little patch of hardwoods up above the creek.

I wouldn't have went to church at all if I hadn't been forced to do it. And I guess maybe Dad wouldn't have gone either if Grandma and Grandpa McNew hadn't forced him to. Grandpa made it part of a loan agreement Dad had to sign when he loaned him 78 dollars to buy an old Ford pickup. Dad went to church for years just because he couldn't get that loan paid off. He'd get it down to 12 or 15 dollars and then something else would come along he had to buy and he'd owe Grandpa another 25 dollars and we'd have to go to church for another year.

So the first 14 or 15 years of my life I went to church fairly regular although on occasion we did miss a Sunday here or there to go hunting or fishing. Dad said my name was on the loan too, but I think he flim-flammed me there. I stood 5 foot 6 inches tall until I was about 17 years old and Dad was 6-3. I wasn't ever very rebellious as a kid, because I never did catch up with him. I grew several inches in college but it came a little late.

I kind of liked going to church because my cousins, Butch, Dave, and Darb went there too, and so did my friends Gary Lawrence and David Fisher. We had a lot of great Sunday afternoons at church dinners and activities which made a couple of hours wasted on Sunday morning seem like a passable sacrifice.

I gave a lot of money to that church over the years, a nickel or so at a time to the Sunday School Class offering plate. And I learned a great deal about life through Bible stories we studied. What happened to Jonah caused me not to swim in deep water for years, and in the seventh grade, enduring a whole year of Mrs. Cranford's math class, I took comfort from the story of Daniel's survival and what Job had went through.

I will always remember the Sunday morning when we studied about Samson slaying the Philistines with the jawbone of an ass. Cousin Darb was only about six at the time, and me and Butch were twice his age, the only time in history you could say that. Eventually, Darwin got within a few years of us, and much bigger than either of us, and he exacted a certain amount of revenge for what we put him through as a little kid.

At home on Sunday morning the McNew boys were helped by their father, Uncle Roy, who was ingrained with a certain amount of irrascalability. No one will ever know what he told Darb about Samson and the Philistines but when our Sunday School teacher asked 10-year-old David Fisher what Samson had done, he had the right answer. "He kilt a bunch of them dad-blamed Phillippistines."

Some of the older girls snickered a little but Mrs. Elliott quietened them with one of those stern over-the-glasses looks. Then she turned and asked Darb what Samson used to slay the Phillistines. He didn't give it a second thought nor a second's hesitation..."He jobbed 'em in the ass!" was his answer, with an air of assertiveness.

It was a small church and there were only three Sunday School classes, all separated by curtains. The laughter went from one to the other and Sunday School class ended early. Uncle Roy laughed the heartiest, in a subdued sort of way.

But all that is neither here nor there. Me and my cousins went to church because we had to, but the front bench regulars, most all of them went to church here and there around our little community and didn't have to. That's why it seemed strange to see them come to the preacher and try to get church services canceled that year on the opening week of deer season.

"It's mostly them city-slickers comin' in here and blastin' away at whatever moves," Charlie began. "We's a figgerin' that there could be danger in it for the women and children if some greenhorn shoots at a deer twixt him an' the church. Logical thing is to call off the church meetin' just that one Sunday, an' then go back to it strong and revigerated the nex' week."

The young preacher was fairly new to our church, and he seemed puzzled. Frankly, I didn't ever think he had what it took to do the job, because he didn't yell much, and he didn't pound on the pulpit hardly at all and he never did point fingers at members of the congregation. If you wanted to sleep, he couldn't hardly even keep you awake. Old Preacher Baker hadn't been like that. He give it a 110 percent every week, fire and brimstone and hell and high water, loud enough to vibrate the stove pipe and scare the field mice out of the cloak room. When Preacher Baker got finished there on Sunday morning, folks went home scared to spit on the sidewalk. Nobody did anything wicked or deceitful 'til Wednesday or Thursday!

But the new preacher was something of a pushover. He was always talking about love and compassion and how Jesus shared bread and fish with folks even though there wasn't enough for everybody, and made it work. He never hardly scared anyone. Suddenly, if you were no-account and worthless, our church was the church for you, because you could get away with anything and not get yelled at on Sunday morning.

Anyway, Alzie picked up on what Charley said about them wild-eyed greenhorn city slicker hunters shooting at whatever moved and allowed as how a .30-30 bullet could travel two miles and still go through a sack of wheat shorts and kill a dog on the other side. He said he heard of it happening in Illinois a year or so before, and Charlie said he remembered reading about it in the Saint Louis Post Dispatch.

Ev Davis said it wasn't just the safety factor. He pointed out that God had said man can't live by bread alone, and that four-day deer season was the only chance for country people to put venison in the freezer. He said Sunday was the best day to hunt because so many city hunters would be worn out and most of 'em headed home on Sunday so's they'd have a day to sober up and get ready to work on Monday.

The young preacher thought about it for a moment, and said he didn't think that kind of decision was his alone to make, but that of the congregation, and many would prefer to let the deer hunters go ahead and miss that one Sunday while those who didn't hunt could attend regular services. He even went so far as to say that he'd ask for special prayer to help Charlie, Ev and Alzie be safe and successful in their hunting.

That wasn't what they wanted to hear! In the pool hall that week, Charlie, the only bachelor of the three, made it plain he had backslid on his religion a mite. He said he had been going to our little country church for nigh onto three years and had been putting a dollar and fifty cents into the offering plate each and every Sunday. He pointed out that he had even backed the preacher on getting the new hymnals. He said he figured he'd be sorely missed if he turned Methodist and that's what he was being pushed into by a preacher who wouldn't consider the needs of his flock.

Charlie had needs all right. He needed that church empty on Sunday morning so he could use the old church outhouse as a tree stand. It sat off into the edge of the woods, overlooking a cedar thicket that would be the logical hiding place of all local deer on the night of the first season, when deer hunters would scare the bejiggers out of them by shooting at every set of antlers and white tail seen anywhere in the open country.

On the second day of the season, the big buck Charlie wanted so badly would surely be in that thicket hunkered down and hard to get to, converted to a nocturnal creature for the next month or better, and if he and Ev and Alzie played their cards right, one of them had a good chance to get him.

But Alzie was pretty much resigned to going to church with his wife Pearline.

Wherever she said he went, he went, most generally. He'd be in church if Pearline was, because she was a foot taller than him, and even though the meek were blessed and in line to inherit the earth, Alzie was too meek to hunt deer on Sunday morning unless Pearline didn't go to church on Sunday morning. There was one chance of that happening, and the preacher had nixed it.

Ev Davis was the smart one. He knew about that big buck and where he stayed. Ev had hunted squirrels in the woods behind the church and some folks thought his squirrel hunting enthusiasm might be the reason the upper window pane in the church outhouse had been cracked by a number six lead shot. Ev figured that with church canceled and Charlie sitting on top of the outhouse from daylight to naptime, he had a good chance of getting that buck. Charlie would take coffee and biscuits and sandwiches and a ladder and a lawn chair, and he'd be late. He'd smell bad, because he only took a bath the last week of each month during the winter, and he'd for sure scare that buck out of that thicket, and Ev would be waiting on the other side, quiet, undetectable and against the wind.

The first Sunday morning of the deer season, Alzie was there singing "Bringing in the Sheaves" in the fourth pew right beside Pearline. Ev was there too, terribly disappointed because he had killed a forkhorn buck down behind his pond on Saturday morning near the salt and mineral block he had put out for his calves. He had nearly fallen off his tractor doing it.

But as the new preacher welcomed visitors and announced that the Thanksgiving dinner was upcoming, there were three great blasts from out in the general direction of the cedar thicket behind the outhouse. Charlie had given up on his idea of using the outhouse for a tree stand, and was sitting on a stump well down in the woods when he spied that big buck, the one every hunter dreams of. He got in a hurry and missed it three times.

Fortunately, those of us in the church could only hear the report of his old .45-70 rifle. We couldn't hear what he said when he was throwing his hat on the ground, nor what he said when he was jumping up and down on it. In the pool hall that week, Charlie was obviously a man who was about to save a dollar and a half a week in church donations. He blamed God for letting him miss that buck. Ev had got his deer, and Alzie killed one on Monday morning, on his way back from taking Pearline to work.

Charlie said he was done with reverence and piousness, he was fixing to cheat on his taxes and lie about every fish he caught from that day forward. God had abandoned him when he needed Him the most, when that big buck was only 60 yards away and his sights were on its brisket.

But there's a happy ending to this story, just like when Jonah said he was finished with going to church himself. In the spring of the following year, Ol' Charlie Foyt was running his trotlines in the Henry Hayes eddy when a sudden storm raised the river and Charlie's boat was swept through a raging shoal and overturned against a snag. Charlie started praying again, as he was being swept downstream toward certain death, and suddenly he seen the arm of an angel extend down toward him in the shape of a stout sycamore limb.

He turned from his evil ways that night and was back in church the next Sunday, from that point on a stalwart in the church, a solid pillar the young preacher could count on for a dollar and a half every week, good times or bad. Charlie became a real inspiration for me and Butch and Dave and Darb especially me. I remember that when he'd miss a crucial shot and lose a close snooker game there in the pool hall, he expressed his disappointment in a much more appropriate manner. He quit shooting snooker for soda pops, and one time when I gave him too much change for a dollar, he gave the extra nickel back to me!

But that's not the happiest part of this story. Oh no, not by a long shot. Charlie Foyt killed a 12 point buck a few years later, just before I went off to college. Up to that time, neither Ev nor Alzie ever got one that big.

Our little country church carried on for quite some time, until eventually most of the old-country folks died off and the kids grew up and went away. But it sits there still today, with the windows boarded up, needing some paint and roof repair. I went past it a year or so ago in the fall, and I couldn't help but think, at the time, what a fine deer stand that old outhouse would still make even yet today.

Author's note...Ninety percent of the above story is about half factual, but some of it is fictitious. It has been so long since some of it actually happened, that I can't really remember what actually didn't. At any rate, please don't tell Uncle Roy about any of this.

Chapter 15

First Trophy

By Jim Spencer

The woods around me were in the middle of the morning shift change. The night prowlers were drifting toward their dens, and the daytime creatures were taking over. A gray-muzzled boar coon, making its way home to some hollow tree in the river bottom, ambled along the draw below me. He passed by so close I could see he had a tattered right ear, souvenir of some long-forgotten battle.

He wasn't in any hurry, and I watched with mild interest as he waddled down the draw and out of sight. I was idly imagining what the other fellow must look like when I heard something to my left, back up the draw in the direction the coon had come from. I cranked my head around slowly, scrutinizing the area, trying to will something to move. Nothing did.

I stayed alert, though. Better hunters than I have learned the hard way that a seasoned, gun-shy old buck can seem to disappear from the face of the earth by doing nothing more elaborate than freezing in place. I'd made that mistake before. I didn't want to make it again now.

I knew there was a big buck in the area; I'd seen him several times during the summer, and his velvet-cloaked antlers were wide and tall even then. If he was coming, I figured he'd do it very cautiously during this early-season, pre-rut time of the fall.

The seconds stretched into minutes. My neck began to ache gently, insistently, but I was sure I'd heard something and I was slow to give up. Five minutes went by, then 10, before I decided nothing was there. I turned my head back to continue watching the downstream end of the ravine...and there stood the old man.

I don't know how he got there without me hearing or seeing him. The woods were as dry as a cactus garden, and the leaves were six rustly inches deep. Still, he came so quietly I never heard a thing, and when I saw him he was no more than 30 yards from me. This was a long time ago, before the days of mandatory hunter orange, and my faded red shirt blended pretty well with the autumn colors in the heavily-leafed treetop I was using for a blind. Apparently he hadn't seen me.

He was close enough that I could see the creases and seams in his weatherbeaten face. He was wearing an old canvas hat that looked as old as he did, and he peered intently from under its battered brim. He wore no glasses, and I got the distinct impression from the casual, unsquinting way he scanned the surrounding woods that he didn't need any.

I kept waiting for him to spot me in my treetop, but his attention was focused on the ravine below and he never glanced my way. I started to speak to him, but for some reason I didn't, and after a while he shoved easily away from the oak he'd been leaning against. He made his way down the slope to the bottom of the ravine, crossed the narrow flat at the bottom and eased up the other slope.

Going uphill or downhill in dry leaves is, for me, an awkward and noisy business. Not so for this old man. He was ramrod straight on both slopes, negotiating each with no visible difficulty, and if he made a sound I missed it. He carried his gun, a wear-silvered Model 94 Winchester, comfortably at half-port, ready to press it into service in an instant.

He moved quietly along the hogback ridge across the way until he was about 100 yards to my right, downstream from my stand. A thicket of young cane grew there, and he backed into it and sat down, his back against a red oak. He cut two or three stalks of cane with his pocketknife and stuck them up in the soft soil in front, and bingo, he was practically invisible.

The November sun sent its first blade of light stabbing into the new day, and that's when I saw how wisely the old man had chosen his stand. While the sun was bright in my face, making me squint and strain to see into the gloom of the deep ravine, my opponent across the way had the sun at his back, and a deer in the wash below him would have the same disadvantage I had.

I debated whether to change locations and decided against it. The sun would soon be high enough to cease being a nuisance, I reasoned, and the old man's presence wasn't worrying me too much. I had him cut off in the direction the buck was most likely to come from, and in my youthful arrogance (I was 17) I figured nothing shootable would make it past me. So I waited.

Deer hunting is by turns one of the dullest and most exciting of sports, and usually the transition from drowsiness to hart-thudding anticipation comes so swiftly it catches the hunter off guard. That's the way it happened this time.

I was fighting hard to keep my eyes open, watching a chickadee standing on its head in the fork of a sapling in front of me, when a flicker of motion up the ravine to my left jarred me back to the business at hand. The movement became a slipping deer, keeping to the brush in the bottom of the ravine.

Just like a smart old buck will do, I thought smugly. The deer kept coming, but I couldn't get a look at its head because of the thick brush and the sun in my eyes. I raised my gun to look through the scope, and when I did the barrel banged into one of the branches of my treetop blind. The dry leaves buzzed like a sack of rattlesnakes, and that was the end of that chance. The still-headless whitetail melted into the brush and went wherever it is that deer always go in situations like that.

I was furious with myself about blowing the opportunity, but there was still plenty of time for something to happen. And it did.

A couple of mostly uneventful hours passed, punctuated once by the quick arrival and departure of two yearling does, and I was getting drowsy again when a pack of hounds struck a cold trail a mile away to the south, away off in the big bottoms toward the river. Again, this was long ago, in a time when Southern deer hunters still used dogs for deer hunting. The dogs trailed falteringly for a while, bawling mournfully every once in a while to let the world know they were earning their keep. Then the tempo changed. One of the dogs evidently got the cold trail sorted out and pushed the deer out of its bed. It sounded like he was running the deer by sight; his voice held too much excitement and the pace was too fast for him to be trailing. By the time the rest of the pack caught up with the jump dog, the pace had slowed a little. But it was still a hot race.

From the direction and distance of the sounds, I was pretty sure I knew where the chase was taking place – in a long, narrow strip of nearly impenetrable cover we locals called the Bear Thicket. It was a good turn of events, because one arm of the thicket ran almost into the mouth of my ravine. It was one of the most-used escape routes for thicket deer harassed by dogs. The only thing that worried me about the situation was the old man; he had me effectively cut off in that direction.

The chase wandered up and down the Bear Thicket for some time before the deer tired of it and beelined for the river. The hounds' yodeling grew fainter and fainter and then faded out altogether, but through it all I kept watching the downstream part of the ravine.

The buck appeared as suddenly and as quietly as the old man had appeared three hours earlier. One second he wasn't there and the next second he was, as if he'd been there all along, standing in the classic pose at the edge of a small cane patch and looking over his back in the direction of the now-inaudible dog pack. His ears were the only thing in motion, swiveling this way and that as he monitored the morning for sounds of possible danger.

It was the ear movement that caught my eye, but it was his rack that held my attention. Even at 200 yards I could tell I was looking at the best head I'd ever seen. The main beams looked as thick as an axe handle, and the points rising from them were 10 inches long and stiletto-straight.

Satisfied he wasn't being followed, the buck lowered his head and started slipping toward me. From the front his headgear was just as beautiful, just as impressive. The tips of his main beams were more than a foot apart. It looked like he was carrying at least 10 points, and even the brow tines were long.

I could have killed him without any trouble. I was above him and 150 yards away, and he had his head stretched out and was walking at a slight angle toward me – perfect conditions for either a neck shot or for sticking one into his chest at the point of the shoulder and letting the bullet range back through the heart and lungs. He'd be dead before he heard the gunshot.

I had the rifle to my shoulder and was smoothing out the wrinkles in the sight picture when the sudden memory of the old man slammed into me like a blindside tackler. The crosshairs wavered, and indecision kept my finger off the trigger.

Did the buck fall into the first-come, first-served category, or did the first chance at him belong to the old man across the ravine? I glanced in the old man's direction. As far as I could tell, he hadn't moved a muscle. The buck came steadily on, now only 100 yards from me and almost directly in front of the old man, at a range of less than 30 yards.

I've never considered myself a particularly noble person, most certainly not when I was 17. But there must have been a little bit of residual Boy Scout lurking in there somewhere. I lowered my rifle and waited for the old man to shoot the monster buck, hating myself for doing it and hating the old man for being there.

The buck passed in front of him, and he moved for the first time since he's sat down. His old Model 94 came up slow and smooth, and I held my breath, watching with mixed emotions. The hunter in me wished for a quick, clean kill, but my selfish side hoped for a miss so that I might have a chance.

Neither of those things happened. The old man tracked the buck with the barrel as it made its way up the ravine, but the shot never came. Finally he lowered the gun and settled back into the cane, still watching the buck as it walked away from him and toward me.

Puzzled, but too excited to ponder it just then, I shifted my weight very slowly as the buck came within 60 yards. I didn't think I made any noise, but when I made my move the heavy-headed old fellow froze in his tracks and looked directly at my treetop.

By then the gun was at my shoulder. I settled the wildly gyrating crosshairs on his chest and squeezed the trigger just as the buck tensed to run. He wilted where he stood.

The heavy boom of the .30-06 was still rolling off through the bottoms when I let out a whoop and charged down into the ravine like a Comanche brave bent on collecting scalps.

That buck made a picture I'll never forget, lying there in a little patch of dusty sunlight in the bottom of that ravine. His rack was perfect. There were not 10 points but 12, all just as long and straight as they had appeared. The main beams were even heavier than I thought. I never did weigh him, but he looked as big as a Duroc brood sow.

I was standing there admiring him when a quiet voice behind me said, "He's mighty pretty, ain't he?"

I nearly jumped out of my skin. In my excitement I'd completely forgotten about the old man, and he had ghosted to within 10 feet of me before speaking.

"Didn't mean to startle you," he said mildly. He watched with quiet amusement as I struggled to regain composure.

"You didn't...I mean...I sort of forgot you were around," I stammered, my eyes gravitating once more to my first trophy.

The old man walked a slow circle around the buck, looking at him from every angle. "I expect so," he said.

He knelt and ran his hands over the rack as if he were blind, letting his fingers linger on the huge, rough-textured butt swells. He crouched there for a long time. Finally he stood.

"Need some help with him?"

I gladly accepted, and we set to work at the field-dressing chore. Adrenaline-fortified, hyperventilated, too excited to sleep for the next two days, I jabbered nonstop while we worked. The old man smiled and nodded and answered whenever I asked him a question, but mostly he kept quiet and let me have the floor.

His name was Earl Bennett, he said, and he was a retired forester. When we finished gutting the buck, Mr. Bennett helped me drag him out of the ravine. It was no easy task, and we were both winded when we reached the top of the slope.

While we were catching our breath, the old man squeezed my shoulder. "You've got a fine buck here, son. As good as I've ever seen."

I couldn't stand it any longer. The question was eating holes in me: "Why didn't you shoot him when he came by you?"

The old man was quiet for what seemed like a long time. Then he said something I'll also never forget.

"I'd tell you the answer if I knew how to put it," he said. "But even if I did, I don't think you'd understand."

"Why wouldn't I?"

Earl Bennett smiled again, and his voice was as gentle as the expression on his face. "If you could understand the answer, son, you wouldn't need to ask the question."

• • •

I never saw Mr. Bennett again, so I never got to tell him this, but he was right. I wouldn't have understood it then, but I think I've got a grip on it now.

In the first place, I'm pretty sure he knew I was in that treetop all along. I think he passed up that huge buck so I could have a crack at it. Maybe he wanted something more to remember of that day than another set of antlers.

If that's what he was after, I sure gave it to him; I was hopping around like a toad on a hot plate. Thinking back on it, remembering his quiet, satisfied little smile, I believe that's exactly what he wanted.

I know one thing for sure: I owe somebody a trophy. It's been a long time since that buck died in that ravine, and it hasn't happened yet. But one of these days, when the opportunity arises, I intend to pay my debt.

Chapter 16

A Bicycle for Christmas

By Larry Dablemont

When I was very young, maybe 11 or 12 years old, my dad got a little angry with me, just before Christmas. It was over a report card that said I was just average, almost all C's.

Dad didn't want me to be average. He was always afraid that's what he was... ordinary and average! He would have given anything to go to high school. No Dablemont had yet finished high school, and he was afraid I wouldn't, because I was so carried away with hunting and fishing, and those old timers in the pool hall, that I didn't do my homework. I was supposed to go to work after school at the pool hall he and my grandfather owned, and spend some of the time there doing homework on a big chest- type soda machine that really did make a good desk. I used it to read the outdoor magazines and write stories.

Dad was beside himself that time just before Christmas when those report cards were issued. He shifted his pipe and told me the way it was... "Stop writing those darned stories," he said, "do you think writing stories is ever going to get you anywhere in this world? You are going to wind up working at a factory like I have had to do, because all you want to do is read these danged magazines and write stories."

He didn't know then what I would do with that urge to write, and the wonderful gift he gave me by putting me in a pool hall with old men who became my closest friends, and helped me to see the difference between intelligence and wisdom. I had tunnel vision at the time. All I could see was the river and the woods; and the experiences those old men related, there on the front bench, was akin to the moose hunting stories I read in those outdoor magazines. And I hated school, because if anyone was indeed less than average, it was me. It seemed as if every teacher knew it. I was the pool hall kid, and in all those years of high school, I never once attended a football game or a social event. I spent all my spare time on the river, and all my working time in that pool hall from the age of 11 to my final year in high school. You couldn't get any more ordinary than me, and I guess Dad saw himself in me.

Dad had to work at a shoe factory during the day. Grandpa and I ran the pool hall until he came home and had supper, then came in to take over. He didn't make much money. How did a dad who would tell a boy who was to make his living as a writer not to write, influence that youngster in a positive way? Well, you just had to know my dad. As fathers go, he wasn't special. He was indeed a common man, ordinary, with all kinds of faults, like other men. But to me, he was the greatest man in the world.

He knew, that Christmas, how much I wanted a nice bicycle, but we didn't have that kind of money. I rode around on a little second-hand bike someone had given me, a tiny little thing with wheels not much bigger than fifteen inches across. If I sat on the seat, my knees kept me from seeing the road! There was a big red and silver bike with 26-inch wheels at the local hardware store, but I never dreamed I could have it. It was for looking at and dreaming. If I had that bike, I could tie my shotgun or fishing rod to the handle bars and ride it down to the river and hunt squirrels and rabbits, or go all the way to Mrs. Kelly's place, borrow her old johnboat and fish 'til dark.

I know that dad figured out a way to buy that bicycle by making some extra money at the pool hall, instigating a snooker league from October to Christmas, charging each entrant a fee to join, and buying three nice trophies which sat in the pool hall to make everyone's mouth water. We had some great snooker players, Junior Blair, Garnett Sliger, Shorty Evans, Jerald Jeffries, and a dozen others. But my dad played snooker all the time, and he was better than anyone. He had the game reduced to a kind of science, and he could do things with a cue stick and a billiard ball that would amaze anyone. Still, the game didn't always come down to who was the best. That league attracted better than 20 of the best shots in our county, and a dozen or so who weren't so good, but loved to play. It came down to those men

I named and my dad, and during the middle of December, he just really seemed to lose his touch. He was out of it by the time the last rounds were played, and I think Garnett Sliger came in first. I could hardly stand it. My dad was the very best, and he didn't win.

I tried to console him one night when we closed the pool hall and I stood there looking at those trophies, with the town Christmas lights shining through the window. "There would be next year," I said.

That's when he stopped brushing the table and shifted his pipe and made sure I understood something.

"I own this place, and I play free all I want…how would it look if I put on a big tournament and won it?"

My mouth fell open as I asked, "You mean you didn't try?"

Dad shook his head. "I didn't say that, a man should always do his best. I just knew I wasn't going to win, because I want these other guys to do well. They are my friends, I don't mind seeing them win. When it came down to one shot making the difference in a game, I just let them make the shot instead of me."

Then he made sure I was listening, as he went on. "I guess there are times you win by losing…you'll see that as you grow older. If you know you are good enough, if you yourself know you are the best…that is all you need, you don't need to prove it to anyone else. And even if you aren't the very best at anything, and you do your very best…that is enough. I have known some great men, the men I admire the most, who just kept on trying, who never quit, and they never were first at anything. But they were satisfied with their efforts because they did their very best. Someday the kind of man you are will be far more important than what you accomplish. I don't know a whole lot…but I know that."

Dad spent a lot of years taking me hunting and fishing, and he didn't always teach me a great deal by what he said. He taught me more by what he did. I watched and learned. He was something special, to me.

I got that beautiful bicycle on Christmas morning, because of that snooker league in the preceding fall. I had it for years and years, and nearly wore it out riding it to the river. And I have thought about it most every Christmas since. Dad passed away on Father's Day this past year, but he will be with our family this Christmas, you can count on it.

Only nine years after I got my bike, my dad was so proud to see my first outdoor article in Outdoor Life, with a story about him and me and an old johnboat we used. It won a national award as the best outdoor story in 1972 and was published in a New York book of award winning sports stories.

As for me, I have never been first in anything, still only average and ordinary and happy being that way. But back when I was a kid, I was ahead of everyone in one category. I had the best bicycle in the whole world...and the best dad!

Chapter 17

This is Why You're a Duck Hunter

By Jim Spencer

First light on a crisp winter morning. To the east, where sunrise will eventually happen, the glow of dawn grows slowly, gradually eating away at the night. The blackness overhead fades to navy, then cobalt, then turquoise. The stars wink out, one by one, like tiny bright fish slowly sinking in clear water. When only Venus remains, you and your hunting companions begin to see high ducks trading across the sky, birds that, until now, had been detectable only by ear – and by imagination.

You're knee-deep in leaf-littered muddy water, one shoulder snugged comfortably into the fluted trunk of a lightning-scarred willow oak. As the light grows, you find yourself scanning the sky like a Londoner during the Blitz, pump gun in one hand and handmade duck caller in the other. The wood of each has the glossy, smooth finish that comes to an implement only after countless hours of handling.

Neither the gun nor the caller appears particularly valuable. In fact, they would probably look decidedly disreputable to the casual bystander. But value, like beauty, is subjective, and to you, both are beyond all calculation of worth. Objectively, you know these two tools of the trade honestly aren't worth much – not if your measure is dollars and cents. Pawn shops are full of guns like the one you're holding, and as far as the duck call goes, there are six or eight more in your gun closet at home that sound at least as good as this one.

The old pump has been with you a long time, though, far pre-dating the nontoxic shot regulations that have in the past two decades redefined the "perfect" duck gun. The old girl sports a new, after-market barrel these days, a choke-tubed version friendlier to steel than the full-choked factory barrel that served you so well through many duck seasons. Even so, she's basically the same gun you bought with paper-route money almost a half-century ago. Jeff Bezos doesn't have enough loose cash lying around to buy her.

The duck call was your Dad's before it was yours. It's scarred and battered, veteran of a thousand hunts. It's a genuine working antique, handmade by one of the old masters in the 1950s.

Your Dad was a wizard with it. He didn't sound pretty, and he'd have been laughed off a contest stage. But when he blew that call, it sounded like duck. And they liked it.

You finger the call while scanning the brightening sky, and you can still hear that ring and raspy timbre of his calling. Your mind's eye recalls the way yesteryear's ducks would crank their heads around when they heard him calling, how they would make that cautious downwind swing, how they would come beating back upwind, looking, looking...

You watch today's ducks against the high blue and think about your father, now gone these 15 years. You've carried his call on every hunt since he died, and somehow it makes you miss him a little less.

No, Mr. Bezos, sorry. The call's not for sale, either.

While you've been remembering the origins and associations of these tools of your trade, legal shooting time has been approaching with all the speed of stampeding snails. The sound of not-too-distant gunfire pops you out of your wandering daydream, and you glance at your watch. Those guys are stretching the clock a little; still a few minutes to go. But the reminder stirs you to action: it's time to load up and get ready. It won't be long.

The final minutes masquerade as hours, but finally Mickey's big hand points to the magic hash-mark on the face of your Timex. Between one second and the next, the law is off the duck.

As if on cue, the morning's first flight of workable mallards crosses the pink-orange-yellow sky 150 yards east, intermittently visible through the naked branches. They're low and they're looking. Your short, sharp hail call, while it doesn't match the raspiness of your Dad's long-gone notes, snatches them around in an abrupt wing-over. They line out and head toward you, but they're still 75 yards out when a barrage from a group of hunters a half-mile southeast flares them.

Pretty much the same thing happens a few minutes later with another bunch, and the first twinges of frustration begin to pick at the edges of your enjoyment of this fine morning. But you shrug it off— after all, those other guys have as much right to be here as you do— and when you turn the third group of working ducks minutes later, they break the magic 30-yard circle. You and your two hunting partners take a greenhead apiece, three clean kills, and all three of you refrain from shooting into the butts of the departing flock. That shot angle has a high probability of crippling instead of killing, and you all know it. There will be more opportunities. No need to push the envelope.

You shuffle through the brown water to where your mallard floats belly-up, and you watch as his orange feet bicycle-pedal a few times, then grow still. Only then do you pick him up.

A wild mallard, brought to hand, has both heft and weightlessness. He's dense and heavy, yet at the same time elusive and ephemeral. Holding a freshly-killed specimen, feeling his body heat through his feathers, is a humbling thing. Sometimes your fingers tremble.

As you hold this one, you notice how the water droplets bead up on the iridescent feathers of his velvety green head. You take a few seconds out of your hunt to think about where he has come from, and what he has gone through to keep rendezvous with you here in this southern backwater.

If you're truly a duck hunter (as opposed to merely a killer of ducks,) this is the point where you may feel a vague twinge of sadness. It's a feeling rooted in a number of complex and basically unexplainable things: that you killed him because you loved him; that you killed him to complete the inevitable cycle of life and death you embraced when you became a hunter; that you wish there could be such a thing as catch-and- release duck hunting, because like a largemouth bass or a brown trout, a wild duck is too valuable a creature to take just one time.

But that's the way we must do it. So, as much as you'd like to, you cannot release this light-yet-heavy, this common-though-exceedingly-rare, this simple-but-complex creature of the wild yonder we know as a duck. And knowing that fact makes you a little sad. It's nothing overwhelming or debilitating; it won't make you curse and tear your hair and throw your gun in the water and quit duck hunting. You just feel a twinge of regret, that's all.

The sadness doesn't leave, but it always ameliorates. And when it does, you brush the water droplets off this handsome bird's feathers and lay him carefully on a nearby floating log, belly down so his gray lower breast feathers don't act as a beacon to warn other ducks.

Then you get back to your calling, so you can coax more of his cousins inside that magic 30-yard circle and complete the cycle again. You do it not because you are callous, or unfeeling, or cruel or bloodthirsty or barbaric or any of the other names hurled at you by those who do not understand nor share this passion of yours. You do it for reasons that are just the opposite of those things. You do it so you can feel once more that curious, unexplainable, indescribable mix of joy, sadness, awe, reverence, love, happiness, regret and heartfelt thanks you feel every time you "reach into the sky with death" – thank you for that phrase, José Ortega y Gassett – and bring down a wild duck.

And all of that, but especially this last part, is why you're a duck hunter.

Chapter 18

Grandpa's Knife

By Larry Dablemont

I picked out that new pocketknife, so proud to be able to be the one Grandma trusted for such an important Christmas gift, a special gift for someone as important as my grandpa. I took it to the counter to give to Mr. Duff. He smiled and said something to me as he rang it up. But I never heard a thing he said. I was reaching frantically into my pocket for that five-dollar bill and it wasn't there. I was about to panic! I had lost Grandma's five-dollar bill while I was crossing Main Street from the pool hall. Ignoring Mr. Duff I ran as hard as I could out into the street, looking beneath the cars, praying that someone hadn't picked it up. But I knew there'd be little chance. I sat down on the curb and tears streamed down my face. Christmas was ruined, and I had ruined it.

A week before Christmas in 1960, I sat in the pool hall, looking at the street light by the corner drug store, trying to see if there might be a flake or two of snow falling through the illuminated darkness beneath the light. I was 12 years old, and I wanted to see a white Christmas more than I wanted a girlfriend. I wanted a girlfriend awful bad, almost bad enough to break down and talk to one of the girls at school, something I had never done before. Almost more than I wanted a girlfriend, I wanted a bicycle. I had never had either. A bicycle was even harder to get than a girlfriend because we were a poor family, and bicycles weren't cheap. Some girls didn't care if you were poor. Not many, but some. However, snow was free, and it ought to be available to folks everywhere, not just those in big cities up north. There were wonderful things about snow. You could hunt rabbits better, there would be new mallards on the river and they'd cancel school.

Grandpa McNew ran the pool hall through the day, and I came in after school, to run the place until dad would get home from his factory job, rest awhile and have supper and come down to take over. I went in and strapped on the money bag, racked tables and collected money when a game was over, and gave my advice on occasion about a tough shot on the snooker table, or whether or not some shooter might scratch on the eight ball in a game of pool. In between those times, I listened to the front bench regulars talk hunting and fishing; a big bass that got away down on the Piney, or monster buck somebody had seen cross the highway over near Bucyrus.

It was an important job, and I was up to it. After all, my dad had left home when he was only 14 and went to work in the city. He told me I was pretty near a grown man, and I could paddle a boat, shoot a pump shotgun and split firewood. Even though I wasn't real big in stature, I could do a lot of big things. I looked up to my dad because he took me hunting and fishing, and gave me responsibility. In the pool hall, sometimes I had to make change from ten or twenty dollar bills, and help sort out arguments between two snooker players and be sure the soda box was kept full of Coke and Pepsi and Jic-Jac...orange, grape and strawberry.

Dad didn't give me many rules, but it was clear that I was expected to do what he said. And he said I was never to lie, cheat or steal, and if I could live by those three things I'd grow up to be a pretty good man. Grandpa McNew backed all those things up, and said other things I have kept with me all these years.

Grandpa McNew was one of the finest men I ever knew. He was a country farmer all his life, not the outdoorsman Grandpa Dablemont was, but a man of faith, conviction and strength. I loved both my grandfathers, but about all Grandpa Dablemont could teach me was about trapping and trotlining, and the woods and waters.

Grandpa McNew taught me things on the other side of life. He was as solid as a rock. He went to church on Sundays, and sang like he intended to be heard in Heaven. He said my dad was right, a man who went through life determined to not lie, cheat or steal, took something with him more important than fame or fortune.

He also taught me how important it was to have a good knife. He had an old Schrade pocketknife with two blades he must have began sharpening before I was born, because they were worn down to almost nothing. He used the little blade to cut his toenails, and the bigger blade to peel apples. He did a lot of other things with them, but I remember those two things because I ate apples he gave me quite often, and I sure didn't want him using that small blade to peel 'em with.

He broke the big blade in the fall of 1960, prying on something, and Grandma wanted to get him a new one for Christmas. The Western Auto store was right across the street from the pool hall, and they had Shrade pocketknives just like Grandpa used for only five dollars. When Grandma gave me that five-dollar bill and told me to get one for her to give to grandpa, I felt about as important as a kid could feel. I had never bought a really big Christmas present for anyone, cause up to then I hadn't ever had any money.

That all changed by the time I was 13, and got into guiding fishermen on the Piney and finding and selling golf balls and trading in pop bottles. By the age of 13, I sometimes had a whole pocketful of money. But at the age of 12, I just SAW a lot of money, there in the money-bag at the pool hall, and in those old men's billfolds when I made change. I guess when I got that five-dollar bill, I just couldn't believe I had it, and I looked at it too much. I took it out just before I crossed over to the Western Auto and looked at it, and didn't get it back in my pocket right, and it was lost. Some rich Christmas shopper got richer because of my bad luck.

As I sat there on the curb crying, Mr. Duff walked out and wanted to know what was wrong. I wouldn't tell him. Then he told me that one of his employees had found a ten-dollar bill on the floor back by the knives, and he thought it might have been mine. My heart leaped and sunk in the same second. I almost jumped up and said, "Heck yes it's mine, give it to me!" Then I remembered what Dad expected of me, and what Grandpa McNew insisted on..."Don't lie, don't cheat, and don't steal."

"No sir," I said, "I lost my Grandma's five dollars I was suppose to buy Grandpa's knife with. Thank you Mr. Duff...but my Grandma ain't never had ten dollars. Now she ain't got five dollars neither."

He sat down on the curb beside me while I sobbed, and handed me that same wrinkled five-dollar bill I had been looking at for two days. I swear, I heard angels singing the hallelujah chorus in the grey clouds above us. No kid ever went from gloom to glory any quicker, or jumped any higher or yelled any louder. Shoppers up and down Main Street in Houston, Missouri must have remembered that Saturday afternoon for years.

Even years later, Mr. Duff reminded me of that day. He always told me I was the most honest kid he had ever encountered. But I wasn't. I wasn't any different than any other kid, except for a dad and grandfather who expected things of me. Give a kid a dad and grandfather who talks about what's right and wrong and what they expect of a boy and most boys will be the better because of it. I believed at a young age in trying to be what Dad expected of me, and I took that edict of his all through my life to this very day..."Don't lie, don't cheat and don't steal."

It did snow that year; the first white Christmas I remember. I didn't get a girlfriend, however, for years, which allowed me to save a little money for many a Christmas to come.

And I guess, to tell the truth, I have not lived by the simple creed Dad gave me as a boy. No man can be that perfect. At times, it has been so hard not to lie or cheat or steal because it is so easy to rationalize that what you are doing is none of those things when it really is. And there are insurance companies you deal with, and ladies who want to know how their hair looks and this and that. But the thing about Christmas is, the baby born in that far-away place grew to a boy who became a man who made it possible that those of us who aren't quite perfect don't always have to be, as long as we keep trying, and recognize who He was. Grandpa's old pocketknife lies on a shelf above my desk. Sometimes when I have trouble deciding what to do when wrong seems like it isn't that far from right, I hold it in my hands and remember when I was only twelve...when it was so easy to figure out the difference.

Chapter 19

The Gift Bird

By Jim Spencer

Some turkeys are more important than others. This one was as important as they get.

There wasn't a turkey gobbling anywhere as I moseyed toward the log landing where Jill and I had agreed to rendezvous at 9 a.m. We'd selected the spot because it was convenient, because we could both reach it with no problem from the widely-spaced places from which we'd started at dawn, and because it was a good place from which to launch a mid-morning, Plan B hunt.

Easing through the greening woods, I thought about how fortunate I was to be sharing this hunt with my favorite hunting partner on this fine April morning. Six months earlier, the odds both of us would be here hovered somewhere between slim and none...

• • •

"Jim, this is Connie, Dr. Wright's nurse," came the voice through the phone. "I don't want to scare you, but you need to bring Jill to the clinic immediately. Don't let her drive. Stop at the drug store on the way and pick up the prescription I've called in. Have her take the pill immediately, and come straight to the clinic. Please do it right now."

Okay, maybe Connie wasn't trying to scare me, but she did it anyway. Not that I hadn't been expecting something. For several months, there'd been a gradual but profound change in my wife – a steady decline in her normally boundless curiosity and energy, substantial weight gain, a noticeable lack of enthusiasm for the outdoor lifestyle we both loved so much. A lack of enthusiasm for anything and everything, for that matter. I'd always admired Jill's work ethic and punctuality regarding writing assignments and deadlines, but recently those had been slipping, too. For the first time since I'd known her, she was missing deadlines and giving editors less than her best work.

But the most alarming thing was her increasing difficulty with short-term memory. "What do you want for supper tonight?" she'd ask, sitting down with her morning coffee. We'd decide on that evening's menu. Before her cup was empty, she'd say, "What do you want for supper tonight?"

I tried to convince myself these were normal functions of aging. After all, we were both pushing 60 at the time, and Father Time is cruel. We all get older, heavier and lazier – or at least I do. But that memory thing was worrisome, and I nagged Jill until she made a doctor's appointment.

After her private appointment with the doctor, I asked for a consultation. When I told him about Jill's increasing memory lapses and recent loss of vitality, he was concerned enough to schedule an MRI the following morning, Tuesday.

Bright and early Wednesday, I held the phone and heard the controlled urgency in the nurse's voice.

. . .

"I know you're not a trained radiologist, but that's not required here," Dr. Wright said when we arrived at the clinic and were ushered immediately to his office. The MRI film showed an image of Jill's head from above, and square in the center front of her cranium was an oval tumor the size of a turkey egg. I am not exaggerating; I can show you the damn film. And the doctor was right. An imbecile could have read it.

My memory of the next couple hours is hazy. Through the blur and buzz of incipient panic, I heard Dr. Wright telling us there were excellent neurosurgery facilities in Springfield and Little Rock, both equally distant. I needed to take Jill to one or the other immediately, he said, while he handled the arrangements as we made the two-hour trip. He said he could arrange for an ambulance, but that would take time and he thought I'd be able to deliver her faster. And time, he said, was of the essence.

"Don't go home to pack," he said, handing me the MRI envelope and ushering us to the door. "Don't stop for lunch. Don't get stupid and have a wreck, but drive as fast as you're comfortable with. She needs to be there yesterday." The one-pill prescription, he said, was a potent anti-seizure drug, and though he didn't say it, he was obviously thinking Jill should be in convulsions already.

Jill and I talked during the drive to Little Rock, but I couldn't begin to tell you what we said. The only thing I distinctly remember is my wife, who could die or start having seizures at any minute, was doing her level best to put my mind at ease. "I'm going to be fine," she said again and again, reaching across to pat my arm. "Everything's going to be okay."

Flashers winking vigorously, we arrived at the hospital's emergency room entrance at 10:30 a.m. A nurse was waiting for us with a wheelchair. At 1 p.m. my wife went into surgery, and I went into a tailspin.

•   •   •

Depending on context and situation, a minute can pass in the blink of an eye or last a lifetime. Jill was under the surgeon's knife for 20 hours. You read that right. Every one of those 1200 minutes was a lifetime, and only the calming presence of our daughter Leslie, who sat beside me almost the whole time, got me through. The only good news in that 1200 lifetimes was the information a scrub nurse brought out – that the tumor wasn't malignant.

But of course, I wasn't the one who had it rough. While I sat in relative comfort in a hospital waiting room, Jill was on a surgeon's table with her head cut open. She was unconscious through the ordeal, naturally, but still it was her, not me, who had a big slice of her skull sawed loose and laid down over her face like a wedge of cantaloupe, while the neurosurgeon used a laser to carefully separate the huge tumor from the delicate tissues of her frontal lobes.

To be brief: Jill survived the ordeal. You already knew that, but here's something you don't know. When they let me into recovery, where Jill was still coming out of anesthesia, I could see in her eyes she was already back. Still groggy, black-eyed as a raccoon, wearing a turbanesque bandage that looked like Marge Simpson's hairdo, she gave me a woozy grin and a wink. "Told you I'd be okay," she said.

And just that quick, I was, too.

Jill came out of surgery on Thursday morning. On the following Thursday I brought her home – appropriately, on Thanksgiving Day. We had Wendyburgers. It was the best Thanksgiving feast I have ever had.

Jill's work ethic and sense of responsibility resurfaced, and so did her love of living. She quickly got back in good graces with her editors, and she started an exercise regime that still astounds me. You'd have thought she was training for the Olympics. She walked, jogged, dieted, exercised – not making a fuss about it, just doing it – and the pounds melted away. She still refuses to let me tell anyone the numbers, but you wouldn't believe it anyway. What's impressive, though, is this: between Thanksgiving and April she lost every pound she'd gained, plus a few more. By the time turkey season opened, she was her old self – slim, trim and in considerably better shape than her husband.

• • •

My morning hunt had been unproductive. As already mentioned, we'd started our morning hunt from different places so we could challenge different gobblers – Jill to hunt a bird she'd worked the day before, me to try for one that had been gobbling near the lake.

My bird was near the lake, all right, but on the wrong side of it. By the time I got to the water and figured it out, he'd flown down and shut up. Except for Jill's gobbler, which I could just barely hear, no other turkeys were gobbling within earshot. She told me later that when her bird flew down it walked away from her, passing near the spot where we'd greed to rendezvous. Then it also shut up.

Hunts like that are par for the course, especially on the public lands we usually hunt. After Jill's gobbler got quiet, I went on a roundabout through some pretty good country, trying to find a turkey to play with.

I didn't find one, though, and about 8:30 I started moving toward our pre-established meeting spot. Jill was already there, reading a book and wearing a smug look. A very nice gobbler lay on the ground beside her. We quietly bantered for a few minutes, like hunting partners do:

"Who gave you that turkey, girlie?"

"Whassa matter, big boy, can't you find a turkey to shoot?"

"I save my tags for big turkeys. But that's a fat one for such a little bitty guy, ain't it?"

After some more trash talk, we decided to go north, where we'd heard several birds gobbling the previous day. But we couldn't get anything going, and with Missouri's 1 p.m. curfew approaching, we decided to drive to a nearby spot that sometimes held a midday gobbler.

We stopped just before we reached the truck to make one last call. It's a little ritual we nearly always repeat, and on occasion it pays off. First I yelped on my old Lohman box and got no response. I gave Jill an exaggerated, now-it's-your-turn finger roll, and when she hit her higher-pitched Black Mystik box a gobbler cut her off. He was close, but not so close we panicked.

He was in a shady little draw south of the truck. We angled downhill to his level, then closed the gap another 30 yards. I set up out front with Jill 15 yards back, and she raked another series of yelps off the top of her box call. The turkey gobbled hard.

But he seemed content to stay where he was, and presently the clock started becoming a factor. We were running out of it. Jill cranked up the excitement and tempo, trying to force the play. That worked the same way it usually does, which is to say it didn't work at all. The gobbler was singularly unimpressed and wouldn't answer the insistent stuff.

But another gobbler did. This one sounded like he was gobbling from the bed of our truck, less than 250 yards away. When Jill turned loose with the excited stuff, he started our way immediately. Then a third gobbler cranked up from somewhere past the truck, and that one started toward us as well. Then another one started gobbling on private land across a nearby county road, maybe 250 yards away. We didn't figure this one would cross the road and join the party, but he was noisy and he got everybody else stirred up. Finally, as if four weren't enough, another gobbler came in silently behind Jill – I didn't know this until later – and started drumming nonstop, practically in her ear.

Rags to riches. From nothing a scant few minutes ago, we were now hip-deep in interested gobblers.

I already had my gun shouldered, but in my haste I'd forgotten to stick a diaphragm call in my mouth. Now it was too late; I was handcuffed. The closest turkey was right there, killable if he'd stick his head up, or take a few steps uphill, or something. The by-the-truck gobbler was steadily getting closer, as was the one just behind him. Jill told me later the drumming turkey was getting closer, too.

That's when the thought hit me like a blitzing middle linebacker: whichever of these gobblers showed up first was going to be the most important turkey of my life. Here I was, sitting in front of a woman who just five months before had been at death's door. Following an ordeal most of us can't begin to imagine, she had without complaint fought her way back to health. Now, after calling in and killing a fine gobbler for herself earlier that morning, she was attempting to call in another one for her husband, who already thought she was Wonder Woman.

When a gobbler is under the gun, it's always important to do things right. The hunt is about much more than the kill, true enough, but the kill is still pretty important. You don't want to screw it up at the moment of truth, assuming that moment arrives. But this kill was so far beyond important it was off the chart. I absolutely had to get this one right.

You think you know something about pressure? Think again. I'm normally pretty cool when a gobbler is coming – sure, my pulse races and the adrenaline courses, but I can usually keep myself under control, if not

quite calm, until the gobbler is down and I'm standing on its head. Only then do I get the shakes and the heebie-jeebies.

Not this time. As soon as I realized how momentous this turkey was, I broke into a drenching sweat and became a quivering mess. My gun barrel, until then steady as a rock, gyrated like a pole dancer on speed. The turkey in front of me gobbled again, and my heebie-jeebies ramped up another notch.

Those 1200 lifetime-long minutes that had tortured me in the waiting room were gone, and in their place were the blink-of-an-eye kind – and there were far fewer than 1200 of them. I knew quitting time was perilously close, but I couldn't look at my watch.

The turkey continued to hold his ground, gobbling hard but refusing to come. Finally, with only a few minutes left, Jill changed her calling strategy. Ignoring the hung-up gobbler in front of us, she started conversing with the gabby one across the road. When the close turkey would gobble she did nothing, but every time the private land bird said anything she was all over him with yelps, cutts and excited clucks.

It drove the nearest bird nuts. After Jill ignored him the fourth or fifth time, he took a few steps up the hill and suddenly there he was, all of him, searching suspiciously for the fickle hen.

When things are that important, they become easy. The sight of the gobbler calmed me instantly, and my world-class case of the yips vanished. The gun barrel quit waving, and I put the bead on the line where wattles met neck feathers. When he ran his head up for a better look, I uncapped it for him. He collapsed, and before I got up to claim him I glanced at my Indiglo. Six minutes of hunting time remained.

I'd killed quite a few gobblers before that day, and I've killed a bunch since. But none of them compare with that one, nor will I ever kill one that does. He wasn't a bad turkey – 22 pounds, ten-inch beard, one-inch spurs if I fibbed a smidgen. Not as good as Jill's bird, but still a good one. But he could have weighed 13 or 30, could have had a nubbin beard or a bell rope, could have had no spurs at all or two-inch hay hooks, and none of it would have made any difference, none of it would have changed the way I felt.

Because this one, this most important gobbler that I will ever shoot, was a present from my hunting partner.

And also a present from God.

Chapter 20

The First One I Ever Heard

By Larry Dablemont

About the time the state of Missouri held its first turkey season, I was an eighth grader, maybe a freshman in high school...I can't remember. I know I had seen my first flock of turkeys the fall before when Dad and I were floating the river hunting ducks. A half dozen had flown across in front of us, only 25 or 30 yards from the end of my shotgun barrel. Talk about temptation!

The next spring, Coach Weaver got himself a turkey tag and began to go out in the morning before school started and hunt gobblers. Then in gym class, he'd talk about what had happened on his latest excursion. Each morning a different kind of close call, but never a turkey to show for it. It was spellbinding stuff to me. I couldn't get enough of it, and I vowed someday I'd get a turkey call and call up a gobbler myself, maybe down on the river somewhere in that national forest land where I had watched that bunch fly across the river.

I think it was the next spring, or perhaps the next, when some of the old-timers in Dad's pool hall started hunting turkeys, and one of them actually got one. He brought it by the pool hall one Saturday morning and the whole place emptied out to go see it. It was the first time I actually saw a wild turkey close up and dead, and what a majestic big bird it was. Ol' Jake Farnsworth saw how interested I was in it, and made me a box turkey call of my own and showed me how to use it. In time, Ol' Jake saw an opportunity he just couldn't pass up. He said by golly somebody ought to take that young kid out and get him in on a wild turkey hunt, and he was just the one to do it. Of course Jake's time was worth a great deal, and he proposed a trade that could have gotten us both in trouble. He said he'd make a fair deal with me! If he got me right up close to an old gobbler, whether we got him or not, I'd be obliged to give him a half dozen free soda pops, and ten free games of snooker spaced out over the upcoming month of April.

It was a calculated risk on my part. True enough, Dad had said that when I was running the pool hall I was the boss and whatever decisions I made was the final word unless he came along and over-ruled it. Ten free games of snooker came to $2.00 and six free sodas, amounting to 10 cents a bottle, was a significant amount. But shucks, I quite often gave away sodas to the front bench regulars on special occasions. And Dad didn't mind if on occasion, I'd just open up the back of the big old soda chest with a crank, slipping out one or two to drink or to reward one of my friends for helping me sweep up or for bringing me a hamburger from the West Side Café across the street.

Naturally I was going to jump at that opportunity Ol' Jake was offering, and the trade was made with the understanding that no one was to know about it but the two of us. Jake said he didn't want it widely known that he was capable of guiding turkey hunters with such a capacity for success or he'd be swamped with others wanting to get the same kind of two-and-a-half-dollar deal. That always puzzled me, because to tell the truth, Jake was one of those kinds of fellows who would do about anything that didn't require any work for a dollar if someone offered it. In fact, he once let the air out of the high school principal's tires for only a quarter, which was all the money I had at the time!

I will never forget that morning when we finally got together for my first turkey hunt. I met Old Jake in back of the pool hall at five o'clock where I left my bicycle. Mom and Dad thought I was meeting Grandpa there to go run a trotline. Common sense told me they'd find out later that I wasn't, but I'd deal with that problem when it happened. I wanted to go turkey hunting so bad I'd just about risk a night in jail for the opportunity.

Jake had a 1949 Ford pick-up with the muffler about knocked off it. You couldn't hear yourself think when it was running, and it shuddered and shook so bad when he shifted gears that you could feel the vibration of a short ride for ten minutes after it was over. We went to his place, a little old farm house about eight miles east of Houston, over close to the national forest land near Big Creek where so many turkeys were, and where almost everyone hunted back then. He loaned me his double-barreled 12-gauge Stevens shotgun, which was only a single-barrel really, because the left barrel had a broken firing pin. Jake told me to be sure I had the right barrel loaded when we set in on that old wild gobbler. He only gave me one shell, so old it had mold growing on the paper, and the brass casing was tarnished nearly blue and partly encased in rust or something, so bad that I had to push it hard to get it down in the barrel.

And right at the beginning of morning light, we headed off down into the woods and across the creek and up on a wooded ridge, listening to barred owls and whippoorwills, kicking the frost off the leaves as we went. It was a chilly morning and if I hadn't been so excited, I think I would have been about half froze.

It was then that Old Jake rested, and as he huffed and puffed he told me that this old gobbler was so old and smart he might never show hisself, and then maybe again maybe he might. Jake said the main thing was, we was gettin' me some turkey huntin' experience to where I was closer to a time I could go out on my own and call up a big old ground-raker. And right then is when I heard him, the very first wild gobbler I had ever heard, clear and clean, from off up the hollow below us, on the high ground of the next ridge over. We were off almost before he got his second gobble sent forth, walking as quiet as we could for a half-crippled old man and a hopped-up excited kid who envisioned the whole town gathering just to ask me how I done it, while I walked up and down Main Street with a giant gobbler slung over my shoulder.

To make a sad long story short and sweet, we got set up about a quarter mile from that old gobbler   and he carried on for a good two hours, gobbling once or twice every minute while old Jake scraped away on that box call he had made me. I said to myself that if a gobbler could get that excited about a turkey call of that poor caliber, I'd soon be the best turkey hunter in all of the Ozarks, because I could beat that with a rusty gate hinge. I kept squeezing that old shotgun and straining my eyes through the greening underbrush, just sure that any minute the gobbler would appear, all strutted up and easing closer. But he never did. The danged old fool stayed right where he was and gobbled for two hours, until we had finally reached the allotted time Jake had agreed to give me, and though I wanted to stay longer and ease a little closer, he insisted we didn't spook the old tom, saying that might run him clear out of the country.

Since we left him gobbling, and apparently unaware of our presence, Jake said we might yet get him on another day, so with my head down and feet dragging, I followed him back to his old pick-up. By 10:30 that morning I was back at work in the pool hall, and before noon Jake had used up two of his free games of snooker and one of his free root-beers.

Despite the fact I had been sworn to secrecy, it was more than old Jake could do to keep quiet about it. He told everyone how close we came to getting a wild gobbler, and insisted that it was an old long-bearded wild tom probably as old as I was, so wary and smart and cunning that he just couldn't be called in. He said it was like that sometimes, you just couldn't get the wisest, oldest ones to budge.

Several days later Grandpa Dablemont stopped by the pool hall and asked if I had an hour or so to go dig some night-crawlers down on the Piney.

I told him I did, after all, we'd be going trotlining that very weekend. But Grandpa knew I'd trade the biggest catfish in the river for that old gobbler. I guess nobody in the world knew the outdoors like my grandfather. It didn't matter whether you were talking about ducks on the river in the fall or big flatheads in the spring or lunker smallmouth in the late summer, Grandpa was the unquestioned authority in those parts of the Ozarks.

He finally got around to telling me about when he had hunted wild turkeys as a boy, and how many he had killed, back before they became almost extinct in those Southern Missouri hills. Now wild turkeys were coming back, and Grandpa said if I was that determined to get one, he'd help me buy a turkey tag and we'd go out and get one. The following spring, that is exactly what happened. When I was fifteen years old, Grandpa helped me get my first turkey, and I wrote about it several times years later after I became an outdoor writer. That story entitled, "The First Gobbler", is found in my book, "Ain't No Such Animal, and Other Stories From the Ozark Hills." You won't find the story about my hunt with Old Jake Farnsworth anywhere. I never wrote about it until now.

Grandpa didn't take me to dig night-crawlers right away. He took me out east of town toward the national forest, off down a little country road where we finally turned off on a washed-out little lane we could barely get down in my old Chevy. I kept asking him what we were doing, and he just smiled, saying he'd show me shortly. We pulled up in front of a little old broken down grey rounded-top trailer which was only about twenty feet long, with several windows boarded up. A skinny little bewhiskered guy by the name of Ernie came out, dressed in old overalls with no shirt, just faded old long-handles beneath the overalls and dirty old socks with no shoes. He seemed happy to see Grandpa, and they went to talking about this and that.

I kept hearing a turkey gobbler just gobbling his head off, and I stepped around the end of the little broken down trailer to peer off down into the woods aways, where there was two hen turkeys and a big old gobbler in a pen. I reckon I should've put two and two together but it took awhile. We weren't very far from the very spot where Old Jake and I had been after that wise old gobbler the very Saturday before.

Grandpa finally asked Ernie if he had seen his old friend Jake Farnsworth lately and the old man said by golly he had. He said Jake had been by a week or so before to ask if he would keep his old hounds inside on Saturday morning, so's they wouldn't interrupt his turkey hunting, down in the woods nearby. Ol' Jake, Ernie said, was a fine feller. Jake had promised that sometime soon he'd take Ernie in to town and treat him to a free game of snooker and a soda pop, just for that one little favor. Ernie said "Shucks, keepin' them two old hounds in the house that Saturday mornin' wasn't no task, they both would druther sleep on his bed than out there under the trailer anyways!"

Ernie sure hated to see us go. He said he didn't often get company. He said Jake came by every now and then, but Jake wasn't exactly company, he was a neighbor. Ernie said he never had knowed Jake to hunt turkeys, and though Ernie hadn't made a big thing of it, he said he didn't think they was one turkey within five miles of his place except that one old tame gobbler of his.

Grandpa and I dug some night-crawlers that afternoon, and caught some catfish that very next week-end. And he took me up on top of a river bluff early one morning and we stood there listening as the world came awake. At the right time, Grandpa cupped his hands over his mouth and gave a long loud imitation of a barred owl. Down below us across the river, a wild gobbler answered, just once. Finally I could really say it was the first one I had ever heard.

Maybe it was the first one I ever killed, a year later when a new April came around. But there have been a lot of them since him, a lot of gobblers, and a lot of Aprils.

And if you are wondering, I never said a word about what I knew to old Jake.

Grandpa asked me not to. He said there wasn't any reason to make light of the old man and hurt his feelings, and I knew he was right. Dad laughed about it, when he heard the whole story, and he said it wouldn't hurt to live up to my end of the deal. After all, Jake did what he said he would do, and I did get to go turkey hunting. And I don't remember many spring mornings that were much more exciting than that one.

I guess I didn't exactly come away from it with nothing. In my box of "old stuff from when I was a kid" there are antique casting reels with braided line, and one of Grandpa's old gigs and his hand-made trotline spool, and the brass handles that came off the front door of the pool hall. And there's also an old hand-made, scruffy-looking turkey call that Jake Farnsworth gave me the first time I ever went turkey hunting. You know, it ain't much for looks, but it don't sound half bad. I'll bet that even today, it would make some old tame gobbler just gobble his head off!

Chapter 21

The Cattle Boat Chronicles

By Jim Spencer

I haven't been there in a while, but they tell me St. Andrew is pretty much like the rest of coastal Florida these days – one tacky high-rise and tacky souvenir shop and over-priced, over-decorated seafood restaurant after another. But in…I'm guessing here, but let's call it 1978… this subsection of Panama City was a sleepy, laid-back little community, the Key West of north Florida, a pastel, quiet nap-town that took seriously its leisurely approach to living and its attitude of *laissez-faire.*

If you were looking for a party in those days, you went to Panama City proper, hub of the bar-disco-night club district in Florida's panhandle. But we weren't there to party. We were there to go fishing, a whole busload of us, and St. Andrew was a dandy place for that. Along the wharf that fronted the water of Grand Lagoon, the pilings were plastered with Polaroid snapshots both recent and old, documenting the good fishing to be had on the charter boats and head boats (also called cattle boats) that berthed there.

• • •

There was another attractive feature in St. Andrew that had nothing to do with fishing. Several small, family-owned oyster bars lined the town's main street, a half-block off the water. Flickering neon Budweiser, Schlitz and Pabst signs glowed in their windows. After the long bus ride from Memphis, we were both parched and famished, so after stowing our gear aboard our big head boat, the Florida Queen, about half our busload of Arkies and Tennesseans descended on one of these places like a swarm of locusts on a field of ripe wheat.

We left behind a weird, straw-haired, cut-off-clad guy. He'd been on the bus, but he wasn't "one of us." He hadn't spoken three sentences the whole trip down, and he showed no more interest in oysters and beer than he'd shown in talking to us on the bus. We didn't figure to miss him much. When we left he was sitting on the portside aft guardrail of the Queen, using a Snoopy rod and tiny chunks of bologna to catch four-inch croakers and pinfish, dropping them into a five-gallon bucket.

It takes all kinds. Me, I had a date with beer and bivalves.

• • •

The little mom-and-pop joint could have used a good swamping out, but the linoleum counter was clean, and there were plenty of swivel stools available. A platoon of condiments stood in ragged formation beside each napkin-holder: salt, pepper, lemon pepper, crackers, mustard, catsup, ReaLemon, horseradish, Tabasco, Slap Yo' Mama seasoning, Worcestershire, Louisiana Hot Sauce, Panola Pepper Sauce, Pickapeppa Sauce, Tiger Sauce – anything an oyster aficionado could desire. One wall was obscured by a messy, haphazard array of business cards, St. Andrew's answer to Who's Who in America. I added one of my own cards to the mess. It pleases me to think it might still be there – assuming, of course, the joint itself is still standing. Considering it's been more than 40 years, that's in question.

Whatever, it was standing on this particular long-ago night, and it didn't take me long to decide it was my kind of place. I took a stool and ordered three dozen. You know. For starters.

Those little Appalachicola Bay oysters weren't as big as my thumb, but they were plump and tasty and the folks who ran the place kept 'em coming. I was somewhere between the fifth and sixth dozen when a stray bit of trivia floated to the fore of my beer-lubricated brain.

"I thought you were only supposed to eat oysters in months that have r's in them," I said to no one in particular.

No one in particular said so what, it was Argust, wasn't it? And that settled that.

Who gave a rip, anyway? Certainly not me, and I proved it by ordering up another dozen and beers all around.

We'd played poker on the bus on the way down. I'd had the hot hand and was, for the moment, flush. My pockets were bulging with other people's money, and that little joint was then and remains today the only place I've ever been where I could afford all the oysters I could eat. So, in the interest of science and gluttony, I decided to see exactly how many oysters that was. Did I mention I'd had a few beers?

But the experiment was inconclusive. I ate nine dozen – one hundred and eight fat little half-shell jewels – but closing time came before I foundered and they chased us out. I think I could have managed another dozen or so, but we'll never know.

• • •

Ho-ho, me hearties, off to the Captain's Lounge we went, bellies sloshing heavily but pleasantly with their loads of oysters and beer. This second establishment, being mere yards from the wharf, was a convenient place to wait for the Florida Queen to throw off her lines and head for the briny deep. Alas, there were no oysters to be had, but they served a potent margarita and an even more potent pina colada, and it was only a stagger and a fall from the bar to the boat.

If you use time as a yardstick we weren't there long, but nobody used time as a yardstick in the Captain's Lounge. We were there for a week, at least. Bob Seger was practicing his Night Moves on the jukebox, and we sang besottedly along. I'm sure we ruined the evening for many of the other patrons, but nobody asked us to leave so we didn't.

Eventually, though, one of the deckhands flew a sortie through the place, announcing in pear-shaped tones that all those who weren't aboard the Queen in ten minutes were "...gonna get your asses left ashore."

We took a vote, decided that after all, we had come here to fish. One more quick (?) round and we pina colada'd haltingly out the door.

Oyster, alcohol and Dramamine-fortified, we came noisily up the gangplank, boarding the boat like pirates on rape and plunder bent. As we settled in for the long ride to the fishing grounds, somebody asked what time it was and somebody else said two o'clock, he thought.

Or maybe it was four.

Nobody had ever sailed these waters before. I was Bligh aboard the Bounty. I was Ahab in search of the white whale. I was Heyerdahl aboard Kon-Tiki, balsa-wooding my way to fame and glory.

I was a little bit drunk, and I was enjoying myself immensely. Standing spraddle-legged forward of the wheelhouse, I flexed my knees to absorb the gentle sway of the boat and watched the moonlit Gulf curl meekly under my mighty ship's prow. I was tasting the salt air, feeling the salt breeze, sobering up fast. Uh oh. This would never do.

Back in a short while with a generous splash of sea serpent repellent over a chunk or two of ice, I found the forward deck crowded with other inebriated Ahabs. The magic was wrecked by these brash interlopers, so I ducked into the cabin and joined a crowd of kibitzers surrounding a booth in which raged a dizzying game of euchre.

• • •

A portly guy everybody called Diamond Jim was walking from player to player, peeking at their cards and holding forth on game strategy, slurring his words and drinking something from a pint Mason jar. Whatever he was drinking was clear as water, but I suspected that wasn't what it was. Offering advice to any who would listen and any who would not, Diamond Jim finally broke up the game through the simple stratagem of giving away everyone's hand. When the booth emptied he crawled onto the table and fell blissfully asleep, snoring softly.

• • •

Came the dawn, ahead of schedule. Ahead of my schedule, anyway. I was snoozing peacefully below decks in one of the Queen's 30-odd bunks when the low growl of the diesels changed pitch, slowed, backed down further, went to a loping idle.

Ding-ding!

Damn! That was the drop-your-lines signal! People were fishing! I bolted up the narrow manway, whanging my noggin on the overhead trimwork in my haste. On deck hung-over and headachy, I plunged into the herd – that's why they call 'em cattle boats – and fought my way to the rail. Most of my fellow fishermen already had lines down, and a few fish were coming up, winched relentlessly to daylight by powerful electric reels that speeded things up quite a bit, considering we were fishing in water more than 100 feet deep, but also took some of the fun out of it. Curses here and there indicated tangled lines or other difficulties, bringing deck hands running.

• • •

I found my spot – position 43, starboard aft. I was two slots down from the straw-haired weirdo who preferred catching minnows to eating oysters and drinking nutritious drinks. I gobbed some cut squid on my two hooks and punched the free-spool button on my reel, but the captain sounded the bell again – *ding!* – before I could get my baits all the way down. That meant bring your lines up, we're moving. And do it now. A few smallish black groupers, a snapper or two and the usual assortment of squirrelfish, triggerfish and beeliners were flopping on the decks. The straw-haired weirdo had caught a 10-pound black grouper on one of his minnows.

Bottom fishing on a cattle boat is bluegill fishing on a gargantuan scale. Either the fish are there or they aren't. Either they'll bite or they won't.

When the bait hits bottom the captain waits for perhaps four minutes. If by then the decks aren't alive with quivering fishes, he sounds the bell and departs for another of his secret holes, which he finds through frequent consultation with Loran, GPS, charts, compass, black magic and genies.

It was a 10-minute run to the next spot, while we sat gazing at the flat, calm Gulf. Flying fish skittered frantically out of the way, sailing across the slick water like silver Frisbees. I'd have sold my kids into slavery for a Bloody Mary.

• • •

Ding-ding! Fifty sinkers dragged a hundred hooks to Davy Jones' locker. Something tapped mine as soon as it touched bottom, and I set the hook into something heavy. I punched the thumb-button and strained against the fish's combined weight and inertia as he zoomed dizzyingly toward the surface.

He came off halfway up.

Both hooks were empty, and before I could get them rebaited the bell said *ding!*

Another boat ride. *Ding-ding!* Fifty splashes, a few scattered yells of success. *Ding!* Those who had caught a fish cursed the captain.

That was pretty much the pattern for the day. Fishing was slow, and the only person who was consistently doing any good was the straw-haired weirdo. He was hauling 20-pound groupers and 10-pound snappers aboard like a Japanese longliner, using those damned four-inch croakers and pinfish for bait. He was weird, all right. Weird like Einstein.

• • •

We covered a lot of water that day. Not surprisingly, it all looked the same. Except for the occasional clump of seaweed, with its inevitable collection of light bulbs, boards and beer cans, there was nothing from horizon to horizon except the flat, ominously calm sea. We were far from any shipping lanes, so there wasn't even any bird life except for one lonely gull that hovered over our stern, begging for bits of shrimp or squid or bologna sandwich. We named him Kilroy. Because he was there.

I'll tell you how bad the fishing was: it was so bad the cook had to go around panhandling to get enough fish to feed us that night. On most deep-water head boat trips, the ship's cook can pick up a spare rod while he's getting the grease hot and catch enough fish to feed the passengers, but not this time. I donated my only edible fish thus far – a nice triggerfish, a pirhana-looking thing that's equally happy severing barnacles, pencils or index fingers with his powerful, underslung dentition. I bought him back later at four bucks a plate. But he was good.

• • •

This is probably the place where I should mention the ship's chandlery, the cramped, sort-of concession stand amidships that was the only game in town for victuals and beverages. Beer and groceries were dispensed here at piratical rates. We could bring hard liquor on board, but not beer – that would wreck the ship's monopoly, don'cha know. A can of beer, in that Year of our Lord 1978 or whenever it was, went for the jaw-dropping sum of six bits – and worth every penny. It was a long swim back to the Captain's Lounge, and anyway, the beer there was almost as expensive.

The only snag was, the chandlery ran out of beer late in the afternoon of the first day out. I guess they didn't have much experience with a bunch of moonshine runners from Arkansas and Tennessee.

• • •

Sometime during the afternoon we hit a school of medium-sized bonito, and 20 or 30 of them came aboard in short order. The bonito is a dark-meated, oily fish, and while he is dandy broiled or smoked not many people can stand him fried. We filleted most of them on the spot and used the fillets for cut bait.

This operation released a lot of blood into the water, and pretty soon a visitor showed up. One of the deck hands said he was a mako, and not a very big one.

That man was lying through his teeth. I know a big fish when I see one. We pitched a couple of fresh bonito carcasses overboard. The shark ate them whole, and sideways to boot. Just opened his mouth and swam up around them, one at a time, in no hurry, as if he did it every week. Which, in retrospect, I guess he probably did.

I was looking right down his throat when he executed this neat trick. No part of either 18-inch bonito touched any part of the shark's mouth when he ate them. That's a pretty sizable mouth if you ask me, and suddenly I knew how Chief Brody must have felt, sitting in the lifeguard's chair on the beach at Montauk. Several of us fools rigged hooks that looked like they came from hay wagons, baited them with bonito carcasses and went after big game. Thank God nobody hooked him, and thank the captain the bell said *ding!*

• • •

The next day was more of the same, except maybe worse. There wasn't any beer, and even Kilroy had given up on us.

Being both bored and immature, we invented a game during the morning. You see, the easiest way to hold those heavy, awkward electric rod/reel combos was to rest the rod on the hip-high railing and stick the rod butt between your legs. Somebody discovered that if you reached behind a fisherman and tapped upward on the rod butt, it felt like a fish pulling down on the other end. The fisherman would jerk. Nothing would be there. Everyone would laugh except him. It was great fun.

We didn't catch many fish that second morning, but we sure did have a lot of bites.

At noon we had to give it up, but by then we were ready to quit anyway. Diamond Jim had a bad case of sore feet from standing on them in wet tennis shoes for 30 hours straight. He had fished all night, impressing the devil out of the rest of us with his toughness and tenacity. Everybody was sunburned, except for one old codger who had stayed in the snack bar the entire trip, stewed to the gills, never wetting a line. He caught almost as many fish as I did.

We all were sore, sticky, sweaty, and smelled bad. The fellowship had been marvelous, the fishing atrocious.

Except, of course, for that weirdo with the croakers. He didn't know the fish weren't biting, and he continued to flaunt his ignorance the entire trip. When we docked, he weighed in nearly 500 pounds of grouper and snapper. Numbskull. I wondered if he acted that stupid all the time.

I was much smarter than him; I knew the fish were on strike. Accordingly, I caught one fish the second day. It was a scamp, the pick of the litter in Florida bottom fishing. The scamp is a member of the grouper family, but runs a little smaller than most species. He's a rich, handsome, brown-mottled color and has little extensions at the edges of his tail, and in profile he sort of reminds you of a '59 Chevy. He is delicious. Mine weighed ten pounds and I was very proud of him.

I gave him to the straw-haired weirdo.

A busted trip? Au contraire. Nobody fell off the boat. Nobody got hooked, bitten or finned. The mako ate nothing except bonito carcasses, and maybe Kilroy. I did not get seasick, nor did I get too badly sunburned. Nobody got mad at anybody else, other than the thing about the rod butt tapping. I met some nice people, some of whom are still friends more than 30 years later. And I ate another hundred or so oysters before we headed home.

• • •

There's more: I wrote the main body of this piece more than 40 years ago, and it was originally published in 1979 in a now-extinct tabloid fishing rag called Pleasure Boating. My memory after more than four decades being notoriously unreliable, I went online to double-check a few facts. Lo and behold, the Florida Queen is still afloat and still taking fishermen out into the Gulf, and her wooden red-and-white hull looks exactly like I remember it.

Therefore, I have made an executive decision: I am going to go back and go fishing again on the Florida Queen. I doubt the little mom-and- pop oyster bar will still be there after all these years, and the Captain's Lounge may be gone as well. But if they're gone, somebody else will have come along to take their place. The Appalachicola Bay oysters will be just as plump and the pina coladas just as coconutty as they were more than a third of a century ago, if considerably more expensive this time around. I doubt I'll hit either delicacy quite so hard this time, anyway; I'm a little smarter now, or if not smarter, at least in better control of my baser urges.

I know St. Andrew won't be the quiet, sleepy little Key West North it was when Seger was young and Night Moves was a new song, but I can always squinch my eyes halfway shut and pretend. It won't be quite the same, I know, but it'll probably be good enough.

This time, though, I'm taking a Snoopy rod. And a couple hunks of bologna.

Chapter 22

Joe's Visitor

By Larry Dablemont

Joe stepped through the front door of his cabin onto his porch and walked right into a spider web, with a spider the size of a quarter running across his face. He noted how hot it was for early in September and cussed the awful humidity. His old hound lay there on the porch scratching away. He could see a half dozen ticks on one ear. For some reason, Joe just had all he could take. He looked toward the heavens and asked God if He had any idea just what he was doing when he made spiders and snakes and fleas and carp.

He sat down in his old rocking chair and nearly jumped out of his skin when he became aware that he was not alone. "Who the dickens are you and where did you come from?" he said with a start, although it was obvious who the visitor was...It was an angel, you could tell by the halo and the wings.

"God sent me to talk with you," the stranger said with an angelic voice. "You complain constantly anymore, Joe, and you once were so happy and cheery. What would it take to make you less grumpy, a little more satisfied with life?"

"Well, you just caught me at a bad time, is all..." Joe answered, "I'm sorta cranky this mornin' because I didn't sleep well last night with this sore back, and that thunderstorm yesterday washed all the gravel off my road and the handle is broke out of the shovel...an' my old hound is full of fleas and ticks."

"Maybe we can fix the flea and tick problem," the angel said, "They've got some stuff at Walmart...or I can send some snow in a week or so and get the temperature down in the twenties for awhile."

"Now see, there's what aggervates me," Joe said. "Everything is so extreme. When it rains it just pours down in buckets, and when it don't, it don't for weeks at a time. Now it's been 90 degrees for a week and you're fixin' to give us a freeze-up and a snowstorm! Why can't there just be a happy medium?"

The angel smiled..."You are thinking of Heaven, Joe. This is the Earth you are living on. Men have made the weather what it is by activities that lacked much wisdom over the centuries. But since you have been a good man, to some extent, over the majority of your lifetime, maybe I can speak to the Creator in your behalf and have some things done to your liking. What are the things you would most like to see changed in your life besides the weather?"

Joe thought about that for a moment, as he glanced at the angel, trying to figure out how this could all come about. He had assumed this visit meant he was about to be escorted to the Pearly Gates to explain a lot of things. Now it appeared someone actually cared what he thought.

"Well," he said as he rubbed his hands over his white beard. "There's some little things I guess, like tomatoes. I'd like to see tomatoes get ripe about the first of June around here and keep growin' 'til about the first of October...I reckon that ain't too much out of line."

"I think it is a reasonable request," the angel said, "because it would be a good thing for many, and I assume you are thinking a bit of your neighbors."

Buoyed by that affirmation, Joe continued. "And it would be nice if we had a couple of years with no snakes nor mosquitoes or fleas and none of these dad-blamed spiders...excuse my language there." The angel nodded, more unselfish things which would be good for everyone in the river valley. He bade Joe to go on.

"Well, they's other things," the old man said. "Like that hole down there in the river where I fish. There's carp in there that'll go 10 pounds, lots of 'em. But I only caught three walleyes last spring and there wasn't a one of them bigger than 18 inches. Seems like if God was payin' attention when he made that river he'd at least of made the walleyes outnumber the carp or made the walleyes big and the carp little."

"But Joe," the angel said, "If you had plenty of big walleye, catching them would not be the challenge you now enjoy, and you would be tired of eating them so much. Why, there was a time long ago that men who lived along this river complained because there were so many fish and not enough chickens! And as for the carp, God didn't put them here in your river, men did."

Joe rubbed his beard again, and thought to himself that whoever brought those carp to the Ozarks ought to have been looked at awfully hard before they were let into Heaven. "Well, that may be," he said, "but how come the chicken hawks outnumber the bobwhite quail, and there's more coyotes any more than they is rabbits? Maybe you could do something about that... for the good of all mankind that is."

"I understand, Joe," the angel said, smiling, "and while I can't promise anything, I certainly will make your feelings known. It is commendable

of you to think of others this way, but what would you have me do just for you?"

Joe thought hard about that, wondering if the angel wasn't just having some fun with him. What was the puzzle? Surely that angel knew how he loved to hunt quail and rabbits.

"I suppose I'd like to get me a good-sized buck this fall," Joe said. "Them neighbors of mine spotlight the big ones ever year, why all I got the last year was a forkhorn and a six-pointer that had ears bigger than his antlers. An' I'd just once like to sneak up over that pond bank of mine about Christmas time and see a big flock of greenhead mallards again... instead of them darn coots. What made God create coots, I wonder?

"And I reckon it'd be a great Thanksgiving if I could get a wild gobbler instead of some little old scraggly hen turkey," he continued. Then, too, maybe we could have one mild winter, with no snow for a change. Last year I was out tryin' to cut firewood with snow up to...my...well... it'd be nice to see jonquils by the middle of February."

"I understand, Joe," the angel said, as the heavenly guest rose and prepared to leave. "It makes it hard for me sometimes. The little Thompson twins have been praying for a white Christmas, you know. But...if you are willing to leave with me, you can have all you wish for and much more in Heaven. It's a nice place."

Joe became a little nervous... "I figured I was still a little young for that," he said, "and besides I got grandkids and neighbors that's gonna need me around here for a spell. I reckon I won't need so much after all, if I stay around here. Things ain't been so bad, if you get right down to it. Most of the time, I'm plumb happy."

"It's good to hear you say that Joe," the angel said with an understanding nod and a smile. "It's just that you complain so much I have been worried about you. And remember, only a few years ago you vowed that if God would let the Cardinals win the World Series you'd be so happy you'd never ask for another thing!"

Later that day, Joe headed for the river with his old hound alongside, and his fishing rod over his shoulder. He was whistling as he went, enjoying that beautiful September day, counting his blessings.

Chapter 23

A Day in the Life of a Marsh Dog

By Jim Spencer

Pintails often don't decoy well, but these two drakes had evidently forgotten to read the book. They made one high, downwind pass, spotted the small decoy spread in the lee of the stand of roseaux cane and heeled over like thirsty crop-dusters at quitting time. They came beating their way back into the teeth of the stiff wind, long necks outstretched, wings laboring.

John the man and Lum the dog watched them come. The two old hunting partners crouched side by side in a modified Cajun pirogue hidden in the edge of the nearly solid wall of tall reeds. The man had stuck an armful of fresh-cut cane stalks into the mud in front of the boat, and the two grizzled duck hunters held silent and motionless behind the foliage as the ducks slowly closed the distance.

At least, one of them did. The big Labrador shivered with anticipation as he watched the pintails approach. He shifted his front feet slightly, whined softly. His human companion smiled; more than seven years of experience as a duck dog, and he was still eager as a pup.

"Shhhh!" the man whispered. "Hold the racket down over there." The black dog glanced guiltily at John, beetle brows forming a frown, then returned his attention to the two big pintails, now hovering at the outer edge of the decoys.

At his end of the small boat, John swung the wear-silvered Model 12 to his shoulder. The move was smooth and efficient, and he'd done it so many times over the decades he wasn't even aware of making the decision to pull the trigger. But it had obviously been made, because the left-side pintail folded and dropped head-first into the bobbing decoys.

The remaining duck flared its wings and caught the wind, rapidly falling away and trying to get clear of the danger zone, but it never really had a chance. The old man recovered from the recoil, swung on the rapidly retreating duck and the Model 12 roared again. The strong wind carried the pintail another 10 yards downrange after the shot, but it was dead in the air.

"Your turn, Lum," John said, but he said it to an already empty boat. The dog was steady to wing, but "steady to shot" was a concept that had failed to penetrate his broad black head. John had never pressed the issue. *What's the point, anyway?* John thought, watching the big dog swim strongly through the chop. *The whole idea of a retriever is to bring back a dead duck, so isn't getting an early start an advantage?* At any rate, neither he nor Lum was interested in field-trial behavior, and the man enjoyed the dog's obvious enthusiasm for retrieving.

Ignoring the nearest duck, Lum struck off downwind after the second bird. John settled back to watch. It took the dog well under a minute to reach the distant pintail, but the return trip against the wind took three times as long. The wind was getting stronger, close to 30 knots now, and away from the shelter of the canes waves were running a foot high across the shallow water covering the mud flat. The big sideways duck created additional drag, but finally Lum made it. He raised his head and deposited the duck over the gunwale of the boat – a behavior he'd learned on his own, John reflected with another smile – before swimming into the decoys for the other bird.

Moments later, ducks and dog were in the boat, and it was Lum's turn to grin as he gave his hunting partner the customary shower of muddy water. John shielded himself as best he could in the close quarters of the little boat.

"One of these days I'm gonna get you your own boat," he told the dog. "Maybe then I can quit having to wear slicker suits on bluebird days." He reached over and gave a light yank on the dog's left ear, and the dog snapped playfully at the offending hand.

"Oh, no you don't," John said. "This boat's not big enough for any rough stuff. Anyway, we got ducks in the breeze. Get your big head down, Lum."

The sky was peppered with ducks, made restless by the worsening weather. They were everywhere – a bunch of gray ducks here, a flock of teal buzzing there, a small, ragged formation of widgeons in the distance. There were enough workable birds that a fellow could afford to be choosy, and John decided this day to shoot only big ducks. Even so, within an hour he'd pieced together a six-duck daily limit consisting of the two pintails, a mottled duck and three drake mallards, a not-very-common species in the south Louisiana brackish marsh.

Lum made a long, laboring retrieve on the final duck, a mallard, while John gathered the decoys, struggling in the knee-deep muck. He nearly bogged down several times in the process, but finally everything was done. Freeing the boat from the canes, he got Lum aboard, endured yet one more muddy shower, and began the long pull across the open flat toward the high-stilted hunting camp to meet his son Bill and his teen- aged grandson Johnny, who had been hunting elsewhere in the marsh. He poled the boat with an ease and economy of motion gained from six decades of experience.

John could never say afterwards just how it happened. Maybe an alligator, maybe a stump, maybe just a momentary lapse of attention.

One second he stood confidently in the stern of the pirogue, knees flexing with the waves as he shoved the little boat crosswind toward the camp, and the next second he was coughing and snorting and struggling to keep his head above the waves, which now were approaching two feet and whitecapping. The swamped pirogue bobbed in the water nearby, and he tried to reach it but his water-filled chest waders made swimming impossible. In the 30 seconds it took him to struggle out of them, the boat disappeared in the rough water.

Knowing it was the wrong thing to do but doing it anyway, John gave in to a momentary surge of panic. He began striking blindly at the water, flailing his arms as if he was fighting a swarm of bees. Almost immediately, one of his windmilling fists hit something firm and hairy, and John opened his eyes and looked into the frightened but faithful face of the big black Labrador. The dog was treading water beside him, whining softly, wrinkling his brow as he'd done when the pintails were coming.

The sight of the dog was a settling influence. John's nerves steadied, and the panic left his as quickly as it had arrived. Trying to think as rationally as possible, he assessed their predicament.

At best, the outlook was grim. The pirogue had overturned in the middle of a large peat-burn lake, two hundred yards from wadable water and another mile across open marsh from both dry land and the camp. Even if he survived the long swim out of the deep water, John was doubtful of his ability to wade that long distance through the deep, clinging mud in the now-pervasive cold. The temperature had been steadily falling since midnight, and now hovered near the freezing mark— very cold for south Louisiana. The combination of cold and wind had the chill factor hovering around zero. Death by hypothermia was as much of a threat as drowning.

All this flashed through John's mind in the space of a heartbeat, and for the space of another heartbeat he almost decided to give up. But another anxious whine from Lum told him that wasn't an option— at least not so long as the big dog, with all his own instincts telling him to strike out for land, stuck beside his hunting partner. Scared as he was, John couldn't help but feel a sudden rush of love and pride for the old soldier treading water at his shoulder.

"Well, knothead," John shouted above the splash and howl of the wind, "let's give it a try!" They set off downwind, staying close together, John swimming steadily but slowly in an effort to avoid exhaustion.

The dog could have easily outdistanced the man, but instead he stayed close, wanting to help but not knowing how. Occasionally he'd nudge John's face or shoulder with his nose, and it was this physical contact as much as John's own strong will that kept the man afloat and swimming. Nevertheless, he was almost spent by the time his feet finally struck mud.

At first it was too soft to provide any support, but as the water shallowed the mud firmed and soon John found it would partially support the weight of his submerged body. He stopped swimming, resting his arms, but soon found that standing still in the thigh-deep muck increased the rate at which his body chilled.

Be a hell of a note to die of hypothermia after swimming that far, he thought, and started struggling through the mud toward the distant dry ground.

Now the cold was a malignant, living thing, eating its way into John's mind and body, numbing his brain as well as his muscles. He'd been in the water nearly ten minutes now, and he felt drowsy. His mind drifting, he smiled faintly, thinking how good a nap would feel...

Lum barked loudly and John's eyes snapped open, the smile giving way to a grimace of discomfort. "Okay, okay!" he shouted fiercely, angry at himself for his weakness and feeling that anger send a little warmth into his leaden limbs. "I hear you, knothead. I'm coming." He continued thrashing across the marsh, fighting the thigh-deep mud, the water still deep enough that waves continued to break over his head. He was near- blind and half-strangled, but for the first time since the pirogue had tossed him, John felt he might just make it. He struggled along beside the faithful Labrador, concentrating on each difficult step with the resolute determination of an ox pulling a plow.

The water was shallower now. Only a few inches covered the mud, and the waves, which were mostly mud themselves, no longer swamped him. But the wind had a better shot at him now, and the chill slowed him even more. His rate of forward progress was very nearly nonexistent as the sucking ooze tried to pull him back.

John felt the panic returning. He started fighting the mud wildly, but this only served to sink his legs deeper into the goo. Drawing on an inner reserve that was just about depleted, he willed himself to stop struggling and lay forward, letting the muck support some of his body weight. Lum, ten feet ahead and struggling himself, looked back and stopped.

"Lum, I ain't gonna make it," John said conversationally, as if the dog was another human and would understand the words. "You better go on without me."

The big Lab barked loudly, then sloshed back through the mud to John's side. He barked again, this time in John's face, made a brief sortie toward dry land, then returned and barked again.

"Get out of here!" John yelled, swatting at the dog's blocky head. "Go!" Then he issued a command he and the dog had learned together nearly a decade earlier, when neither his beard nor the Lab's muzzle had had any gray. He's quit using the command when he realized that "steady to shot" stuff was counter-productive for a water dog.

"Back, Lum! Back!"

The command was vaguely familiar to the dog, and he cocked his head, puzzled. He knew he was being given an order, but failed to grasp it. He came back toward John and bumped him with his head, his brown eyes searching the man's face, looking for clarification.

"Back, knothead, back!" John yelled again, this time motioning with his right arm the way they'd practiced in the back yard all those years ago.

Understanding came with the suddenness of an electrical circuit closing. The light went on, and Lum's head snapped to attention. He barked once more, then churned away through the mud and shallow water, never looking back, heading for the pass bank, the natural levee along the tidal waterway that always constitutes the highest ground in a Louisiana coastal marsh. The dry land was 200 yards distant, but the powerful dog covered the distance in less than two minutes, his wallowing lunges changing steadily to yardage-eating leaps as the water grew shallower and the mud firmer.

On firm footing at the edge of the willow thicket on the pass bank, Lum looked back across the 200 yards of mud and water separating him from John. The man gave the hand signal again, and Lum's answering bark was barely audible over the howling wind. Then the dog was gone, a black speck headed toward the hunting shack a mile away down the pass bank.

"Well I'll be," John said aloud, flapping his arms, continuing to struggle toward dry ground. "Like Rin-Tin-Tin or Lassie or somebody."

In his exhausted state, John found it almost impossible to make any more headway through the deep mud, and after a while he quit trying. The deadly chill crept deeper into his body, and he tried to keep both mind and muscles active to ward of the drowsiness he knew was coming. He started talking aloud, hoping the sound of his own voice might help keep him awake.

"Yeah, just like Rin-Tin-Tin. He sure was a runty little fellow, though, when Bill gave him to me. Had a touch of mange, too. Didn't look like he'd ever amount to anything, but he sure fooled me. Fooled a lot of other people, too. I know Bill gave him to me as a joke, but it backfired. Best damn dog in Louisiana."

John stopped talking, his thoughts turning inward. Then he started again: "How long ago was that? Eight years? No...nine? Yeah, nine. Johnny was five then, and he told me at breakfast he'd be fourteen next week. Fourteen already, and already taller than his daddy and me."

The old duck hunter's voice faltered, then stopped, as the cold continued its deadly way into his bloodstream. His resistance to the deadly drowsiness was slipping more with each passing minute. But his brain continued its wanderings...

Funny, John thought, the little things you remember. Like the sight of the puppy and the little boy asleep together in the doghouse. Or the time Johnny came back to the house mad as a billy goat because... because Lum went fishing with him...fishing with him...and kept sw...swim...swimming out after the...cork...and...bringing it back...

Sleepy, getting sleepy...hope they...hope they find me...won't find me, though...somebody gets lost...out here...don' nobody ever...

"...find him."

The words penetrated the fog in John's head, and with some difficulty he managed to open an eye. Hovering above him were two worried faces, one belonging to his son, the other to his grandson. The muted growl of a diesel engine and a feeling of rolling, steady motion told him he was aboard a powerful, rapidly-moving boat.

"What...?" he tried to ask, but his son cut him short.

"Be still, Pop. You're going to be okay. We're on a crew boat, heading up the river to Venice. Before you know it you'll be in a warm hospital bed."

The words came pouring out of his son in a flood of relief, and the old man smiled in spite of the pain in his cold-tortured muscles when he heard how Lum had brought Bill and Johnny, in true wonder-dog fashion, to the mud flat where John lay unconscious and near death.

"The crew boat came by just as we got you to dry ground," Bill continued. "In just a minute or two we had you aboard and now we're almost to Venice. It was like a miracle that..."

John held up a hand, interrupting his son's excited monologue. "Where's my Lum dog?" he demanded, some residual strength still showing in his voice.

At the sound of his name the big Labrador bolted up from the deck, cramming his head and still-muddy forequarters into the cramped berth where the old man was laying. Bill tried to drag the dog back.

"Leave him be." John's voice was stronger, authoritative, and his son stepped back.

Heedless of the mud, John wrapped both arms around Lum's great noble head and buried his face in the grimy coat, holding tightly while the dog slurped noisily at his ear. "Thanks, knothead," John murmured against the dog's warm neck.

When man released dog, it was hard to tell which of them was muddier. John grabbed a handful of the hair and hide covering Lum's muscular flank, gave it a twist and a pat, and received a tired but contented grunt in response. And in just a few seconds more, the two old hunting partners were sleeping peacefully.

Chapter 24

The Legend of the Dutchmen Brothers

By Larry Dablemont

On a summer evening on the river, Grandpa told me the story behind a mystery.

We were on our way downriver to the Bell Rock. Just above the Cow Ford Eddy was where we were going, Grandpa and I. We meant to camp out there on the sandbar below the old Bell place, beneath the yawning maw of the big cave, where we could go if'n it stormed bad in the middle of the night and lightnin' came to be a danger, or if the river was to come up. We were goin' to set two trotlines, one in both eddies, and figured on catching a big flathead or two.

But we wasn't there yet when I looked up on the high ridge to the left above the river and asked Grandpa if he had ever seen the old rock chimney, what was left of it, up there on the peak of the hill.

"Yep" he said, "they call this here stretch of the river the Dutchman's eddy, and that there old fireplace and rock foundation is where the Dutchman's old cabin stood."

"They was outlaws," he said, "brothers! And they was bad thieves that'd steal a widow's last pig if they didn't have to butcher it. Low down, lazier men you'd not find."

About that time the old johnboat drifted into a shoal where Grandpa wanted to seine chubs and sunfish for trotline bait, so he told me he'd tell me more about the Dutchman brothers later.

It was blacker that night than a crow in a coal mine, just the way Grandpa wanted it, to make the big flatheads come out from under the bluffs and big rocks to feed. There were sparks rising into the air above our campfire and a whippoorwill whistlin' over and over in the timber above us, close to the cave. We had us a nice canvas lean-to set up and blankets waiting beneath it, with soft sand to sleep on. Grandpa wouldn't want to stay up very long after it got dark because he'd want to run the trotlines and re-bait them about two in the morning. I don't know how he always could wake up in the middle of the night whenever he wanted to, but he always did, and at that age I was always so excited about the prospect of a 30- or 40-pound catfish that it wasn't hard to crawl out from beneath the quilts and put on those wet shoes. But before we turned in and let the fire burn down he told me the story of the Dutchman brothers as he had promised.

How well I can remember his voice from 60 years ago. Grandpa had no equal when it came to telling stories about the river and the outdoors and the people of his past.

"Nobody really knowed 'em well," he started out. "That old house had set empty for awhile and they just moved in it. Course it needed fixin' up as I 'member, cause it had cracks between the boards. Onc't I was runnin' a dry land trapline in the winter and when I went by it was started to snow and blow pretty good. They seen me and axed me if I wanted to come in and warm up. Reg'lar enough fellers I reckoned at the time.

"I had just got back from the war so I was likely twenty or so then, and times were hard for everyone. But them two brothers seemed to be doin' good. They had a couple hogs and some chickens and three nice- lookin' horses. Boy I'd a give my left ear to of had me a horse like one a them. And they had put that old house in good order with a new shed out the back door. They had on good overalls and cowboy hats, and had sugar for the coffee, and I had to wonder what they did to live that good. So I just up and axed 'em and they claimed they went aroun' and broke horses and butchered for folks and built sheds and the like, just a doin' whatever come up.

"Course I was young and green and I believed 'em. But lots of other folks didn't. Up at Venable's store, some of the fellers that came in and played checkers in the winter said I hadn't been too smart goin' in to talk to them culprits. They held that the Dutchman brothers had robbed and killed an old couple over towards Licking on t'other side of the river, and then burnt down their cabin after they robbed 'em.

"So about March a year or so later, I was driftin' down the river a ways below Mineral Springs when I seen two horses cross a shoal below me in one heck of a hurry, splashin' water up near their saddles, and I could see it was the Dutchman brothers leant for'ard and kickin' those horses on at a good pace; set a trotline in the Cathcart eddy that afternoon an paddled back up to Mineral Springs, tied up the boat and headed up the old road toward home when I come across ol' Porky Smithson's wagon and team. He was layin' in the dirt and mud behind 'em, with his head bashed in and blood all over. His pocket book was layin' there on the ground, empty, and I found out later that his boots had been took. They was near about new and ol' Porky was proud of 'em. He was showin' them off up in Houston a few days before and braggin' about the money he had come into cause he had sold a good mule.

"I run up towards Houston and found a feller on his horse and he went an' got the sheriff who got together a posse. Several of 'em came down and loaded ol' Porky up and took him up to town and I went with 'em. The sheriff axed me all kinds of questions and I told 'im what I had seen. He wanted me to take 'em across the river the next morning to the Dutchman's place, and I told the sheriff the best way was to cross right there at Mineral Springs and take that long ridge down to the creek holler below their place, then just sneak up the hillside and be on 'em 'fore anybody could know we was a comin'.

"Well I was there at the crossin' at daylight, cause I didn't sleep good at night. Hope you never experience it, but when you've seen a man you know with his head and neck and legs all twisted up and his face white and scary lookin' with blood all covering where he normally had hair, an' all puddled up around his head, you can't hardly sleep for a week. But what I was about to see was about as bad.

"We got together that next morning about daylight. All of 'em had horses but me, so one feller I didn't even know told me to just get on his horse behind him. It was a rough ride, 3 miles or so down the river, but I held on. There was the sheriff and likely 6 or 8 men he made deputies of. They were well armed, pistols and rifles and a couple of shotguns. Scared me a little. I didn't know many of 'em but one had a team and wagon, and he was going to go all the way down to the Sand Shoals crossin' and try to come up from down river on the old dirt road that went up to Bucyrus. Wa'n't no way we'd all get to their place 'til near noon or so.

I will always remember that early spring mornin', bein' scared makes things that happen kinda stick in your mind. It was fairly cold, with just a little bit of frost in the valleys and I was glad when we got off the horses finally, tyin' them up along the creek. I took 'em all down to that little point that comes down to the river right there at the head of the Dutchman eddy shoals. "Everbody strung out an' headed up that slope through the woods and I figured I was about to see a gunfight. It woulda been bad if the brothers had chose to fight, but they wa'n't able to. We wasn't even out'n the woods afore you could see the two of 'em hangin' there from the limb of the big oak tree by the house, hung up off the ground by their necks, not even stiff and cold yet. A sort of bench was kicked over beneath them and their feet was 2 feet off the ground, I reckon and their hands weren't tied. I looked up at 'em and I can't forget what they looked like, even today. I never will. One of 'em had his tongue hangin' out and his eyes kinda wide open and bugged out. I could tell you more but you don't wanna hear it. I didn't look at the other'n, 'cause I'd seen enough."

Grandpa stopped his story for a while and threw a couple more limbs on the fire. But I knew he had more to tell, so I waited patiently, a little spooked by the seriousness of it and the darkness. A barred owl was hooting downriver and bull frogs were bellerin' around us. The whippoorwills had stopped for a while.

"Some folks say they got wind of the posse on the way and kilt themselves," Grandpa said as the fire flared up with the new wood. "But I never was sure, 'cause they was a broke winder and some spent rifle cartridges on the floor inside, but no rifle of the same kind to be found nowhere. What I think is, somebody got to 'em before the posse did, 'cause ol' Porky had a lot of friends. Word of what I had seen got around town, and I think somebody got there before the posse did. Course it got aroun' that they had hung themselves. Maybe they did!"

Grandpa slept good that night, snorin' whilst I laid there and dozed, off and on, a little bit uneasy, wonderin' if the ghosts of the Dutchman brothers really did haunt the river bottoms below Squire Lee's place like some of the front bench regulars in the pool hall claimed.

You know, I can't remember what catfish we caught that night or whether we caught any at all. I do know that as we paddled back up river, Grandpa told me that when he had been inside that place where the outlaw brothers had lived, they showed him a white, chiseled-out tomahawk they had found earlier, hoein' up a garden. He said it had been there on a big rock ledge sticking out of the fireplace. That fascinated me so much I had to go look for it, and I did. There was nothing there on that hilltop of course but a hint of rock foundation, and the rock pile remains of the fireplace. I spent much of a summer day tossing rocks out of the way hoping I wouldn't surprise some holed-up copperhead, but by golly I finally found it, a six-inch, white flint Indian tomahawk, which I have been told was actually some kind of hoe.

I look at it on occasion and wonder what the man who made it might have been like. Was he just a big old hairy-lookin' feller, or someone who looked like Sittin' Bull. It's likely he had a family living in one of the nearby caves.

Wouldn't it be wonderful if we could just see what those people were like, and maybe talk to 'em? Because of Grandpa I know a lot about what the Dutchman brothers were like. I can't say I'd like to meet 'em, because it takes evil men to do what they did. Up to now, if I have ever been around evil men I didn't know it. I think though, that this summer I would like to go back to that gravel bar below the Bell Rock where Grandpa told the story, and where just maybe, there's really the spirits of the early men who made that tomahawk. Maybe there is too, the spirits of the old Dutchman brothers who found it. Maybe the two of 'em is sorry for what they done! I reckon that they were startin' to get that way, when whoever it was throwed that rope over the limb up there on that ridgetop, on that day way back there when the Dutchman brothers first started becomin' a legend along the Big Piney.

Chapter 25

The Old Mallard

By Jim Spencer

C lose your eyes and see him there in the north country: sitting on some nameless prairie pothole in southern Saskatchewan, sharing his tiny kingdom with muskrats, grebes, and an assortment of other water-oriented birds and mammals. This old greenhead is a veteran of several migrations already. He doesn't "know," in the sense that you and I know, that fall is coming and another migration is imminent. But his instincts have been preparing him for the arduous trip ahead, and all summer and early fall he has gorged himself on aquatic vegetation, macroinvertebrates and the ripening wheat crop that has been the ruination of many of the potholes on which his ancestors summered in centuries past.

The Old Mallard knows nothing of these things. There is this pothole in this year, and for now that is enough.

He has spent the last several weeks living as unobtrusively as possible. He's been flightless during the annual molt, and therefore much more vulnerable to predation. But thanks to camouflage eclipse feathers and an extra measure of caution, he has made it through yet another molt without incident.

Now, the camo feathers have mostly been replaced by his new winter plumage, and once again he is easily recognizable as a greenhead. A few patches of brownish feathers persist on cheeks and throat, and a stray brown feather peeks here and there through the herringbone gray of his breast. But these will soon be gone and he will once again be decked out in all his gaudy splendor.

Already he has regained the ability to fly, and over the past several days he's been making flights of increasing duration in an instinctive body-building regime. He must be in peak condition for the long flight south.

It won't be much longer.

• • •

There's a lot involved in getting ready for duck season, even when you hunt them as simplistically as we do. Some duck fanatics spend months of their afternoons, evenings and weekends camo-painting boats and outboards, rigging frames on their boats for portable blinds, painting and patching and re-rigging hundreds of decoys, working their Labradors (springers, Chessies, Irish water spaniels, Boykins, shorthairs) over and over, ad infinitum.

But we don't bother much with that stuff. We keep it simple; we hunt south Arkansas style, in flooded fields or (preferably) green timber, and we travel light. You won't find any camouflaged boat and motor in my yard, and while I do own a few decoys, they're in a pitiful state of repair and don't see use one day in three seasons. I doubt that more than half of them will even float.

My Labrador? Don't make me laugh. Her name is Casey, after an old girlfriend, and while she's a fine, companionable beastie and sleeps in front of a fire as well as I've ever seen it done, she's hopeless as a retriever. Which is fine with me. Dogs are handy on a hunt when there's a cripple on the water, but in my system of values the return is not worth the investment. Like I said, we keep things simple.

Still, there are things that need doing.

There are waders and hip boots to patch; it doesn't sound like much of a job, but it is. There are duck callers to tune and practice with. There are woods to scout.

That last thing is pointless and I'm fully aware of it, but as the days shorten and summer's heat fades, my instincts begin to spur me to action as surely as those of The Old Mallard on the Saskatchewan pothole. I know he's coming, and I must be ready. Part of that "being ready" stuff is mental, and scouting the woods is part of it. Without several pre-season reconnaissance trips to relieve the mounting pressure of the approaching season, I'd be loony as a...well, as a loon, by the time Opening Day finally arrived.

Now the autumnal equinox is long gone, and most of the scouting is behind me. The days are cool, the nights cooler still, and in a week or two there'll surely be a frost.

It won't be much longer.

• • •

The Old Mallard is now in full breeding plumage. The vestiges of brown from the last eclipse feathers fell away last week, and his flight muscles are firm and ready from his daily regimen of warm-up flights. Even between flights, he spends a good bit of time standing on his tail and vigorously flailing the air with his wings, strengthening and stretching his muscles even when he's not flying. He is at the peak of physical and mental conditioning.

If he was a falcon instead of a duck, he would be said to be in yarak – that in-the-zone peak of conditioning and fierceness all falconers strive for with their birds. But the falconer has no counterpart in the world of waterfowling, so there's no one to develop the language necessary to quantify and glorify the conditioning of this bird. Even the most ardent waterfowler would balk at calling a mallard fierce. Certainly he is beautiful; certainly he is fit. But fierce? Think of Donald. Think of Daffy.

So, we must therefore simply say he's in excellent shape and let it go at that. It's good enough.

For the past few days, The Old Mallard has been associating with others of his kind, mixing indiscriminately with drakes and hens alike. For the present, there is no conflict or rancor. Later, when the mating instinct begins to take hold, he'll become interested in hens and competitive with other drakes. For now, though, companionship and the safety of numbers are all he needs.

Migration is close at hand. For the past four nights, a skim of ice has crept out from the edges of the larger pothole The Old Mallard has moved to. Many of the juvenile mallards and almost all of the earlier-migrating species – teal, pintails, gadwalls, widgeons, shovellers – have already left. But The Old Mallard is a "red-legs", an adult veteran now into his sixth year, and he and his fellow senior citizens tend to remain as far north as temperature and snow cover will permit. In two of his five previous migrations, in fact, he never got any farther south than central Missouri.

This particular winter, though, already hints at being a bad one, and it may be The Old Mallard's ticket for his first look at the hardwood swamps of north Louisiana. That remains to be seen. Only one thing is certain at this point:

It won't be much longer.

• • •

The Arkansas duck season is now 47 days old. The first half of the split was unspectacular; abundant sheetwater in the fields and flooded woods have made for a wide dispersal of ducks, and the threat of a harsh winter stalled out somewhere north of the Missouri River. So did the bulk of the mallard migration.

The second segment of the season has been equally mediocre, but finally there's weather on the wind. A strong Saskatchewan Clipper is roaring through the Dakotas, a January blizzard the like of which hasn't been seen in that country in several years. The weatherman predicts this wicked storm will arrive in Arkansas in two days, bringing sleet, snow and near-zero temperatures to most of the state.

It's a terrible forecast for a golfer or a highway department crew member. But I'm neither of those, and I'm smiling. Like 50,000 other fools in the state, I can hardly wait.

• • •

The Old Mallard is restless. He rides the chop of a secluded backwater of the Mississippi River in Pool 26, just upstream from Alton, Illinois. He's been here since the cold fronts of mid-December pushed him this far. But the winter has been mild, and there's been no snow cover on the corn and soybean fields nearby, and The Old Mallard has been living the good life – short flights, abundant food, closed hunting seasons.

But trouble rides the north wind, and this old duck senses it. Ancient instincts are at work, instincts understood neither by the bird nor by the men who hunt him. Six hours before the brunt of the storm hits Pool 26, The Old Mallard and a hundred of his kin lift from the water and head south across the darkened landscape below, climbing to nearly 3,000 feet as they fly.

They notice, but do not need, the man-made landmarks below – the massive Lock and Dam 26 at Alton; the impossibly huge sprawl of St. Louis; myriad smaller villages and individual night lights of rural residences. They need only their internal compasses and the glittering, serpentine channel of the river itself to keep themselves on course.

They put 50 miles behind themselves each hour, running before the storm, flying down the valley of the Father of Waters.

• • •

The sky is still clear at 4 a.m., but the wind raises goose bumps on your neck as it flirts with your collar. You can smell the front coming. We all went back to our closets and cedar chests for extra clothing before meeting at the café for the ritual pre-hunt breakfast. You'd expect grim faces in the face of such weather, but there are smiles around the table this morning as we gulp strong coffee and gobble greasy eggs.

We know what's coming, and we expect it to be memorable.

• • •

The Old Mallard is tired. The new day is two hours old, and the flock crossed the Missouri border into Arkansas air space at first light. They sensed at that point they were far enough ahead of the main storm for a rest stop, and they started losing altitude above the confluence of the White and Cache rivers near Clarendon.

Some of the members of this migrating flock had been in this country before, and The Old Mallard has been content to let these birds take the lead. Still losing altitude, they passed over the flooded bottoms surrounding Red Cat, Horseshoe, East and Forked lakes, then sailed on nearly motionless wings over the long, serpentine channel that is the Crooked Lakes. Holding to the east side of the White, they passed several expanses of inviting-looking flooded timber before dropping to inspection altitude over a stretch of similar-looking flooded stuff sandwiched between the river and Maddox Bay.

• • •

It's been a disappointing hunt. We'd launched at St. Charles and made the long boat ride upriver to Maddox Bay Chute, eyes watering and faces burning from the bitter cold. But the waves of ducks we hoped would be riding the front haven't materialized, and the best our party of four has been able to do is scratch down a lone greenhead and a pair of wood ducks. The temperature has been steadily dropping since before first light, and the wind is a living, malevolent thing. Standing in the waist-deep water is a bone-chilling business even on a mild day; when the air is colder than the water, it's brutal. We take a vote: another half-hour, and we'll call it a day.

Wait, though. There's a good-sized flock, low over the woods to the northwest. A hundred birds or so, looks like. We punch a quartet of loud hail calls into the wind, and they seem interested. As we continue to call, they swing downwind and beat their way back to check us out.

If they hold their course and altitude, they'll be low enough on the first pass, and we'll take them then rather than try to make such a big flock come into our tiny opening. They look like flight ducks rather than locals; they're noticeably bigger than most of the birds we've been shooting at around here this season, and somehow they look weary, as though they've flown a long way in a short time. A hundred red-legs, fresh from the north.

The three guys with me are from Kansas, hunting the green timber for the first time. I'll let them shoot first. Being rookies, they'll no doubt pick birds from the first wave of the flock. To avoid confusion and to keep all of us from shooting at the same duck, I'll pick a bird farther back.

In fact, as the flock approaches, I have my eye on one already. Even at this distance and through the trees, it's easy to see he's bigger than any of the ducks around him. He'll be old, no doubt, and maybe tough, but he'll be a treat rubbed with sage and wrapped with bacon and baked on a bed of chopped celery, onions, apples and mushrooms. The taste of a Saskatchewan pothole, miraculously delivered to me here in Arkansas.

My mouth waters slightly, and there's a quiver in my voice as I coach my rookies in a hoarse stage-whisper: *Here they come, guys. Alan, you take the birds on the left. John, the middle ones are yours. Robbie, take the ones on the right. Nobody move yet. Here they come.*

It won't be much longer.

Chapter 26

Old Lures and a Christmas Memory

By Larry Dablemont

Some folks say that God works in strange and mysterious ways, and I reckon they are right. I wonder if sometimes even He isn't surprised at the way things turn out. When we were boys, Rusty and I were closer than brothers. We both loved the outdoors so much because our fathers were fanatics about hunting and fishing and they took us along.

We spent our boyhood days fishing the creeks and ponds around our little Ozarks community and finally got the use of Johnny Hackett's old V-bottom boat down on Schuster's Lake. From that day on we spent most of our free time catchin' bluegills and catfish and bass from the lake, or rummaging for worms or crawdads for bait.

I thought Johnny was old then, but I guess he was only in his 50s. He lived in an old farm house just a quarter mile or so from the lake and he had no relatives anywhere close that I ever knew of. So he seemed to get a kick out of Rusty and me stopping by to show him our fish and borrow something from time to time.

Once we set up our tent down on the lake to stay overnight and run trotlines, and it came up a big thunderstorm late in the evening. We got on our bicycles and hot-pedaled it up to Johnny's place and spent the night sleeping on his floor. But we went to sleep late that night, listening to the wind blow and the lightning crashing and the thunder rumbling while old Johnny told fishing stories from long ago experiences of his.

We were only about 11 or 12 then, but by the time we were old enough to drive, Johnny's place had become a regular stop for us when we were on our way to the lake or river, or on our way back with a prize catch. He'd give us fishing tips or fix a fishing reel for us or give us some old lure he had either found or grown tired of using.

When we got out of high school, Rusty joined the army and I went off to college. I finished two years of it before I flunked out. My mother always liked to say I just didn't apply myself and that I was plenty smart, but I wouldn't study hard enough. She was partly right. The other half of the story was, I wasn't quite as smart as Mom thought. Guess I took after Pop's side of the family. But I married a girl I met in college, came home and got a good job. I wondered if Rusty would return home someday, and finally he did, with a wife and two kids.

It was great, the two of us hunting and fishing again just like the good ol' days, but it didn't take long to notice that Rusty had changed some. He was a little bit wild-eyed on occasion, prone to use some of that atrocious language he learned in the army, and just a little bit ornery. But we still stopped in to see old Johnny every now and then, we took him on a squirrel hunt early in the fall, and helped him get his wood supply in, stacked up on his back porch.

Johnny was indeed getting old. I'd pick him up on Sunday mornings and he'd forget to shave, and sing too loud and go to sleep during the service. But everyone liked him, and he liked getting together with people...that is until that awful Sunday morning when he was standing in line waiting to shake hands with the preacher and he started telling one of our neighbors about the bass he had seen down at Schuster's Lake. Talking loud like he normally did, since he couldn't hear real well, he said that old bass was a "big sonofa..."

But he came right out and said the whole word, and everyone heard it. A few people snickered and some others laughed out loud and Johnny was so embarrassed that he decided not to go back to church anymore.

I talked to him about it, and couldn't change his mind. The preacher dropped by his place, and told him that even he had used a bad word or two on occasion, and he knew that everyone in the congregation had slipped up now and again and said something they weren't proud of. He reminded Johnny that Jesus had chose to spend his time with sinners and imperfect people...but it was to no avail. One thing Johnny couldn't live with, and that was embarrassment.

It was about then that Rusty spent an afternoon helping Johnny get rid of some junk around his place and found an old tackle box in a back shed. It had about 20 old lures in it, and Rusty found two in the cardboard boxes they came in, back in the 1930's. Johnny said some of them were his daddy's fishing lures. Rusty bought the whole bunch for fifty dollars, and Johnny was tickled. Fifty dollars was a lot of money.

Rusty and I went rabbit hunting in a little skiff of snow in early November, and he showed me a new compound bow he had bought at the pawn-shop for a hundred dollars. It was then that he confided in me that he sold three of the lures he had got from Johnny for $300.

That kind of ate on me, so finally one day when we were having a cup of coffee at Ruby's Roadside Cafe, I spoke up..."Rusty, I gave Johnny a ride home not long ago with a couple sacks of groceries, and helped him put them away. There was a couple of bags of beans and some potatoes and a loaf of that two-day-old bread they sell for a dime. And I remember there were a half dozen cans of dog-food, an' he ain't got a dog."

Rusty didn't say nothing, so I went on. "I ain't saying it wasn't a good thing for you to sell those lures and all, and chances are Johnny would never have sold any of them, he likely would have given them to you if you had asked. There's nothing wrong with taking something for selling them, but Rusty, that old man hasn't had a new pair of over-alls or boots for years. He gets all his clothes in the commodity room for indigents in the basement of the courthouse."

Rusty took another big slurp of coffee and listened while I went on. "That old TV of his gets two stations, and the other day when I was there you could only see about two thirds of the screen, the rest was black. He just listens to it..."

"Alright, alright," my old friend interrupted, and you could tell he was more than a little irritated. "But I gave him fifty dollars at least...all you do is go down there and haul him to church and back."

We both got a little hot under the collar and had a few words. It ended with the two of us stomping out and not speaking for a couple of weeks. And then one morning my wife came into the store and told me Rusty was in the hospital in the city, pretty bad off. Doctors thought he might lose the use of his legs. It was a blow, something I never expected. I kept thinking about those two little kids and his wife.

Come to find out he had gone bow-hunting for deer with his new bow down behind Schuster's Lake, and found an old tree stand someone had built years back. It seemed solid, so Rusty climbed up in it, about 10 or 12 feet off the ground, and sat there for a couple of hours. Eventually he saw a deer coming toward him, and he shifted around and got his weight over some rotten boards or rusted nails. Later he said it had happened in a split second, and he was falling. I guess he was knocked unconscious for a minute or two, he had some broken ribs, dislocated shoulder and a slight concussion.

But he came to, aware that he had no feelings in his legs and lots of pain everywhere else. He nearly panicked, and then began screaming for help. Somehow, old Johnny Hackett, with all his hearing problems, heard the screams faintly, and found him within an hour of the fall. Johnny had been in the woods roaming around with an old sack looking for pecans.

Rusty told me all about it as I sat by his bedside that afternoon, tears welling up in my eyes, trying hard to tell him how sorry I was about what I had said earlier. I sat there with my hand holding one of his, and his wife holding the other, realizing that I had never even considered holding a man's hand before. Rusty was hurting, and groggy from the pain medicine, but he smiled a little and answered. " Nobody ought to be sorry for sayin' what's the truth. You know who saved me don't you...it was old Johnny."

I tried to say I knew all about it, but obviously I didn't. Rusty quieted me and "I was layin' there hurtin, and went on prayin' and screamin' an' I hear a rustle and looked up to see Johnny. His eyes were big as saucers. I could tell right off it wasn't an angel, an' that was a relief."

You could tell Rusty was getting a little emotional himself, but he went on. "You know what that old man did. He knelt down there and took off that old coat of his and put it under my head, and said he'd have help in just a minute. There it is about 35 degrees and he went without his coat to give me a little more comfort."

It was quite a story. Even at his age Johnny must have ran all the way back to the Cranston place, a mile or more away, and they had an ambulance down into the woods as close as they could get. A half dozen men came to carry him out on a stretcher, and old Johnny was trying to help. He kept telling everyone that boy was like a son to him...be careful. By Christmas, Rusty was on his feet again. His spine had been bruised, but not damaged. He had some stitches in his forehead, his arm in a sling and his ribs wrapped as they healed. Thank goodness he had some good insurance and unemployment benefits where he worked. The community had a little bake sale and collected more money for his family.

And I heard he sold his bow over the local radio station.

I spent more time at his place than mine for a week or so. Judy and I got to keep the kids for awhile, and it made us decide we'd have our own baby before the next Christmas came. Little did we know that our little boy, and Rusty's third child, also a boy, would be born about three months apart.

When Christmas came, it was one to remember. Johnny Hackett got a new TV set, and a new coat, one that was warmer than anything he had ever seen. Rusty bought both. He told me that when he lay there on that cold rocky ground, two things came to him that he will always remember, one was how thin that old coat was, and how bad it smelled.

Of course, I had to do most of the work putting up that TV antenna, while Rusty, stove up too bad to do much physical work, was trying to teach Johnny how to use a remote. There wasn't a way in the world that was going to be an easy job. It took two or three weeks of daily visits and repetition. But we both got a kick out of it. And there were new stories we couldn't recall hearing when we were kids. Well, heck, some of them were stories you wouldn't want to tell a kid!

By the time it was over, Rusty had spent way more than the sale of Johnny's lures had brought him. And he told me that what I had said really had weighed on him, about the dog food and the coveralls and boots.

"I lay there that day in the woods promising God if I could ever walk again I'd do things better," he told me. "not only for Johnny, but for everybody in my life, my folks, my family, everybody I work with. Hell, by the time they came and got me, I had enough time to promise everything you can think of..."

We both had a good laugh out of that. It reminded me of that time when we were kids when I got a hook in my ear and promised God I'd never again fish on Sunday. That didn't last long.

Rusty told me of an idea he had. He said that there were more tackle boxes in that old shed of Johnny's, and some old reels and steel rods. There was a Mercury outboard motor in there that would still run, must be 60 years old. And there were a pair of old double-barreled shotguns in his closet, and one was a Parker Brothers, maybe worth a thousand dollars. The two of us, he figured, could find buyers for a lot of what Johnny called his "junk". And we could get him signed up for some government programs to help him have a better life.

Well we did that, over the years. The whole thing would make a good story in itself, how Rusty and I got into antique dealings and eventually opened up our own place out on the highway, kind of a country store where you can buy about anything.

It's still there, and doing well, with an old pot-bellied stove inside to sit around, and a couple of domino tables, and a porch with rocking chairs for the summer. Old Johnny did his share of story-telling from those rocking chairs over the years which followed.

We got him going back to church that very Christmas, by folks telling him what a hero he was and how bad the church needed him. And boy that was some Christmas. We had a big dinner up at the church and everyone drew names and Rusty and his family, and Johnny too, was right there in the midst of it. That's what surprised me, Rusty came back to being the kind of person I remember as a kid. I don't know that he kept every promise he made back then when he was lying hurt in the woods, but he did pretty good on most of them. I can tell you this, Johnny Hackett never bought dog food again.

Our boys are about eleven years old now, and starting to get interested in hunting and fishing. Last year we had another country Christmas, but it was a little sadder than most. We laid old Johnny to rest on a glorious sunny day in late November, warmer than any we could remember for that time of year. He died in his sleep, with the TV on, a re-run of his favorite western playing.

It snowed on Christmas day, and Rusty and I stood by his headstone, behind the church, watching the fresh earth slowly covered with white. Both of us could have cried, if the other hadn't been there. Rusty said what I was thinking. "You know, we'll get to see him again someday, if Christmas means anything at all."

"You say that like you wonder," I replied.

"Naw, not really," Rusty answered. "I'm sure of it. I remember when we'd have the Christmas plays at school when I was a kid, and Jesus was just a baby in a manger. I never paid much attention to what it was all about... just kids you know. But you get to looking at what Jesus said when He was a man, about our age. Until my accident I never thought much about it.

"But Johnny told me he prayed that day after he found me...that God would be there with me 'til he got back, and make me good as new again. I think maybe that day He made me better than new again!"

Neither one of us said anything, as the snow rustled the leaves in the stillness. Then Rusty put his hat back on and as we walked away he said, "I seen a monster of a buck at the back of my place last week."

Then he looked at me and grinned..."He was a big sonofa..."

Chapter 27

Why I am a Trapper

By Jim Spencer

T hey tell me I was born too late, that I should have been a mountain man, that I would have fit right in with the buckskin-clad loners who explored this land in their relentless quest for beaver plews. They tell me I'm an anachronism, that the day of my art has come and gone, that I'm a practitioner of an old-fashioned, outdated form of outdoor activity that has no place in the modern world.

They tell me, too, I'm a social misfit, that I'm a cruel and bloodthirsty perpetrator of an inhuman and inhumane activity, that my fellows and I should be thrown into jail like the criminals we are.

They tell me these things because I'm a trapper. They're wrong.

First, I was not born too late, and I would not have made a good mountain man. Sure, I'd love to have seen the Ozarks as Friedrich Gerstacker saw them in the 1830s, with elk and bison in the cedar glades and a turkey behind every bush. And sometimes I daydream about the things Messrs. Lewis and Clark saw as they ascended the Missouri more than 200 years ago. John Colter doubtless saw a great many things I'd give ten years of my life to see.

But I'm too fond of flush toilets, air-conditioning and Gore-Tex to wish I'd been born in the 1700s instead of the 1900s. Take away my insulated waders and my pickup truck and I'd wimp out on you in a hurry. I'm a Baby Boomer, born into the lap of solid middle-class comfort, and I simply wouldn't be willing to pay the necessary price to step into H.G. Wells' time machine and turn it back a couple notches. Nope. No mountain man here.

Second, I'm no more anachronism than anaconda. It's true that trapping, like prostitution, is an ancient profession. It's also true that trappers, like modern-day hookers, still use the same basic equipment their predecessors used a thousand years ago. Those opposed to trapping are quite correct when they claim there have been few significant changes in the basic leg-hold steel trap since its invention in medieval times as a device for catching poachers on the lands of European royalty. A Yankee blacksmith named Sewell Newhouse brought quality, consistency and mass production to the trap-making business in the 1820s, but the basic steel trap is much the same today as it was when days were old and knights were bold.

Rather than use that as a condemnation, though, view it instead as proof that trapping achieved state-of-the-art technology long before most other forms of outdoor recreation. The fact is, Mr. Newhouse merely refined an already efficient machine. If he could come back and go with me on my trapline this winter, he'd have no trouble recognizing the tools of the trade, because they've changed so little in appearance and function. It's hard to improve on perfection, and so the leg-hold steel trap remains the most efficient – and, in many situations, the only – method of regulating populations of many species, or of removing specific problem animals from otherwise non-problem populations. The proverbial fox in the henhouse, for example.

In fact, far from having outlived its place, trapping may now be more important than ever in terms of protecting human interests from nuisance animals and regulating populations of some species to keep their numbers within the capacity of their habitat. Man has intruded upon the natural world in a big way, and out-of-control wildlife populations can no longer be tolerated in many areas because they disrupt or inconvenience our human way of life. It's an arrogant attitude, but there it is anyway.

But so far, what we've been talking about here are differences of opinion, and differences of opinion have never bothered me much. That's why Baskin-Robbins has 31 flavors; that's why lawyers will always be with us.

What does bother me, though, is that last set of things "they" tell me: that I'm cruel, bloodthirsty, inhumane and worse. I've been accosted at parties, at work and other places by people who called me things they didn't know me well enough to call me.

It's not the name-calling itself that's troubling. What scratches going down is the fact that these people who berate me are mostly good, mostly decent, mostly intelligent people. They're not members of that lunatic fringe like the Animal Liberation Front. They don't go around blowing up research labs and lurking around shopping malls throwing red paint on fur coats. Such felonious, wacko behavior is as far removed from them on the one hand as trapping is on the other.

But they sincerely believe trapping is cruel and inhumane, and they're very concerned about the whole thing. Else they wouldn't accost me at parties and meetings. They wouldn't tell me they think I'm participating in cruelty when I trap. This concern shows through in their voices, in the earnest look in their eyes. They want me and my kind to cease and desist. They want trapping outlawed forever.

The general population of middle-class America being what it is, it's a good percentage bet that you, reading this in your easy chair in front of the fireplace, are a non-trapper. And even though you're probably a fisher or hunter or both, it's entirely possible you're anti-trapping as well.

But before you unfriend me on Facebook, give me a chance to explain the whys and wherefores of my side.

First, understand that most of us who are still trappers are not in it for the money. Picking up aluminum cans on the side of the road pays better than trapping.

There are professional trappers among us, sure, and there are also opportunists who come out of the woodwork and join the ranks only when fur prices are high. But even when the market is good, not even the best of the best can make enough from their traplines to support themselves and their families without working another job during the long off-season.

Getting paid for prime, well-handled furs is a nice perk of an enjoyable outdoor activity, but slinging fries at a fast-food joint is more profitable and less aggravating than trapping. In a recent season, my records show I spent $418.72 on supplies, equipment and gasoline, trapped for two weeks and grossed – grossed, mind you – less than a thousand dollars.

That's hardly CEO wages, but I've already told you I'm not out there for the money. I'm out there for...well, read on:

Please take note. I am not cruel and insensitive. I am not barbaric and bloodthirsty. Don't hang any halos on my head, because I assure you they don't belong there. However, the reasons they don't belong there have nothing to do with my being a trapper. My level of bloodlust is no higher – or lower – than that of the millions of my predecessors who have hunted, fished and trapped for both recreation and livelihood down through the years of this country's birth and development. It's no higher or lower than yours.

I am a professional wildlife biologist. Just as your professional training may be in business, law, farming, medicine or engineering, mine is in the management and control of wildlife populations – both upward and downward. Even though pro-trapping groups sometimes use this argument where it isn't justified, there are indeed many instances when trapping with snares, leg-hold traps or killer-type traps is the only way to control certain problem animal populations.

The beaver is a prime example of a species that needs control, not only for its own good but for the good of the humans who live in proximity to beavers. As proof that trapping is an effective control on this species, consider that the beaver was exterminated from most of North America because of over-trapping. Here in the Southeast, beavers were gone from large areas by the beginning of the Civil War, and the extermination was nearly complete by the beginning of the 20th Century. A few isolated colonies hung on in remote regions of Alabama, Mississippi and the Florida parishes of Louisiana, but for the most part southeastern beavers existed only in tales told by grandfathers.

After a 50-year hiatus, they came back. And they came with a vengeance.

From a standing start of zero animals in most places, beaver populations climbed swiftly to epidemic proportions. The increase was unimpeded by predation, since natural predators such as bears, cougars and red wolves had also been exterminated and were never effective agents of beaver control anyway.

Since the frontier way of life was gone, and since beaver fur had become a cheap, barely marketable commodity, there was little trapping pressure. Beavers rapidly re-colonized their old home grounds, and beaver dams now span streams and block ditches in virtually every county in every southern state.

Sorry if it offends your sensibilities, but the only way to control beaver populations is trapping. You can dynamite beaver dams until your ears ring like a church bell, and all you'll do is inconvenience the beavers. Go home

after a hard day of blowing dams, and the beavers will repair the damage while you sleep – cutting down some more of your trees in the process.

Same thing with muskrats. They don't build dams, but they burrow like hyperthyroid gophers, and they give farmers, road builders and pond owners fits.

Again, there's no way to keep these prolific little fellows under control besides trapping them.

Otters in catfish ponds, skunks in chicken houses, raccoons in suburban attics – all these and more are instances were trapping is the only effective solution.

However, as we've already mentioned here, this old population control argument isn't always valid. In many instances, furbearer populations cause no problems and remain fairly stable and healthy, whether they are trapped or not. Mink and bobcats are examples. These are territorial, mostly solitary species, and the biology of their kind doesn't allow them to overpopulate except in the most unusual circumstances.

But note what I just said: populations of these animals would remain relatively stable *whether they are trapped or not.* Trapping is a consumptive use of these furbearer resources, no denying it. But when it's done legally, within guidelines established by wildlife resource agencies, trapping doesn't deplete populations of these animals. Natural reproduction replaces those individuals taken by trapping, just as it replaces those taken by predation and disease, and the circle of life rolls merrily on.

Most of us make every effort to trap as humanely as possible. No fooling, we do; humane trapping is also efficient trapping, and it's just plain good business to do it humanely. But in addition, most trappers realize the potential for pain and suffering, and we do everything we can to minimize it.

Most trappers use drowning sets or killer-type sets where possible, and we run our traps daily as the law prescribes when these type sets can't be made. The result is not only less discomfort for the critter, but also a higher percentage of catches. The trapped animal doesn't have as much chance to fight the trap, injure itself and possibly escape.

There are slob trappers out there, sure. But there are also slob drivers, and we don't all need to be banished from the highways because some fool wants to drive a hundred and weave in and out of traffic. Neither should all trappers be penalized because some other fool sets an illegal trap with teeth on its jaws. Traffic regulations exist to control the dimwits, not the right-minded. Trapping regulations have a similar purpose.

I am no dimwit, or at least I don't think so, and therefore I try to follow not only the law but also my conscience. And that's why I have no problem, biologically, morally or ethically, with being a trapper. I'm comfortable in the role of predator, and I don't feel ill at ease when I insert myself into the life cycles of various furbearers. On the contrary, I enjoy it; it makes me feel closer to the land. It turns me into a player, not a spectator.

I do my best to make each and every set as humane as possible, so the trapped animal will drown or be quickly killed, or will be securely held in a trap of the proper size, strength and configuration to minimize injury and discomfort. Almost every other trapper of my acquaintance does these things, too, and I know literally hundreds of them.

I'm no Pollyanna. I realize that when the jaws of a steel trap snap on the foot of an animal, it hurts. I've caught my own hands and fingers in traps hundreds of times, so I know what I'm talking about here. I'd be lying if I said it was pleasant.

But natural death isn't too pleasant, either, if you happen to be a muskrat. Substituting a quick drowning for being ripped to shreds by a great horned owl or eaten alive by a coyote, or dying slowly from internal parasites, doesn't seem like such a bad deal. The muskrat might not take the deal if he had a choice, but it's the best I can offer. At least when I catch the muskrat in a trap, its fur gets used for warmth and beauty rather than as binder in a coyote's scat or a horned owl's pellet. In the process, I get to perform my chosen role of predator, of player, of participant in the web of life.

And if all this doesn't convince you, I don't know what else there is to say.

Chapter 28

The Buck That Got Away

By Larry Dablemont

There's a beautiful buck deer head hanging over my fireplace, with a set of antlers like I ain't never seen the equal to. Maybe you've seen better, if so I don't care and I don't want to hear about it. If you were sitting in my living room, you wouldn't be able to see that deer head over my fireplace, turned just a little so it looks like he is distracted by something off to the left. You can't see it, but I can. Sometimes when I am lying on my back on the couch napping a little and there's a warm fire burning in the fireplace and the lights are low, I look up there at those widespread antlers, ten points regular and one more if you count the little weird tine coming off the right beam hanging down toward his ear.

Granted, the rocks in the fireplace up above the mantle would look bare to anyone else, but to me, he's there. He's my buck and I can see him just like I saw him that day in the sights of my old .54 caliber muzzleloader.

My friend, Jim Watson, gave me that muzzleloader. I didn't know him all that well back then. At the time I thought he must be nuts for giving me his muzzleloader. Well, if you know Jim, he is a little nuts, but in a good way, like big-hearted, old time country people are. He didn't want anything in return, he said he had read my newspaper column for some time and noticed I had borrowed a muzzleloading rifle from a friend of mine to hunt with.

He said I needed to have my own rifle and he didn't use that one because he had better ones. The one he gave me seemed awfully good to me, it was a Thompson Center Hawken rifle and it made me feel like a mountain man. At sixty to seventy yards it would shoot as straight as my aim would allow it, and my aim is good. I've got eyes like a sharp-shinned hawk and a hand as steady as sunset on a calm day.

At 100 yards or so, a muzzleloader isn't the most accurate rifle, and the bullet loses some velocity and wobbles out of twist and may not hit where you are aiming. The answer to that problems is, don't hunt where you can see that far! Don't hunt where you can see any farther than 60 yards or so. I usually wind up hunting bucks in heavy cover and can't see more than 50 yards, because after the carnival we call the November gun season is over, the bucks don't hang around much in open country.

I always wanted to hunt old man Farley's place, because nowhere on his place can you see more than 50 yards. I don't know if you remember him... old Joe Farley has a place down on the river, where he grew up with his brothers, Charley and Harley Farley, always said he glad he was the youngest, or he would have had one of his brother's names, and already been dead from the strain of it, like they were. He's sort of a rascally, cynical, pessimistic-natured old coot, but I like him because he don't put on any airs, and he says things like it is.

He was sitting on his porch that first time I met him, he said he had read that book I had left him and didn't much like it. I told him I hadn't much liked writing it, and he said he could see why. He said it sounded like a bunch of baloney to him and about half of it probably was made up. I told him the whole darn thing was made up, but I couldn't make a living selling true stories because my life had been too boring. He grinned a little at that, and I asked him, if I was to float down the river and camp on the gravel bar below his place if I could hunt deer on his land in the muzzleloader season.

"Hell no," he said, "would you let me come over and camp in your lawn and shoot your rabbits?"

I thought about it for awhile and said I probably would let him shoot the same number of rabbits out of my lawn as I would shoot deer out of his woods. We argued about it for awhile and he said he knew my grandpa and never liked him until he got to know him, and then he only liked him a little. But he said because my grandpa had brought him catfish on occasion and made him a johnboat once for half price, he was inclined to let me hunt. We shook hands on the deal and I told him, deer or no deer, I'd bring him some catfish.

Come muzzleloader season, it was too cold to camp on the gravel bar, and old man Farley told me he had an old bed and stove in the little broken down cabin on the little hill above his place that I could stay in. I came in and had coffee with him that evening about sundown and in the light of a kerosene lantern we swapped stories until bedtime. He finally told me where the big buck hung out, and said if I saw that buck I'd likely wet my pants. I huffed up at that, told him I had seen big bucks before, and most likely I'd pass one up to get some good venison. I knew better, but he didn't.

"He won't be fit to eat," the old man told me, "because he's old...but he's got a heck of a headgear. Like I said, if you see him you'll likely pee all over yourself...or worse!"

Later that night, I got a good fire going in the little broken down old house, then zipped up in my sleeping bag and got warm. I woke up about

The Buck That Got Away

two in the morning when a mouse ran across my face, got up and restoked the fire and threw a couple more split oak chunks in the stove. Got a drink, visited the porch shivering in the cold and got back in the sack. I slept a little later than I intended to, but hurried around at dawn to drink some coffee and get out there on the rock ledge overlooking the deer trail going down to the river. I was bundled up pretty good but it was still cold.

I had one heck of a spot. It was a little like being in a tree stand, because I was up above the trail on that ledge, and my scent was above any deer which might pass that way. Of course if one came up behind me, my chances would be slim-to-none or worse. That's a little less than my best chances are if I have one in front of me.

I don't know if I have ever told anyone this, but I don't much like deer hunting. It is hours and hours of uncomfortableness, aching butt and boredom with only a few minutes of heart-pounding excitement. Anyone who claims to be a hunter and has to wear a blaze orange cap and vest is going to be a little disgusted with deer hunting. The woods are full of city slickers and greenhorns and ATV riders and target shooters with high-powered rifles and I don't much cotton to it.

Muzzleloader season is different. Up to a few years ago, if a man hunted deer with a muzzleloader you knew he was a pretty fair hunter, an outdoorsman, not just a would-be-er out once a year. When you hunt with a muzzleloader you can take off the orange monkey suit and hunt a little because there won't be any game wardens out in the woods, they'll be somewhere warm, likely watching figure skating on TV.

You can spend a few hours walking slowly into the wind, and stopping every now and then to watch and listen. And it IS enjoyable to sit out in the woods and see the day come to life and watch all the birds and wildlife around you. It is that time of year that young male squirrels make fools of themselves chasing young female squirrels which they can't seem to catch. I guess eventually, the females get slower or the males get faster because in late February and March, there are a bunch of little squirrels beginning to be born that are certainly not a result of all that "you can't catch me" nonsense.

Well so much for philosophy! What I did was, I got bored and went to sleep about mid-morning and fell off the ledge I was sitting on, landing in a pile of wet leaves just off to the side of the little trickle of water, and I slid down the hill about 15 feet, catching myself by hooking one leg around a redbud tree just in time to avoid going over the next level right onto that deer trail.

My heart pumping and one elbow throbbing, I righted myself and realized that I was more wide awake than I had been all morning. I heard a crashing in the brush to my left and before I knew what was happening, old man Farley's big buck was right there in front of me, not fifteen yards away.

I still had my muzzleloader, and what followed didn't take as long as it seemed, but it is going to take awhile to describe it. I cocked it and brought the old .54 caliber Hawken rifle to my shoulder and put the sights on his heart. The old buck just stood there, that tremendous set of antlers lowered a little, a look in his eye as if he was thinking, "what the heck is this?"

And for a moment, I realized that the gods of the hunt had smiled on me. I was in the best situation I have ever been in as a deer hunter accidently of course, but still there I was with one leg locked around that redbud tree, that trickle of water seeping down the other leg and the biggest buck I had ever seen right there where he couldn't react quick enough and I couldn't miss. I knew I had him and he knew I had him.

I could see him saying to himself something along the lines of "OH !"

And then a funny thing happened. You could see he was just too old to give a darn. He looked at me as if to say, "O.K. You got me, I ain't gonna break my neck trying to get away...I've had a good life, fought the good fight, had a long reign."

And for a second, I thought to myself, "*Do I want to do this? He's an old veteran, like old man Farley, a part of these woods, deserving of a hunters respect, a patriarch, a monarch, a piece of heritage.*"And then I looked again at that wide heavy rack and thought, "What the heck, he'd look just as good over the fireplace as he would out there in the cold and the mud."

And then I squeezed the trigger!

Braced for the explosion, I have no way of

telling you what it was like to hear the pop of that cap, with no powder charge 'ka-whoom' to follow it. A primer cap sounds like a really small firecracker, like a kid's cap-gun, like a pellet gun. And then it was my turn...I said to myself, "OH!" He looked at me a moment longer, grinned a little and turned to lope down the trail, flashing that big white flag, gone forever. I moaned and cussed and cried a little, and it wasn't because my elbow was all skinned up from the fall, with my back hurting and that cold rivulet running through one pant leg. It was because of seeing that buck leave!

He was gone, and I knew what had happened. I had been practicing and cleaning that rifle so much that I had forgot to reload it after the last target-shooting session. I had intended to ram a powder charge down it and then follow with a mini-ball the night before, but I had got to talking to old man Farley and forgot it. That morning, I had put a primer cap on the nipple and never thought about it being unloaded. The gods of the hunt weren't smiling on me after all, they were rolling around on the ground laughing and holding their sides.

But if you think I am going to moan and groan about it here, you are wrong. I ain't. I am used to being the most unlucky, misfortunate, down and out misfit I ever knew of. I was born under a black sky, and I'm not one to carry on about it. That's just the way it is. But my foot still hurts from kicking rocks and stumps all the way back to old man Farley's place.

We ate dinner there, squirrel and gravy and biscuits and some other things I can't put a label on, but when you're hungry, enough salt and pepper and butter makes anything edible.

Old man Farley said it was as it should be. That old buck deserved a better fate than I could offer him, and he was so old his steaks would have tasted like a coyote's scent post, and been nearly as tough. He said I ought to be glad I didn't remember to load my gun like a normal, medium-intellect type of deer hunter would have.

Sitting out on the porch later in the rocking chairs, drinking hot cider and watching another squirrel chase, he went on to say, "If you'd have kilt that big ol' buck, you'd be down there right now up to your ankles in mud with blood up to your elbows, gaggin' whilst you tried to get the entrails out. We'd have to try to pull him up that hill by the horns and I might have a stroke or a heart attack and you'd feel awful. Then you'd have to buy a hunnert pounds of pork and pay a processor a small fortune just to have something mixed up with the meat so's that you could eat it."

Chapter 29

The Last Trophy

By Jim Spencer

Howard is a retired farm implement dealer. He's 76 and is a charter member of the One Shot Hunting Club, which he and six other young men started more than a half-century ago. He is the last man standing from that original septet.

Throughout that half-century of his membership, Howard has borne more than his share of the responsibility. Despite his age, he still does more than his share of the work necessary to maintain a hunting camp. The other members, all Howard's juniors by at least 20 years, unanimously agree One Shot wouldn't be half the club it is without his continuing efforts.

One Shot owns a little better than a thousand acres and leases twice that much from an adjoining paper company. With their more than 4-1/2 square miles of land, they're the largest deer club in the county. It's a prime mix of piney woods, thickety cut-overs and bottomland hardwood timber, with more than 20 well-maintained food plots. Guess who plows and plants most of them.

Most of One Shot's 22 members have two permanent stands, but Howard has only one. "When you've got the best stand on the property, why would you want another one?" he always said when asked about it. And it was arguably true, it probably is the best. The stand itself consists of a roomy, roofed shooting house eight feet off the ground, built around three sides of a big white oak. It's a quantum improvement from the old plank nailed in a fork that served as Howard's stand for the first 10 years. The tree overlooks the juncture of piney woods and hardwoods, where two brushy draws come together at the edge of the pines. One of the club's food plots is both within sight and within rifle range.

Behind the white oak, a 60-acre pasture of bahia and dallisgrass is bisected by a brushy fenceline that runs straight as a ruler for 400 yards, from Howard's stand to a timbered block of more than a thousand acres leased by the Six-Gun Hunting Club, One Shot's friendly rival in the area. The fenceline provides the only protected travel route for deer moving between the two clubs, and it is heavily traveled.

Howard has covered this stand every year since the club was formed, and less than a dozen times in all those years has he failed to tag a nice buck on opening day. For only three years has he hunted the entire season without making a kill – the last three.

Because, you see, Howard has gotten old, and he knows that each passing season might be his last. He has decided that his last buck, if he ever kills another one, will be a trophy that will be talked about around the camp for years to come. He has passed up almost a dozen nice bucks in these past three years, but so far that big one hasn't come along. Howard has been content to wait.

This particular opening day dawned dewy and clear, but a little too warm for good deer hunting. At first light, Howard had already been in his stand for a half-hour. The mosquitoes were hungry, but he didn't seem to notice. He was as immobile as the oak tree itself, letting the bugs drink their fill. The only movement he made was a slow, almost imperceptible sweep of his head as he scanned the area. His faded but still sharp blue eyes didn't miss much.

Half-light brightened to full-light and the resident squirrel population came to life. Branches shook. Acorns fell. At one point, Howard had eight of the hyperactive little rodents in sight, and there were at least two more in the white oak above him. One of them, a young fox squirrel, dropped onto the roof of the stand and hopped from there to the shooting port, less than three feet from the old man. They made eye contact, and the startled squirrel beat a quick retreat. Howard took it in with amusement, but never moved so much as an eyebrow.

A mile south, One Shot's collection of deer hounds – mostly Walkers, with a few redbones thrown in – struck a hot track and the chase was on. Howard pulled his attention away from the squirrels, feeling a momentary twinge of guilt at having let his attention slip.

Minutes later, Six-Gun's dogs struck paydirt in the woods across the field to the north. Howard grew even more alert. Something was likely to happen soon.

The chase on the Six-Gun lease went quickly in the other direction, but the One Shot pack grew ever closer, and Howard focused most of his attention in that direction. All around, at varying distances, shots were fired as first one hunter and then another had their chances. Howard sat, still as a tombstone. An observer might have thought the old man to be asleep, but Howard's every sense was tuned.

The dogs were still a half-mile away when Howard caught a hint of movement in the brush of the west draw and two does appeared. They came steadily on toward the crossing, covering ground quickly but without panic, and passed within rock-throwing distance of Howard's stand.

The old man had already quit watching the does and was instead looking behind them, at the west draw they'd come out of. His reward was quick in coming. A nice eight-pointer stepped into view. He was a shooter, with a spread of about 18 inches and thick main beams, and Howard watched him with interest although he'd known at first look he wasn't good enough to be the last trophy. He let the buck come and go, putting the crosshairs on his neck and silently mouthing "Bang!" as the animal stood watching his back trail at the edge of the woods. Then he was gone, following the does along the fencerow into Six-Gun's holdings. The dogs came through a few minutes later. Four of them, all Walkers, and they noisily followed the trail along the fencerow and into the other woods. Now both chases were north of the field, and Howard shifted most of his attention in that direction.

It took longer this time, but again his vigilance paid off. A flicker of motion at the edge of Six-Gun's woods caught his eye, and a deer materialized. The animal was slipping, keeping inside the edge of the brushy woods, and it was hard to keep track of. But then the deer reached the fencerow and started south across the field, and Howard finally saw antlers. They seemed promising to the naked eye, and when he raised the rifle for a closer look through the scope, he whistled softly through his teeth.

This was him. This was the one he'd been waiting for, the one that would hang on the clubhouse wall. This one was worthy of being chosen for an old man's final trophy. This one was Boone and Crockett material. On the big buck came, never faster than a walk, stopping often. He carried his head low, the way many old bucks do. At 200 yards he stopped to study his back trail, and Howard settled the crosshairs on the base of the gray-brown neck. At this distance and angle, a shot there would range down through the heart and lungs, and it would be a DRT – dead right there – kill. But a thin screen of brush made the shot uncertain, and Howard held his fire.

Satisfied he wasn't being followed, the buck resumed his sneak-walk, drawing closer with every step. The range was inside 150 yards now, and the old man had picked out the opening at 125 yards where he'd take the shot. He put the crosshairs on that opening and waited.

Murphy's Law says whatever can go wrong will go wrong. The buck entered a cane thicket on the fencerow and failed to reappear. Howard held the crosshairs on the opening for 15 minutes. When his eyes began to water, he lowered the gun. Evidently the buck had bedded down in the cane.

Howard was weighing his options when Mr. Murphy made another appearance, this time in the form of a lone black-and-tan hound. Howard watched in frustration as the bony animal came out of the hardwoods, crossed beneath the stand and started along the fencerow, heading north toward the cane thicket.

The inevitable soon happened. Dog met deer and they were off, headed rapidly north, the monster buck utilizing the cover for maximum effectiveness. Howard tracked the buck in the scope, and though several times he had opportunities to shoot, he was never certain of a good hit. Deer and dog entered Six-Gun territory and the old man lowered the rifle. Two minutes later, a single rifle shot ended the chase.

Howard didn't realize he'd been holding his breath until it came out of him in a long sigh, the loudest sound he'd made since before daylight. He smiled to himself, amused that a geezer like himself could still have such a juvenile reaction, and then he rose creakily to his feet, knee and hip joints popping.

"I hope you died quick, old fella," he said, looking across the yellow field. He unloaded his battered old .351 Winchester, lowered it to the ground on a piece of rope, and climbed carefully down from the white oak stand.

• • •

The members of One Shot were shocked and saddened the next morning when they discovered Howard had died peacefully in his sleep. By common agreement there was no hunting that day, Tuesday, but it was decided Tuesday night that the hunt would resume Wednesday. Everyone felt, correctly, that Howard would have wanted it that way.

Thursday, the entire combined membership of One Shot and Six-Gun drove 150 miles to Howard's hometown for the funeral. A week later, there was a new trophy on the common-room wall of One Shot's clubhouse, bracketed by the nearly identical ten-point mounts that were the club's mascots.

The new addition consisted of a handsome walnut plaque with an unfired .351 cartridge affixed to it. The round had come from the pocket of Howard's hunting pants, and although nobody knew, it was the same one that had been in the chamber of his rifle the day the big buck got away. Howard had never told the story.

The inscription under the cartridge was simple: "In fond memory of Howard G. Barnes, who never shot just for the sake of shooting."

Howard's grandson is a member of the One Shot club now, and he has inherited the old man's white oak stand. The location is as good as it ever was, and the grandson kills a decent buck or two there every year.

But no one, not even young Howard, covers the old man's stand on opening day.

Chapter 30

The Kid Who Went to War

By Larry Dablemont

It was the day before Thanksgiving in 1939. There was a knock on the door and a boy stood outside, waiting for the old man to answer. When the door opened he tipped his hat politely and said, "Mr., I reckon you don't recall me, but I'm Joe Roggins' youngest boy Jimmy...and I come to ask if I could shoot me a couple of mallards off'n yore pond." Before the old man could answer, the boy went on... "My Pa's been feelin' poorly and he allowed as how he'd like a big ol' mallard duck or two for dinner tomorrer, an' they's a bunch of 'em on yore pond. He'd be thankful to eat one of 'em on Thanksgiving."

Charley Claymon and his wife were in their early sixties. Neither knew the young seventeen-year-old kid who stood there before them in ragged overalls and an old patched suit coat probably made ten years before the boy was born. His overalls were two or three inches too short. Charley couldn't help but smile at the sight of him. But heck, it was Thanksgiving and he and his wife Eva had grandkids coming and Charley felt good that day.

"Oh hell boy, them mallards ain't mine," he said, "they belong to the good Lord, an' I 'spect He made 'em to feed folks, so if'n you shoot a couple, I don't care. But shoot some on the water and bring me one too. They's a long cane pole on the backside of the barn and you can use it to fetch 'em to the pond bank."

"That was nice of you, Charley," his wife said as they watched the young man walk through down the gravel road with the cane pole and an old hammer double-barrel twelve gauge.

"Well I felt sorry for the kid," he grumbled. "Joe is just an ol' drunk, I ain't seen him in a long time...figgered he was dead. Never knowed he had a boy that young."

A little later in the day, they heard two distant shotgun blasts, but the young man who had promised to come back with a mallard was not seen again.

On Thanksgiving Day, his daughter brought a traditional turkey with her kids and her husband, and Charley bemoaned the fact that he didn't have a baked wild mallard to go with it. "Never even thanked me, that boy, and he never brought back that cane pole...reckon that's the new generation for you." Then he added, "But what could you expect from the son of ol' drunk Joe?"

On Christmas Eve that year, the Ozarks was cloaked in an inch of snow, and it was cold. Migrating ducks were on every pond. Charley Claymon had his chores done and was shaving when his wife Eva said there was someone knocking at the door. Charley hadn't even had breakfast yet! No wonder he was a little cranky! But he cheered up when he opened the door. Before him was Jimmy Roggins in that flimsy old coat and the ragged overalls.

"Good God in Heaven kid," Charlie said, "Get in here out of the cold before you let all the heat out...whatcha got in that bag?"

"Well, I owed ya some mallards Mr. Claymon, so I brung you some for Christmas and I brought back that pole I had a yourn," the boy said as he handed over the bag. "I got 'em plucked and gutted with the head and legs cut off. Ready for b'ilin."

For the Claymon family it was a day to remember. Mrs. Claymon wasn't about to let the boy go without coffee and biscuits and gravy. It was at the table that Jimmy teared up just a little and told why he hadn't returned a month before.

"Pa et ever bit of them mallards," he said as his eyes moistened, "But it was two days later he came down sickly while we was splittin' some firewood. He just up and died on the front porch of what the doctor from Licking said was a heart failin'. We buried him at the graveyard behind the church at Plato on the seventh of this month, the day I turned 18."

As it turned out, Jimmy Roggins had a cousin in the Navy, and the young man had sold what little his father had owned, some chickens and a milk cow and a rangy old hog, and then joined the Navy. A neighbor was to take him to catch a train on Christmas Day to California. But not before he got a Christmas present from Eva Claymon; some socks and an old coat that she insisted he take.

"Well, I got that old shotgun of Pa's out on the porch and I would like to give it to you for a Christmas present," the boy said. "Maybe you could get somethin' fer it somewhere and buy yourself a new cookin' pot or something like that." And with that he was gone, up to the country store at Bucyrus to catch a ride to the train station in Cabool.

The Claymons placed the old shotgun in a closet with that worn suit coat, thinking about the boy at Christmas time in 1940, hoping he was doing well. He would have turned 19 two weeks before Christmas, certainly no longer a boy. Then Christmas drew near in 1941. With it, there came awful, horrible news from Hawaii and a Naval installation at a place called Pearl Harbor. All across the Ozarks, every radio that worked was in use. There was word that the Japanese bombers had attacked and sunk several American battleships and that there were thousands of servicemen dead.

A somber Charlie Claymon went to his barn to work that night while his wife cried. He said nothing to her about the 7th of December being Jimmy's birthday. He knew that the boy was likely among the dead.

The Battle of Midway came months later, and the United States Navy decimated Japanese destroyers and aircraft carriers, nearly wiping out the enemy navy. The years passed and on a golden September day in 1945, Japan surrendered. What a wonderful fall that was as Ozark boys who had become part of the greatest fighting force the world had ever known began to come home. What a Thanksgiving that was in the hill country of Missouri and Arkansas. But there was so much sadness too, because many Ozark families never saw again the young men they watched go off to war. Charley Claymon was slowing down, beset with arthritis. He needed help around his small farm, but he had never had a son. He thought of old drunk Joe Roggins who had had 3 or 4, and on December 7th, he particularly thought of Jimmy, who he would have been so proud to have raised. He knew that Jimmy's body might be in the sunken hull of one of those warships in Pearl Harbor.

And he was shaving again that Christmas morning when there was a knock on the door. He complained because Eva couldn't leave the kitchen and he had to go off half shaved. He opened the door and a tall young man was standing there, a young man who looked so much like young Jimmy Roggins had looked standing there years ago. But his voice was deep as he said with a big smile on his face, "I've come for my shotgun... I'm wantin' some mallards for Christmas dinner!"

If there was room here, I could tell you about that wonderful Christmas day in that little house back in the woods along the main gravel road a few miles west of the Big Piney River. But I don't need to do that...you can envision it yourself. I WILL tell you that Jimmy Roggins went to work on his old home-place, a nice little cabin with a fireplace and six acres of hard-scrabble ridgetop with a four-acre clearing below. Oh yes, a half dozens chickens and a pair of calves and two or three hogs. And during the summer before the Christmas of 1946, Jimmy had met a local girl at the skating rink in Houston. They were married before Thanksgiving. And for years after that, Charley Claymon, as December came around, boasted that the coming

Christmas day was gonna be the best ever. He often said that he and his boy Jimmy was gonna get some mallards for Christmas dinner. He said he never had favored turkey!

Chapter 31

Meditations on Squirrel Hunting

By Jim Spencer

There was only a suggestion of a sound, a faint whisper of claws against bark. If the same thing happened now, I'd never hear it.

But my pliant 10-year-old eardrums, uncalloused by the accumulated hammering of the tens of thousands of rounds of ammunition I've burned in the decades since, picked it out. I cranked my head slowly to the left, remembering Dad's admonition to make all my movements in waltz time...and there he was! Big as a house cat, red as a barnyard rooster, the fox squirrel spread-eagled head down on the trunk of a Nuttall oak a scant 15 feet away, glaring suspiciously at my blue jean-clad form.

He was just right to be wrong. I shoot left-handed, and the squirrel was 15 degrees behind my left shoulder. Even from the abyss of my inexperience, I knew I wouldn't be able to shift far enough to shoot left-handed without spooking him, so I determined to try him from the wrong side.

Inch by agonizing inch, I finally got the gun around and pointing in the proper direction, the squirrel eyeballing me all the while. The old Stevens .22 autoloader weighed a short ton, and I was a skinny kid, and I was hyperventilating. When I tried to line up the iron sights, the barrel wobbled like a leafy branch in a stiff breeze. In desperation, I finally slapped at the trigger as the front bead passed by the squirrel's head.

It won't surprise you to hear that I missed. But the squirrel gave me an undeserved second chance by leaping four feet to another tree trunk and freezing again, head up this time, trying to figure out what had just happened. Somehow, the act of shooting and missing had calmed me a little. Cool as a cucumber (not true, but that's the way I remember it,) I drilled him through the ears on the second try.

In all probability, there were other squirrels in and around that stand of red oaks that day. But if there were, they were safe from me. That cat-sized fox squirrel was my first one, and I had eyes that day for no others but him. When Dad came back late that morning to pick me up, he found me holding my squirrel in my lap, playing with it like it was a toy soldier – examining its tail, peering into its black eyes, smoothing its fur, carefully dabbing away any stray blood that threatened to mar the beauty and dignity of my first trophy. I can close my eyes and see that squirrel still, plastered against that tree trunk and piercing me with one fierce, beady eye, tail curled over his back in that familiar *give-me-any-lip-and-I'll-bark-at-you* position. Years later, I had a similar-sized fox squirrel mounted in that identical pose in honor of Old Number One, which, despite my protests, we ate. We weren't exactly poor folks, but we lived pretty close to the paycheck, and there wasn't any spare cash laying around for silly frills like taxidermy.

Old Number One's flesh is many years digested, but his memory remains. And it's not because of his surrogate hanging from my office wall, either. I remember that squirrel because he was my introduction to the world of the hunter. His blood was the first I ever spilled; he was the prey that proved me a predator.

Squirrels have fulfilled that role for more of us older hunters than not, at least those of us who grew up in the South. Squirrel hunting, in the days when deer and turkeys were scarce, was the most popular form of hunting there was. The typical hunter from the 1940s through the 1990s cut his teeth on squirrels, and many of us have never managed to shake the habit. Nor have we ever wanted to.

It's a thing steeped in tradition, this squirrel hunting, and the tradition dates to the earliest settlers. Before the Civil War, our great-great-great grandfathers were being sent out with the family muzzle-loader and told to bring back a mess of squirrels for breakfast. It was a duty, sure, but an enjoyable one, and the tradition persisted through successive generations. My own father, who grew up in the heart of the Great Depression, was the last of the Spencer clan to be sent out to fetch breakfast from the hickory trees on the back forty, but he wasn't the last of the Spencers to enjoy squirrel hunting.

Today, living in the country with a huge expanse of national forest literally at my back door, I'm fond of following in the footsteps of my ancestors. No one sends me out there to fetch a mess of squirrels for breakfast, but sometimes I go anyway. Not because I have to, but because I need to.

Affluence, a higher standard of living and a more urbanized population have all conspired to largely do away with subsistence hunting. My father and his before him hunted to put meat on the table; I hunt to fulfill an atavistic inner need. The economic incentive has not only gone away, it has reversed. Given the cost of equipment, gasoline, licenses and ammunition, wild meat is pretty spendy these days. I can eat steak much more economically than squirrel or duck or venison.

In the final analysis, of course, economics has nothing to do with it. Originally it did, sure, but not now. My grandfather and my father are both gone, but during their lifetimes their circumstances improved to that point of reversing returns; it became cheaper for them not to hunt than to hunt. But neither of them quit, because neither of them wanted to. My dad was even once known to drag my mother away from an East Coast vacation and drive a thousand miles in two days to get back home in time for the opening day of squirrel season. It doesn't make a lick of sense, but there it is anyway.

No doubt you've noticed I'm struggling here, trying to explain something I don't understand myself. But there's something about being in the woods, rifle or shotgun in hand, that can't be replaced by the so-called non-consumptive outdoor sports like hiking, canoeing or wildlife photography. These activities are pleasant and enjoyable, and I do all of them from time to time. But not during squirrel season.

It's not as though I feel like I absolutely have to kill a sackful every time I go out there. There was a time when I measured the success of the hunt in terms of body counts, but not any more. I'm longer in the tooth and grayer in the beard now, and I no longer feel that overwhelming blood lust most of us feel when we're young and just beginning to hunt.

Maybe I'm flattering myself, but I like to think this is because I've gone beyond learning how to hunt and am now learning how to be a hunter. Learning how to hunt is merely a process of accumulating skills and habits – stealth, patience, alertness, patience, marksmanship, patience, woodsmanship. And, of course, patience. Anybody with enough of that and enough coordination to keep from tripping over his or her own feet can eventually learn how to hunt. Learning how to be a hunter, though, is largely a matter of attitude.

Fulfilling man's ancient role as the Ultimate Predator is my professed reason for being out there, but it runs much deeper than that. I hunt from necessity just as surely as did my great-grandfather, but while his necessity was rooted in economics, mine stems from another source. Great-Granddad was duty-bound to bring down as many bushytails as he could, and furthermore to do it quickly, with the smallest expenditure of powder and shot as possible.

There is no such urgency when I hunt. Breakfast is not at stake, and so my hunting is born not of economics but emotion.

This profound difference allows me much more freedom than Great-Granddad ever had. As a modern-day squirrel hunter, I am free of those old pressures. It's nice to bring home a mess of bushytails, but nobody goes hungry if I don't. Therefore, I can extract a greater measure of enjoyment from my hunts, if a lesser measure of meat. The only pressure I feel is what I've put there myself, and with each passing year that self-imposed pressure grows lighter and lighter.

From long-ago talks with my father, I know he felt the same way. He remembered those old pressures, and told me he was glad they were gone. Despite their absence, though, his urge to hunt remained strong until he died. Strong enough, as I've already mentioned, to pull him back on a forced march all the way from the Eastern Seaboard, towing in his wake an Airstream trailer and a protesting mate, so he could go sit with his .22 against a familiar log in the White River bottoms and shoot three squirrels through the head on opening day.

The urge remains strong in his son, too, and I've tried to pass it along. When my daughter Leslie was 10, I took her on her first solo squirrel hunt the same way her grandfather had taken me when I was that age. I left her sitting in a grove of red oak trees, with whispered instructions to watch the trees, stay put and wait for me.

She did. When I came back to pick her up a couple hours later, I found her right where she was supposed to be, holding a dead gray squirrel in her lap.

Playing with it like it was a toy soldier.

Chapter 32

Firewood for Christmas

By Larry Dablemont

I f any man had a right to be a recluse, it was Calvin Maggard. He had lost some of his productive years while serving time in prison in the 1930's. While he was in prison, his wife left him. When he got out, he retreated to the little homeplace and 160 acres where he had been born and raised just below Cooper's Ridge on the hillside above the river. There, over the years, he just sort of built a shell around himself. He had retired early because of a bad leg, which he had injured on the job, and it earned him a modest pension. The few people who knew him knew he was a fine man at heart, but not many got to know him well. He kept away from people and he kept people away from him. Cal Maggard was as ordinary and common as dirt. That was his opinion of himself.

Billy Richards came home from World War Il, just an ordinary, common war hero like all the others who had fought overseas. He was only 24 years old when got married and in no time at all he and his young wife had three small children to raise. A hermit he wasn't. Billy never met a stranger and he had a swarm of family and friends. He showed up on Cal Maggard's porch one Saturday morning just after Thanksgiving with his hat in his hand and never hesitated one bit to come in and have coffee. Cal Maggard didn't know what to make of the visit.

"Grandpa said he knew your folks," the younger man said, "liked 'em both. Said you was a wild one when you were a boy."

The older man turned away without saying anything.

Billy went on, "Well now shucks that ain't nothin' to be ashamed of I don't reckon, I was that way some myself 'til the army got ahold of me."

Maggard turned and looked at the young guy sitting at his table, and bit his lip. When he was younger, he would have shown the brash young man the door and told him to stay away. Age made him more tolerant, and his curiosity wouldn't let him do it. "What in the world brought you here, boy?" he said. "I don't reckon I ever even run into you except that one time at the pool hall."

Billy nodded his head. "I don't want to make you mad at me, but I've noticed you got a bad leg and I figgered maybe you might need some

firewood for the winter if that's the case I'm your man. I need to make a few extra dollars fer buyin' a Christmas present or two for my kids."

"I ain't got the money to be hirin' nobody, or buyin' firewood or worryin' about..." Maggard was saying as the young man interrupted him.

"I ain't made my offer yet, you best wait 'til you hear it." Billy told him as he nervously bounced his feet beneath the table and finished his cup of coffee. "I'm ready to fill your front porch with firewood on weekends, haul it in my old pick-up and only ask two dollars an hour. 'Cause you got that strip of woods up there on the ridge where the tornado went through last spring, and there's downed trees that need cuttin', lots of 'em. And there's brush needs stackin' an' I'm the man to do it...I'm a bargain at two bucks an hour, an' I won't lie about my time neither."

The older man looked hard at the visitor, and sat down at the table to think. "I've thought some on trying to clean it up, but I want the good trees that are left standing to stay. There's quite a few ricks of wood in that mess. Reckon we could clean it up a little, and leave the brushpiles for the rabbits."

"See there," Billy said with a grin, "I told you you was gonna be happy I stopped in." He looked into his empty coffee cup and shook his head. "I'd have another cup of this if you'd make a fresh pot...this last one was a little stale. Then I reckon I ought to get up there and get at it."

Cal Maggard couldn't help but think to himself that he might really regret this agreement, but he reached across the table and the two shook hands on the deal. By late afternoon he was beginning to feel more comfortable with the idea. The kid was a bundle of energy, and even while he worked there was a smile on his face. He wasn't big, but he was wiry and strong and he cut wood and split it with a never-ending fervor. Cal noticed that Billy's chainsaw was old and small and inclined to stop running on occasion. So he loaned him his own bigger chainsaw which had set in the shed for a couple of years. In little time, with a few adjustments, it was running like a top. The young man had a way with mechanics. And so, when the front porch was filled with firewood, and Billy Richards was paid for his work, Cal Maggard suggested he keep the chainsaw. After all, the older man couldn't work much as he grew older, with that bad leg, and Billy would need the saw to do the job that needed doing.

The young man wouldn't hear of it. He said it would get broke, or stolen, and he didn't want the responsibility of looking after it.

"Well, I respect a man for feeling like that about someone else's belongings," Cal Maggard said, as they watched the sun set on a late November evening. "But you could rent it, sort of, or maybe trade for it outright by just cutting a few ricks of firewood for some folks in need around these parts. Take the widow Smithson for instance, down just past the old church."

Mrs. Smithson had lost her husband in a car accident almost three years before and could surely use the wood. So Billy said he'd cut some extra, and asked if Maggard would mind hauling a load in his old pickup. "I'd do it in a minute," Maggard said, "but that old pick-up is like the chainsaw. I can't keep it runnin'."

That's where Cousin Joe came in. The next day, right after church, Billy showed up with his cousin, and they went to work on Mr. Maggard's pick-up, over the older man's objections. They went on about how they wanted to enlist Maggard's help in delivering a little more wood to some needy families in the valley, and there was little he could do but go along with it. Before dark, with an overhauling of the old carburetor, the ten year old pick-up was running better than it had in years, and the following evening just before dark, the two younger men were loading it with firewood to be delivered. And that's how it happened that on Tuesday, three days after Billy Richards knocked on his door, Cal Maggard was driving up the lane to the home of a neighbor he had never really met, Allie Smithson.

He had noticed her before in the crossroads store, and he had wanted so badly to speak to her, but he just couldn't. When she glanced his way, he looked away, but she noticed his attention. The sadness in her eyes hurt him. Here was a woman of unusual beauty, with dark hair and dark eyes, much like his wife had been. Finally, with a load of oak-hickory firewood, he had the chance to speak to her, and it wasn't as difficult as he had thought, after he got up the nerve to knock on the door, and explain what he was there for.

He hoped she wouldn't notice his hands were shaking just a little. She protested just a bit, said she intended to buy some wood before Christmas and hated to impose on others. But finally she agreed, as long as she could help with the unloading of it. It was a little tense at first, but she laughed a little while they were unloading the wood, especially when the visitor jokingly remarked about his bad leg not feeling so bad after dropping firewood chunks on his feet.

For some silly reason, he asked if she needed a Christmas tree, and then he couldn't believe he invited her to come and help pick one out, up in the little clearing below the tornado's path, where cedars grew in abundance amongst sumac thickets and patches of brome sedge. But he could scarcely conceal his happiness when she accepted his invitation. If Mrs. Smithson was surprised at how outgoing this neighbor of hers had become after so many years of not having much to say, she wasn't half as surprised as he was.

Billy and Cousin Joe were hard at work cutting firewood that second Saturday of December when Cal Maggard and Allie Smithson went to find a Christmas tree. Maggard had to be amazed at the job the two young men were doing, utilizing the downed timber and salvaging the oaks and hickories which had survived. Small openings here and there had brush piles stacked, and a few big den trees with limbs lost still stood strong despite the damage.

Allie Smithson smiled that morning, and said she thought the ridge would be beautiful again, when spring and summer helped heal the scars. Cal realized he hadn't thought about that, how time would heal where the storm had been, and that so much good could have come from it. At the time, he could not have envisioned that the twisted, downed trees which seemed to be an impenetrable mess could be slowly changed to a forest again, where there were birds and squirrels and rabbits and raccoons, just as before. It seemed miraculous that so many stacks of wood could come from the dead trees. Somehow it brought to mind the Bible story about the basketful of fish used to feed a multitude.

At the little country store at the crossroads, just across from the church, folks were talking about how Billy Richards and cousin Joe had traded a rick of firewood for a sled and an old bicycle, and Jack Langley, in his fix-it shop, cleaned both of them up and was holding them for the little Parker boys, whose folks were so poor the boys had never had a Christmas present larger than a pair of socks in their entire life.

The third Saturday of December, Billy and Joe were at Cal Maggard's place early, and Joe brought an apple pie that Ol' Lady Johnson had made. He said she had baked six or seven of them from apples in her orchard that were just going to waste, and was having Billy and Joe deliver them, as a way of returning something for a load of firewood they had brought her. That was the day that Maggard went up in the woods to help load some wood, and he noticed his leg seemed to be getting better. It was a mystery... he couldn't understand the change.

"I think as I get older I appreciate this place more and more," he told the two woodcutters. "I remember seeing a few deer here when I was a kid, then they just seemed to disappear forever. But now they've stocked some across the river and I think they are coming back. I saw two sets of fresh tracks crossing the ridge early in the fall. Can't wait to see one sometime."

"Grandpa told me about huntin' deer not far from here when he was a young man," Billy said. "Wouldn't it be somethin' if they got to be so many of 'em we could hunt deer again!"

That evening, when they all stopped for a cup of coffee back at the cabin at dusk, Cal Maggard brought forth two ten dollar bills, and asked the two young men to find something more for their families at Christmas. They objected a little, but the older man was adamant.

"I've had no one to buy Christmas gifts for until this year," he said, "and you have both worked far above what you have been paid for. My pick-up runs again, and I have new friends in the community, and my ridge-top is beginning to look better than it did before the spring storm. I want to put something under a Christmas tree for someone again, so you two take this and do that for me."

He saw them again the next Wednesday, when the country school held its Christmas play and a brief church service which followed. He had never been there before, and he went grudgingly. But then again, Mrs. Smithson had never invited him before...well, she hadn't exactly invited him, she had insisted. Her six-year old grandson was in the play, standing there behind the manger with a robe that was way too big for him. And her little granddaughter sang "Silent Night" with a couple of other little girls. Cal noted to himself that the kids weren't all that good, and all in all, it was sort of a boring evening, but the local folks made a big deal out of it, and the parents and grandparents were all beaming. He also noticed that Allie Smithson was prettier than he had ever seen her, and she smelled wonderful all crowded up next to him with so many people there to fill the pews and all. And he hated to see it all end.

The minister concluded the service that night by recognizing visitors and he ended with Cal Maggard, the good friend of young Billy Richards and Cousin Joe, who had teamed up with them to donate so many loads of firewood to those in the area who were in need.

"It is seldom that we have had so much Christmas spirit in our community," he said, "I don't remember when so much has been given, when so many have been busily helping others and meeting needs, heeding the words of our Lord who urged us to love and serve those around us.

"On the night of his birth, Jesus was given gifts of frankincense, myrrh and gold as the children have shown us here tonight," the preacher continued. "A month or so ago He was given a chainsaw to go with willing hearts, strong backs and hard-working hands. God has done much with that gift, and we are all truly grateful!"

On Friday the preacher was there at the crossroads store while Cal Maggard was putting gas in his old pick-up. It was an uncomfortable meeting. "I guess you know I was very pleased to see you in church the other night," the preacher said to him with a big grin, "after...how was it you put it?...that it would be a 'cold day in the desert' before you'd be caught in church. I kind of wondered if I showed up at your place again if you'd still threaten to run me off like you did a few years ago."

"I still ain't no church-goer, preacher," Maggard said, obviously uncomfortable, "but I've often wished I'd been in a better mood that day. I didn't mean a lot of what I said. I regret some of what I done years ago. I guess a man changes as he gets older."

"I know," the preacher answered. "I've changed some myself in the years since we last talked. It has been a long time, and I bear no grudges. Fact is I did some praying for you at the time, not really believing it would do any good. That was a lack of faith on my part. God works overnight sometimes, and sometimes he works slowly, but he works in strange and mysterious ways, and maybe one of his greatest miracles is the changes in men that we see from time to time. I have a feeling we will see more of each other, and get along better, now that you will be coming to church on occasion."

"I didn't say I was, you know," Cal said as he finished filling the tank. "Less'n you know somethin' I don't?"

"Maybe I just have a feeling," the preacher said with a smile. "You know it actually does get cold in the desert this time of year after the sun goes down, and I know Allie Smithson well. She's a good judge of character and she thinks you are a fine sort of fellow. I think maybe she's right. I'll bet you a five dollar bill against a rick of firewood for the church stove, that you'll be coming to church with her again one time or another."

Cal Maggard walked close to the preacher, and there was a somberness in his face, "Don't you know I spent time in prison? Don't you know I was a thief? I can't sit there on the front pew and sing hymns and act like I'm somethin' different than I am."

The preacher answered, and the levity gone from his voice as well "You ARE something different than you were, what you have been doing the past few weeks in this community proves that.

"Our Lord knew about thieves," he said. "He hung beside one on the cross and took that thief to Heaven with Him that very same day. We have no room on the front pew anyway, and you don't have to sing. What I need is a good man to sit in the back and tip me off as to who is sleeping during the sermon, and make sure nobody steals my hat off the back shelf."

They looked each other in the eye, and Cal Maggard finally spoke. "I might could do that," he said. "We'll have to see."

It was a beginning, the old preacher sensed that. A beginning brought about by a little-used chainsaw that needed repair and a change of heart. Maybe it indeed began with dark clouds on a muggy ominous day the previous spring. Maybe there was a beginning in the strong roaring winds which swept across Cooper's Ridge.

Only God knows, He who indeed works in strange and mysterious ways. But like the birth of Christ they celebrated in the old church that night with the children's play, it was a beginning which would have longlasting consequences.

There was no wind on Christmas day. Big flakes of snow drifted down on the little Ozark community that morning as Cal Maggard's old pickup made tracks along the white country road which led to the Smithson home. He had a couple of Christmas gifts all wrapped up on the front seat beside him, and it was the first time in 30 years he was dressed up for Christmas and not staying home alone. He had promised Allie Smithson he would take her to church so she wouldn't have to drive in the snow. Humming an old Christmas hymn as he drove along, he noticed that his leg didn't hurt much at all.

Chapter 33

Bobble Your Stopper and Wiggle Your Piminnow

By Jim Spencer

"I got one, Daddy! I got one!"

That excited pair of sentences burst from the lips of my tangle-headed nine-year-old daughter on that long-ago spring afternoon in 1986. We were fishing a small oxbow lake in the lower White River bottoms in southeast Arkansas. What got Alicia all worked up was the appearance of a very respectable crappie flopping wildly on the otherwise calm lake surface near our small boat.

The crappie was firmly (I hoped) attached to the gold hook at the end of her line. Evidently that was indeed the case, because Alicia landed it per her usual technique – hauling back on her limber pole until the fish was airborne, then derricking it over the boat by brute force, yelling her head off all the while. After three abortive tries, I managed to grab her line as the frantically flopping critter sailed by my face yet again.

"It's a big one, Daddy!" Alicia screeched from her position approximately two feet off my right ear. "It's a lot bigger than yours." It's an exaggeration, but not much of one, when I say you could have heard her in downtown St. Charles, seven miles away across the vast bottomland forest.

She was right, though, on both counts: It was a big one, a heck of a lot bigger than the eight-incher I'd caught ten minutes earlier.

While I strung this piscatorial giant and rebaited my daughter's hook with another lively shiner, she regaled her brother and me with a spirited, detailed account of how she had managed to single-handedly overpower this burly, outsized fish that now tugged futilely at the frayed piece of nylon ski rope we were using for a stringer. (I had forgotten to bring a store-bought stringer; I almost always do, although over the course of my fishing career I have probably purchased a mile of them.)

When I finished restoring her rig to fish-catching condition, Alicia picked up the pole and complacently flapped her hook back into the water. Then she started giving Geoff and me a detailed course of instructions on how to go about trying to duplicate her feat. The following is a sampling (by no means a complete one, either) of the things she told us: "Look. You don't have to fish up close to trees and stuff to catch a big fish. I caught mine right out here in the middle."

"Hold your pole up high like this, Daddy. You're holding yours too low, and it takes you too much time to raise it up when you get a bite."

"Move your stopper up higher on your string, Geoff. The fish can see it if you don't, and they get scared and swim off somewhere else."

"If your piminnow doesn't want to wiggle, then bobble your stopper up and down like this, to make it look like he is." (Back then, Alicia called minnows "piminnows," Still does, come to think of it. I don't know why.)

"You have to be a real good fisher to catch a big fish like that one I caught. I'll bet there aren't any more big ones like that left in this lake."

She was wrong about that one, though, because shortly after she spoke those words, her stopper bobbled and disappeared, and more screeching commenced. In a very few seconds, I was making grabs at another crappie that was the twin of her first one. And if Geoff and I thought Alicia had been lording it over us before, then we, too, were wrong.

"I don't believe I ever saw even a picture of two fish as big as those two are," she smugly informed us as I strung her second crappie on top of the first. "I don't think anybody ever, ever caught two fish that big on the same fishing trip."

More from the motor-mouth of Alicia the Super-Fisherwoman: "Daddy, if you'll just move your pole back and forth a little, like this, you might catch one. But it won't be as big as my two are." "No, no, Geoff. Your stopper is still too far down on your string. You're not ever going to catch a fish that way." "If you two would stop losing so many piminnows, maybe I could catch a big

fish for each of you. But not if you use all the piminnows up." "Daddy, you're still not paying attention to what I'm telling you. You're still holding your pole too low. Hold it up high, like this. And move it back and forth a little."

She sat there placidly, my bright and lovely daughter, casting these pearls of wisdom before us two swine with all the calm confidence of Billy Graham addressing a football stadium full of sinners. I wanted to drown her. By the time the sun sank below the treeline and it was – mercifully – time to go, Geoff and I had even managed to catch a fish or two ourselves. Geoff even caught a channel catfish considerably bigger than either of Alicia's two slab crappies. However, Alicia was quick to ask how big a crappie could get, and how big a catfish could get, and so on, until she had determined her one-and-a-half pound crappies were actually much bigger, comparatively speaking, than Geoff's three-pound catfish.

I caught nothing but runts, so all I rated was a better-luck-next-time pep talk from Alicia as I wound the line around her pole at the boat landing. It reminded me of several dugout speeches I've heard various baseball coaches make during my youth, usually just after we'd blown a crucial game.

But who knows, I thought, maybe I actually will have better luck next time. After all, thanks to Alicia's coaching, I now knew what I'd been doing wrong.

I was holding my pole too low, for one thing, and I think my stopper might have been too far down on my string. My piminnow wasn't very lively, either, and I neglected to bobble my stopper up and down or move my pole back and forth. On top of all that, I fished too close to trees and stuff.

I think I've got it all sorted out now, I remember thinking as I drove home that night, while Alicia slept peacefully in the back seat. *This fishing stuff is a lot more complicated than I thought.*

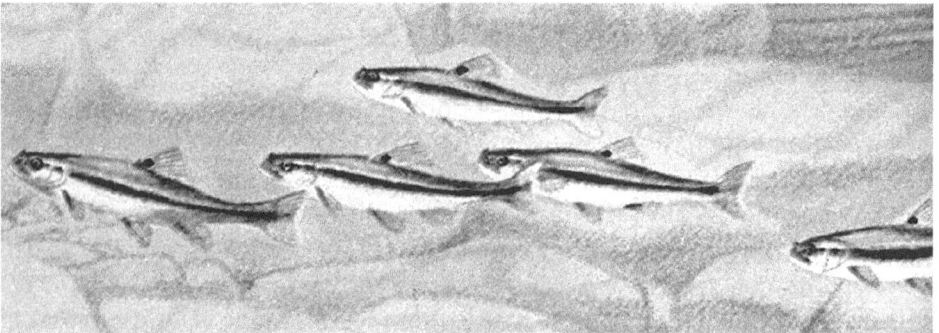

Chapter 34

The Christmas Hunt

By Larry Dablemont

It must have been about 1956 when we had the big snow just before Christmas. We lived on a little farm out on Indian Creek, but we sure weren't farmers. Mom's family was. Most of the McNews raised gardens and had cows and chickens and fruit trees and a cellar full of canned goods. They were Scotch-Irish in ancestry and prone to such things. Me and Dad were French-Indian. We were outdoorsmen... hunters, trappers, fishermen and the like.

I can't remember any Christmas before then. My life didn't amount to much until I turned eight or nine years old, and got my Iver-Johnson single-shot 16-gauge. Dad bought if from a neighbor, a real bargain with a box of shells to go with it. Mom had a fit!

Mom didn't hunt and she didn't see any reason for me to start so early. She was ten inches shorter than Dad and you'd think that alone would resolve the matter in my favor, but you'd had to have known my mom. If I was going to get to go out and hunt up something for Christmas dinner with Dad, we'd have to accomplish it with some trickery. But Dad was good at that sort of thing. He was awful smart. So smart that he and Dick Schmidt, one of the neighbors from down the gravel road aways, had figured out how to watch the World Series without buying a TV set. They went into the Western Auto back during the summer and was admiring one when the store-owner suggested they take it home and try it for a few days...figuring that would give him a sure sale. Televisions back then were only little black and white screens about the size of a bread-box, and there was only one or two stations you could get. But in October, one of those stations carried the World Series and the Friday Night Fights.

So Dad and Dick Schmidt went back in there in October and started admiring one again and that time when the store-owner suggested they give it a try at home, they reckoned it might be a good idea, just to see if it would work way out in the country. It did, and I never saw anything like it. It was amazing. Dad said he couldn't believe you could nearly see the ball when they'd throw it. But eventually they took the TV back, and Dad said it was a waste of time because the dad-blamed Yankees won the World

Series. If he and Dick would have known the Yankees were going to win, they would never have gone to the trouble to haul it out there and back in the back of Dad's old 1949 Ford.

As smart as Dad was, he hadn't gotten much schooling. He had to quit and move off to make it on his own when he was only in the 9th grade. He took a good job at the shoe factory to support me and my two sisters, but his heart was in the woods and on the river and so was mine. Mom sort of done us both a favor when she arranged to have some of her family come for Christmas dinner. We were too poor to have a big feast unless Dad and me went out and hunted something to go with the potatoes and gravy and biscuits.

Mom had in mind serving up old Ike. Ike was the big tom turkey Dad had won at a turkey shoot over towards Raymondville back before Thanksgiving. That's something else Dad was awful good at. Besides being so smart and knowing how to outfox Mom, he was one heck of a shot with a shotgun.

When he took his old '97 Winchester to a turkey shoot, some of the other shooters wouldn't even put their dollar in until he quit. Dad would push his pipe over to the corner of his mouth and throw that old pump- gun to his shoulder and holler "pull" and they'd throw one of those clay pigeons out over the sedge grass and he'd blow it to smithereens. You could hear the crowd *ooh* and *ah* when the shooters would move back thirty yards from the hay bales and Dad would just keep clobbering those yellow clay birds. He might win two or three turkeys in a row, and then again he might win one and lose one, just because he was so fair minded and wanted others to get a turkey every now and then too. Dad was just as good-hearted as he was smart.

One thing about it, if you had a good '97 Winchester, you could eat good in the winter, even if you were poor. We ate lots of rabbits and squirrels and quail and ducks, and Dad said we were lucky to eat like that when most folks in town didn't get much besides chicken and pork and beef. We ate one of the turkeys Dad won in November for Thanksgiving dinner. And Mom figured the other one was destined for the Christmas table. But the other one was old Ike, and Dad and me had gotten kind of fond of him. Dad traded a coon dog puppy for two hen turkeys and we were planning on raising a bunch of young turkeys the next summer. Dad said we wouldn't be able to do that if we had Old Ike for Christmas dinner.

His solution to the problem was rabbits and squirrels and quail and ducks. He said that I could go with him on my first hunt with my new used Iver-Johnson 16-gauge single-shot and we'd come back with so much meat

Mom could invite all my aunts and uncles and cousins, even the ones from Iowa.

Mom had another fit. She said I was too little and too young and it was too cold and the snow was too deep. Dad bit down on the stem of his pipe and said by dang he'd be the judge of all that and he had made his decision. It might be he should have been a little more diplomatic!

But when the yelling was finally all over, and Mom had got down to the point of trying to win the argument by crying, I figured my chances of going on my first Christmas hunt had shrunk down to about the same chance old Ike had of celebrating New Years Eve.

But I hadn't calculated on Dad's trickery. He winked at me as he puffed on his pipe, peering over the top of Mom's red hair, hugging her and saying she was right and he just wasn't thinking. But he wondered if she'd agree to just let me go along, if we'd only go out an hour after the temperature got to 30 degrees, and if we'd leave the Iver-Johnson at home. And he said if we didn't get more game than all the McNews could eat in two meals, he'd personally lop off old Ike's head, strip off his feathers and have him ready to bake before Santa Claus ever left the North Pole.

Dad was smart, but like I said, he was tricky. Mom figured she won the argument, and went to figuring on how to bundle me up so I wouldn't get the new-mown-ya. About that time, he was sneaking my Iver-Johnson out to the barn.

The next day it warmed up a little, and the skies were gray again, with a little bit of a north wind and little bits of snow spitting down. By mid-morning it was in the mid-thirties and Dad and me headed for the barn. It was a glorious day for a hunting trip. Old Ike ran off aways and kept an eye on us, as if he knew Christmas was only days away. He should have been cheering us on. His chance of survival had dwindled to the likelihood of Dad and me finding quail and rabbits and squirrels.

Dad stuffed my jeans pockets with shotgun shells, and broke my shotgun down so he could hide it up under his coat. From the barn we headed down into the timber above Indian Creek, with Mom watching from the window, and Dad trying his best to keep the stock and barrel and forearm of my 16-gauge where it wouldn't show.

When we got down into the woods, well hidden from the view of our little house up on the hill, Dad put the shotgun together and we rested a bit while he lit his pipe. He went over all the safety points again, and then told me I had to keep the gun open until he said I could load it.

That kind of dampened my spirits. No hunter I ever heard of went out with an unloaded gun and hoped the game would wait 'til he got a shell out of his pocket. But there wasn't any arguing the point. Dad was awful smart, but he was pretty hard-headed and not inclined at all toward compromise unless Mom forced him into it.

Down through the woods and across Indian Creek we went, where the snow was deepest and where I began to realize that hunting could get into work. Up the far hillside and across the fence, into the brome sedge fields of Mr. McKinney's place. Mr. McKinney had a really big farm, and the hunting was good there. There were deer tracks coming along the fence row past the cedar glade, and Dad stopped and showed them to me. I had never seen a deer. Back then they were scarcer than perfumed polecats. When Dad was a boy, there wasn't any at all. Now there were starting to be a few here and there. I had heard Grandpa Dablemont say they were awful good to eat, and I thought to myself that if we could get a deer, we could probably have enough meat to keep old Ike safe throughout a whole year.

Grandpa Dablemont had told me that when he was a boy, there were more wild turkeys than tame ones. He told me how he had killed hundreds of them. I never could figure out why there weren't any left but there weren't. A wild turkey hadn't been seen in those parts since before Dad was born.

But there sure were lots of quail and rabbits. Dad killed a rabbit right off. It jumped from beneath a patch of sumac, and went skipping across the snow like a flat rock thrown across the pond. I heard the old pump-gun roar, and I knew that rabbit was headed for the Christmas dinner table.

I hadn't even reached for my shell pocket. I knew I didn't have a chance to get off a shot at a running rabbit. Dad said we'd see one sitting somewhere and he'd let me nail him. I had proven to be a pretty fair shot on coffee cans and cardboard boxes. Dad had taken me out target shooting before and I had figured out the fine points of scattergun shooting. Keep your eyes open, lean forward, hold the stock tight against your shoulder, hold a deep breath, squeeze the trigger firmly and get up and try it again. But I hadn't shot anything in snow up to near the top of my galoshes, with a cold wind making my eyes water and a shawl wrapped around my neck so tight I couldn't hardly find my chin. I struggled to keep up with Dad and not get my shotgun barrel in the snow.

We were headed to Mr. McKinney's place when a big covey of quail flushed. Dad shot twice and got one. I had seen lots of rabbits around the house, and quail crossing the gravel road below the barn, but never a covey rise. It was one of the most unbelievable thrills I ever had up to then, and they scared me half to death when they came up with a flurry of wings and feathered bodies going every which direction. I realized then that I would never be able to hit a quail. They were too fast. But they were beautiful. I hoisted up that rooster bobwhite, looking at the soft brown hues and feeling how plump he was. Even without any bright colors, he was absolutely beautiful.

I was cold and tired and disappointed, but I was really enjoying myself. Dad was disappointed too. He said if he could have seen that whole covey running down a fence row, we could have had enough quail to feed half of Mom's family. "The game," Dad said, "gets all the breaks!" I had heard Grandpa Dablemont say that before.

We walked up to Mr. McKinney's house with one quail and one rabbit, and I realized that Old Ike was a dead turkey. It would take a miracle to save him now, and it seemed unlikely that there could be a miracle when the game gets all the breaks.

Mr. McKinney made me take off my coat and sit on his couch while his wife made us hot chocolate. He jerked off my stocking cap and tousled my hair and went on about how I was growing up so fast. He told Dad I sure was a fine looking boy. Even back then, I didn't put much truck in that. He would have told Dad I was a fine looking boy even if I was the ugliest kid he had ever seen. I wasn't interested in being a fine looking boy, I wanted to be a hunter. I wanted to walk up a big covey of quail with a bullet in my shotgun, and get three or four of them in the air...or even on the ground for that matter. I just wanted to kill something we could eat.

Halfway through the hot chocolate, Mr. McKinney brought up the ducks.

Boy did Dad's ears perk up when he heard that. Dad loved to hunt ducks. He and Grandpa would float the river in the old johnboat and sneak up on mallards and wood ducks, and sometimes even get some squirrels on the same trip. We ate a lot of ducks in the winter time. Dad would pick all the feathers off, and Mom would save them for stuffing pillows. He'd pick the feathers off those ducks right up to the base of the skull, and down to almost the ends of the wings and right to the knees. I never could figure that, because the neck of a duck didn't have enough meat on it to feed a house cat. But Dad would always gnaw on that neck and go on about how good it was.

I hadn't got to go float the river yet and hunt ducks. I had floated with Dad and Grandpa when we fished or set trotlines and seined bait, but I hadn't been on a duck hunt yet. I hadn't even seen a wild duck except the dead ones Dad brought in.

Dad and Mr. McKinney talked for awhile about his big spring-fed pond to the south of his place and how many ducks had been flying in to land on it, right next to his cornfield. When we headed that way, I thought I wasn't going to be able to keep up. Dad seemed to be so excited he forgot I was along. We headed up the drainage area below the pond, with snow starting to fall a little harder.

The pond bank was high, and we sat down at the bottom as a half dozen big ducks circled around over head and settled in on the open water. Dad said to be quiet and still, so I did, but I watched those ducks and it was about the most beautiful sight I had ever seen. Their wings made a swishing sound like a sudden wind when they passed overhead, and you could hear one just quacking like the dickens. Up on the pond, three or four others were quacking back at them.

Dad left me at the bottom and he went up to peek over, through the weeds and willows along that end of the bank. Then he slid back down and told me I could take a look. I remember peering over that bank and out onto the water through the high reeds, and seeing what looked like hundreds of mallards, maybe even thousands. They were packed in there like rats in a feed trough, splashing and flapping their wings and quacking and sticking their heads under the water. It was a sea of green heads and blue wings loafing in the lee side of that high bank out of the wind.

Back at the bottom of the pond bank, Dad told me I could load my gun, but then he loaded it for me, and told me how we were going to do it. I'd sneak up the bank, and he'd come up behind me and we'd raise up and give 'em what for, just like Davy Crockett and Jim Bowie at the Alamo, just like

Doc Holliday and Wyatt Earp at the O.K. Corral. Dad was smart alright, and sort of poetic at times. He knew just what to do and when to do it and how to do it.

My heart was beating so hard I could feel it even through all those clothes, and I was so excited my ears weren't cold and my toes weren't numb anymore. Finally we were at the high point in my life. Finally I was on the verge of becoming a hunter like Dad and Grandpa. I was about to pull down on something besides a cardboard box. It didn't get any better than this! I figure Old Ike was back home in the barnlot praying for something like that pond full of mallards.

I goofed up when I snuck up that snowy bank by sticking my gun barrel up in the air, so excited my hands were shaking. But Dad had figured on that. He was ready and that '97 Winchester began to roar. It was chaos and confusion from that point on. I cocked the hammer and there was a sky full of mallards, fighting for altitude over that pond, climbing high into the sky above me, into the north wind at our backs. I aimed at the whole bunch, not 30 yards straight above me, and I squeezed the trigger. The next thing I knew, I was sliding down the pond bank on my back, with snow down my neck and my heels pointing toward the gray clouds into which wild mallards were rising, my shotgun sliding along side of me.

Then I saw it as plain as day. Right above my right boot was a big old greenhead, folded up and hurtling down on top of me, falling from the flock with a heavy thud into the snow beside me, stone dead.

I could hear Dad up there on the pond bank whooping with joy. I heard him reload and dispatch of a couple of cripples. But I was preoccupied with my first mallard. I picked him up and looked at that beautiful bird, his gleaming green head and bright yellow beak, the glowing red feet and black curls in the tail. I had killed something, and the feeling was strange. It had been a real live creature only minutes before and now it was dead as a hammer because of me. Well not exactly because of me. That drake was a victim of circumstance. He had flown into the area where my shotgun was pointed. A million ducks in the world and this was the very one destined to be my first taste of success as a hunter.

I sat there and basked in the moment as snow fogged down around me, and I could hear Dad up there splashing around at the edge of the pond raving about the gods of the hunt smiling on the patient and the deserving and the desperate. He came back and sat down beside me and went on about that big mallard while he lit his pipe and the pleasant smell of tobacco permeated the winter cold. It was a moment of great magnitude, and we savored it.

I don't know how many ducks were on old man McKinney's pond that day, and I don't know how many flew off. But I know how many didn't. Ike was a lucky turkey. There were eleven awfully unlucky mallards left there on and around that pond. Dad had lined up a passel of them on the water with his first shot, thinking about how the McNews loved to eat on Christmas day.

If it hadn't been for me, we would have only had ten. He talked about that the next day while we were in the cellar picking mallards almost all day long right down to the skulls and knees. And he said it again while we were eating ducks on Christmas day, ignoring the fact that Grandma McNew said she'd about as soon eat a pigeon. Aunt Margie and Uncle Roy said they sure did like the way Mom cooked mallards, and me and cousin Butch just concentrated on the pie.

It's strange how things happen. A great horned owl got Old Ike before spring, but he didn't eat much of him and we had most of what was left for Sunday dinner one day in late March. Mom never trusted Dad again, but she finally admitted it was going to eventually come down to me being a hunter and carrying my shotgun loaded.

She'd have to accept it... after all, I was a Dablemont, and Dablemonts were outdoorsmen, born to hear the song of wind in the pines and flowing water over river shoals. Born to roam and wander the woods, following the baying of the hounds, drawn to the distant sunset. Kin to the wild geese, blood brother of the wolf, descended from Canadian Cree hunters and French trappers. That was me. I was a Dablemont. Unfortunately Mom was still a McNew!

She hid the old Iver-Johnson for awhile, and me and Dad had little to do but go along with it. Dad was awful smart, I'll admit that. But I don't know that he did such a smart thing bragging about how I killed that duck and how we had outfoxed Mom by sneaking off with that shotgun hid in the barn.

There'd be a time, she said, when me and Dad would learn to listen to her, and give up our sneaking and deceitful ways. Until then it was back to shooting coffee cans and cardboard boxes in the barn lot, thinking of that wondrous day when a cloud of mallards soared above Mr. McKinney's pond in the snow...that wondrous day when I killed my first duck and figured out what made life worthwhile.

Chapter 35

A Curmudgeon's Take on Fishing

By Jim Spencer

This is supposed to be a piece about fishing. But it's also, I'm afraid, going to be one of those "things aren't like they used to be" diatribes.

The thing is, things aren't like they used to be. I use some pretty sophisticated tackle nowadays, as almost all of us do, but when my fishing career got its start more than a half-century ago, that wasn't anywhere close to being the case. Until I was approaching my teens, my entire fishing tackle arsenal consisted of maybe ten feet of braided fishing line, a few hooks and whatever beat-up old cane pole happened to be available at the time. Bait was worms almost always, dug by my own hand along a little ditch that ran not too far from our house.

Seriously, that was the extent of my stuff. If I needed a weight to get my worm down deep enough, I tied a long, thin pebble into the line above the hook. If I got hung up, I waded or swam to get my hook back because hooks were unimaginably precious. I brought my fish home (mostly six-inch bullheads and pint-sized bluegills) on a forked stick cut from a willow tree.

None of the group of ragamuffins I ran with had tackle any finer than mine. We got by with the most basic of basics. It took me a long time to work my way up the ladder, first to cheap Chinese/Japanese spinning tackle, then to slightly better stuff, then to the muscle rods and powerful reels so popular with bass fishermen today. Except that our rods were fiberglass and not the space-age stuff rods are made of today. Nowadays I usually use lighter tackle, but it's even more sophisticated and expensive than the heavy stuff.

These days, though, kids don't have that primitive start. Kids today start out with sophisticated equipment, taking it as much for granted as they do the $150 Nikes they all seem to wear. It's quite a change. And in my opinion, not a change for the better.

"In fishing, the way to gain full appreciation is to begin at the beginning," wrote Harold F. Blaisdell, one of the best fishing writers of the 20th century.

Blaisdell was singing the same song I'm singing here when he wrote *The Philosophical Fisherman* in 1969. Blaisdell's beginning as a fisherman was even more primitive than mine; he said he caught his first fish (a minnow) on a bent pin, a piece of heavy cotton thread and a willow switch. My own beginnings, primitive as they were, were at least ahead of Blaisdell's; I never used a bent pin or a cotton thread. I did resort to a willow switch every once in a while, though, when cane poles were in short supply.

This next part is difficult to explain, but here's a stab at it: Having to do our fishing with this extremely primitive equipment, I believe, taught kids like Harold Blaisdell, like the ragamuffins I ran with, like me, how to cope. It taught us self-reliance. It taught us, in short, how to fish, and taking it a step farther, how to cope with difficult situations in life.

Today, all the inherent difficulties that are part of fishing (except the instinctive wariness of the fish themselves) have been, to the extent of human ingenuity, eliminated. No effort has been spared to substitute artificial advantage for skill and savvy. Invisible lines, spinning reels that will cast a country mile, side-scan fish-finders, spot-lock trolling motors, spray-on scents for your baits and lures. The list is endless, and they come up with more new stuff every day.

I have an 11-year-old nephew who says he loves to fish. And sure enough, he does, but only if someone will take him. He doesn't seem to have any desire to just go fishing on his own, and I think part of the reason for that is because we've spoiled him by equipping him too well. He has a tackle box as big as a small suitcase, stuffed with several hundred dollars' worth of gear. His rod and reel cost more than I once paid for a used pickup truck.

Although a fair portion of the tackle in his box has come from his Uncle Jim, I'm pretty sure equipping my nephew that well has not been a kindness. Cody has never had to improvise. He's never had to put together any of his own tackle. Therefore, I think I might have cheated him out of a large portion of the real value of fishing.

Fishing is not just about catching fish. It's about becoming a self-starter; it's about learning to solve problems. It's about learning to improvise.

And because he has all that expensive tackle, Cody has never once had to figure out how he was going to get his hook back when it was hung on a tree root under five feet of muddy water, because he's never in his life had a hook inventory that could be expressed with a single digit. He's never had to look for just the right willow limb or river cane stalk, because he started his fishing career with that space-age spinning rod I gave him when he was eight. I doubt he's ever held a cane pole in his hands.

Don't misunderstand, I'm not advocating that we all go back to low-tech stuff. I like my graphite rods and my tackle boxes full of lures (and extra hooks) as well as you do, and I'd hate to have to go back to using oblong pebbles instead of split shot. But I truly believe we'd serve our kids better if we started their fishing careers a little farther down the equipment curve than we're doing these days.

And, to borrow a line from the famous philosopher Forrest Gump: "That's all I have to say about that."

Chapter 36

Conversations With a Coyote

By Larry Dablemont

The fire was burning low...the remaining embers lighting up an area of only a few feet on that sandy, river gravel bar. It was too early to go to sleep, so I decided to just lay down on my sleeping bag and relax awhile, then rebuild the fire. It was then that I saw him, or rather his eyes. They shined yellow, only a few feet on the other side of my fire, where I had thrown the bones of a good meal I had enjoyed at dusk.

"I can't see anything but your eyes," I said to him, "but I know you are there...you cowardly coyote!"

"When what you refer to as cowardice insures your survival, it is a wise choice over reckless indifference," he said with something of a snarl. "I noticed you this afternoon, leading your boat around that log jam where the swift current would have surely swamped you. Was that cowardice?"

"I see your point," I answered, "but you have nothing to fear from me or my fire... I have no gun, I am a threat to nothing but the fish I catch." "I cannot be anything but what my ancestors were," he said. "I like that word, 'cunning' over cowardly. The caution learned by my great grandfathers and theirs, remains in me. We are not like men, we do not throw away great wisdom and change with each generation to be less than what our ancestors were."

"Not all of us have done that, Coyote." I told him. "I still value what my grandfather taught me, or I would not be here on this gravel bar when there is a soft bed at my home." He said nothing to that, and I could hear him crunching one of the bones I had left him. It was quiet otherwise, only the slight sound of the flowing water over the river shoal, and one whippoorwill across the river.

In time the crunching stopped, and the eyes were gone.

"Don't go, coyote..." I beseeched him, "it is lonely here and I'd like to talk to you about some things."

In his snarly, gravelly voice from beyond my campfire, he answered, "I have hunting to do. Perhaps you should have fed me better. The bones were excellent, but not enough to fill my hungry belly. I will never understand why you men throw away such a thing as a delectable crunchy bone, the very best of the kill."

"You have some wisdom, and much cunning, Coyote," I said, "but not so much understanding. Men do not have the teeth you have to crush and reduce a bone to small pieces as you can so easily do."

At the edge of the campfire, I could now see much of his face, his mouth spread in a wicked-looking grin. I had talked to this coyote on other occasions and I knew he loved nothing more than to argue. "I hear you talk of understanding, Man." he said to me. "And yet you have so little of it. Your kind has lost most of its understanding of those things which exist away from your cities. You understand very little; certainly nothing about how the water and the land gives life, for you destroy both as you increase in number. You do not understand that the earth will find a way to take away your great increasing populations if you do not do it yourself. And when that time comes, your people will cry and moan and ask why these awful times come upon you, even though they are times of your making. The biting cold, the wide floods, the killing droughts and the great heat; the mighty tremors in the earth, the strong winds which take all in their path. It is the earth telling you, this is enough!"

I lay there and thought of ways I might argue with him, but it was hard to come up with something. "How did you gain so much awareness of man?" I asked him as I peered over the campfire. "You spend so much time avoiding him, except when there are bones he leaves behind."

"And each year there are more of you to avoid," He said. Your leavings are often the litter of your progress, too few bones and too many cans and bottles and bags. Now there are rubber tires thrown into the river which last forever, instead of the wooden wagon wheels which brought your grandfathers here."

"I know," I told him, "my grandfather made nothing that he did not use again and again. He discarded almost nothing, and what he did, quickly was reabsorbed by the land. His boats were made of wood, and were gone before he was. My boat is metal, and long after I am gone, it will be a blight upon the land somewhere."

The coyote seemed to resent me agreeing with him. "Men's numbers grow to become a plague upon the land, and you change too quickly. The men whose seed you sprang from were not like you. You are not enough like them, in the ways you should be. The understanding you speak of is not the way of man. Knowledge is your way, and you do not understand that knowledge is grown in both light and darkness. Some is good, and some is evil and destructive."

It was quiet as I thought of what he said. Even as the fire burned lower, it seemed his eyes glowed brighter. "But you are right," he said, "there is much I too do not understand. It is a hard thing for me to understand man, because He who made man made him in His own image, with another place to go where all is not as it is here on earth. A man has a distinct soul, and when he dies, and leaves the body he lives within, he goes away from the Earth. Every man has that soul, and he alone possesses it. It comes with him when he is born, and it leaves as he dies."

A barred owl hooted along the bluff across the river, and the coyote looked toward it, then spoke, "With my kind, and that owl and his kind, and all other living things, it is different. I have the same soul as my great-great-grandfather, and I am like him in all ways because I am just an extension of him. When the body I live in dies, my soul continues in a younger body, and in that body I continue, as I am now, and I live on in many many bodies, all are exactly as this one I am in now, until there are no coyotes, and we do not exist. It is that way with all things. So why do you men become so upset when I take a spotted fawn or a rabbit to eat? It does not cease to exist, it comes back in another body. You talk of understanding, but you cannot understand that, can you?"

"No, I guess not," I told him. "I do not mind seeing you eat what is left of a deer I kill, and I am not bothered if you kill a snake or a rat or even a possum. because I know it is nature's way that predators must kill and eat. But I must admit, if I saw you trying to kill and eat a small baby deer, it would trouble me. I have a hard time accepting such a thing because there is such a brutality in it, such an example of weakness against strength.

"Those men who do live in cities would try to stop you." I told him. "They would see the fawn as innocent, and see you as evil. It is the way we are, us men, and nothing can change that. Even though God made us, we cannot see things through His eyes, of course. What He called perfection, you live with, Coyote, and are a part of. Men cannot accept perfection unless it is the perfection we create and perceive to be right. To men, perfection means comfort and ease and fairness."

At that, the coyote laughed louder than I ever knew him to laugh. I never expected such a thing from him. "You talk of comfort and ease and fairness, and yet among men there is no such thing except for a few," he said. "Greed has created greater brutality among men than ever found among wild things in wild places. Man wants fairness for himself, not for others just like him. It is greed which does that. No wild creature understands greed. Survival has nothing to do with such a thing here on the river."

I began to get tired. "This conversation is beginning to get beyond us, Coyote" I said. "We started out talking about how I discard the bones and you find them to be so delectable."

"If you did not put them over a fire, they would be even better," he said. "Why do you men insist on putting what you eat in a fire before you eat it? What a horrible thing fire is. And yet men seem to have to have it, always."

"As my teeth cannot do what yours can Coyote," I said, "neither can my eyes. Fire allows us to see in darkness, and keeps us warm, because we cannot live in the cold comfortably as you can."

With that the coyote began to talk in calmer tones. "The owl does not like the light, because he cannot see well when it comes," he said. "And the small flying squirrels which live in hollow trees, cannot see when there is light, they must live in darkness. I feel so good when it is cold, and yet the big-toothed ignoramus you call a groundhog crawls into the earth and dies for awhile when it is cold, and comes back to life as the warm days return. How strange it is that we all have been placed together on this earth by the Great Being who made all things."

"I have thought often as you are thinking now, Coyote," I said. "Why did God make some men who thrive in a land of ice and others who live in a place where there is little water and the sun burns the earth? I know you know of no such places, but you have tasted a little of each. And you don't know this, but there are places filled with men who never grow as tall as me, and other places where all men are taller. There are men who have different colored skin, and speak a language other men cannot understand. And there are men who want to kill other men because they do not look or believe or speak as they do. I ask myself, did God do this all intentionally, or did He just let it happen? Has He turned away from what He made to let man destroy it all, or is He controlling it all from some other place...and if so where is that place? Does He yet have a plan, does He have an answer? A small number of men believe He does, through someone else who lived long ago. But more and more, men of our sort are overruled and laughed at for believing that."

It was quiet for a moment, and the Coyote spoke in a quiet, reflective manner you would not expect from a coyote. "Maybe we should not think of such things," he said. "Once I knew a coyote who tried to count the stars... but she never did get it done. Her children starved while she was trying to do it.

"He who made us did not make us to count the stars."

I heard the coyote sigh a little, and it was quiet. Then he continued. "I too have wondered, why did He make a creature whose sole purpose seems to be damming the river, though every flood seems to destroy all their works, and yet they try again to do it when the river gets low, because they seem worried there will not be enough water if they don't." I realized he was speaking of the beaver. "Why did He make the groundhog able to dig a hole and die," the coyote asked me, "and then come back to life, while the mouse must gather and store seeds and nuts all through one season just to survive another. And why is man such a fat creature, and why are there never any fat coyotes? Why can you catch fish, and I cannot, when I need them much worse than you?"

I chuckled at that, and the coyote heard me. I forgot that he was being serious, and I apologized for laughing. "I can't tell you the answer to those things, but I will go back, and I will tell other men who are like me that I talked with you, and that you had much to say that is wise." I said. He replied in a growling, snorting sort of manner. "You will go back and say you talked with a coyote? You might as well tell them you talked to God. You will sound just as foolish!"

And with that he was gone. He had much to do in the night, I knew, to just get enough to eat. It was a life I didn't want to think about. I would sleep and as I did that night some creature somewhere not far away would lose its life so the coyote could live. I closed the cover of my tent, wrapped myself in my sleeping bag and drifted off to sleep. Tomorrow I would catch some more fish and tell my readers how to lure a bass from beneath a rock with a spinner-bait. It is a simpler thing to do than to get them to listen to the words of a coyote. I have tried before to say such things and men do not so much want to hear it.

Maybe after all, we should just live day by day and not think of such weighty things. Maybe we should let God take care of the things of which He is in charge.

Maybe we should just try to spend our time enjoying life and trying to make life better for those around us, and paying attention to doing what is right, above all other things. Maybe it does little good to count stars when there are other things we need to concentrate on.

But I can't help but think that God gave us great knowledge to use in good ways. Just because we can make a multi-million dollar rocket doesn't mean we should crash one into the moon when all that money would help so many of those around us who are sick, or hungry. Maybe we should work hard, as a species, to heal the land we seem bent on destroying. Maybe we should fix our rivers, and clean the air, and work to leave the land strong and healthy for all living things tomorrow and in years to come. Maybe we should control our numbers so we can use the forests as they replenish themselves, and maintain beauty on the earth rather than turn it into an expanse of sameness to provide food for us.

Maybe we should let the coyote have a fawn or two, knowing so many more will survive and live and create more deer at times than we need.

Maybe...and then again, maybe you shouldn't put too much credence in the words of someone who sleeps on gravel bars and talks to coyotes.

Chapter 37

Hunting on the Shady Side of 70

By Jim Spencer

That first turkey hunt is a long time gone, but the memory stands fresh as this morning's biscuits. I didn't kill a bird that morning, of course.

I was green as a sack of July apples, and I had no more idea what I was doing than if I'd been a ballet instructor. But it was on that fateful morning in the late 1970s, when I stood on a ridge not far east of Natchez and listened to seven gobblers sound off one after another, that the trajectory of my life was drastically altered.

It took, at most, nine or ten seconds for those seven gobblers to complete their overlapping serenade. In the instant before the racket started, I was not a turkey hunter. By the time the woods were quiet again, I was.

Just. That. Quick.

In those days, turkey populations were in the early to middle stages of their remarkable comeback. Turkeys weren't even legal game in many states, and even where these big birds were lawfully hunted, it was a new experience for practically everybody. Most of us were still pretty far down the learning curve. There weren't all that many of us hunting turkeys back then, either, so the birds were pretty safe. Sure, there were some good turkey men even in those days, but they grew few to the hill and most of them were tight-mouthed as snapping turtles. They weren't much inclined to offer advice to us newbies, and when they did it was usually deliberately wrong.

We found ourselves in a fix: bitten by the bug but not knowing how to scratch. So we attended calling contests and turkey hunting seminars when and where we could find them. We read the few books and magazine articles then available on the subject. And because it's true that misery loves company, we sought out other neophytes who shared both our enthusiasm and our ineptitude. But most important of all, we hunted. At every opportunity, we got out there and embarrassed ourselves in front of turkeys.

Early on, we lurched through turkey hunts like drunken sailors through Singapore. We wallowed in our own ignorance like pigs in slop. We made horrible, comical, disastrous mistakes, then doubled down on them. We called inappropriately and inexpertly. We moved when we shouldn't, and were too scared to move when we should. We changed set-ups too often, or conversely, not often enough. We skylighted ourselves on ridgelines; we blundered into food plots and fields without first checking them for turkeys. In short, we did everything wrong except wave a white flag and holler "Here, turkey turkey turkey!" It wouldn't shock me to learn somebody somewhere even tried that.

Not surprisingly, we ran off turkeys in wholesale numbers, educating far more birds than we killed. But the beauty of the situation was that turkeys were increasing faster than turkey hunters, and there were so many birds and so little competition from other hunters we could afford to make those mistakes. And slowly, gradually, we begin to learn.

It was the polar opposite of the situation our fathers and grandfathers had faced a half-century earlier. In those discouraging days before the cannon net and modern wildlife management, things looked bleak indeed for the future of the wild turkey. In most of the country they'd already been pounded out of existence with the double bludgeons of habitat destruction and year-round unregulated hunting. Even where turkeys remained, they were generally so scarce that just hearing one gobbling made it a good hunt. Most of the few remaining turkey hunters were convinced these birds would soon be extinct in the wild. Therefore, they hunted them for the same reason ornithologists and museum curators of that era were shooting ivory-billed woodpeckers: because they wanted a specimen or two for their collections before they were all gone.

When opportunities come that rarely, you learn to hunt conservatively. The common premise during those days of scarcity was that if a turkey answered your call, he'd eventually come looking. You just needed to be patient, give the turkey time to be a turkey, and not get in a rush and do anything that would alert the bird and spook him – such as call more than once or twice an hour. These guys learned to take patience to a new level.

Not me and my fellow neophytes, though. Nosiree Bob. As mentioned, turkey numbers were on a steep upward curve by the time many hunters of my generation got started. Where I hunted, in the Ouachita Mountains of western Arkansas and eastern Oklahoma, it was common to hear a dozen or more gobblers on a given morning. If you stubbed your toe with this one, no problem; go to the one gobbling over thataway. If you messed up on him as well, there was more than likely another one gobbling farther down the ridge.

And so we stumbled along from one gobbler to the next, spooking birds, leaving ranks of educated turkeys in our wake but not taking many of them home. Many (if not most) of my fellow low-information turkey hunters operated in similar fashion through the '70s and '80s. This was partly because we didn't know any other way, and partly because of the video craze that hit the turkey hunting subculture during that time span. To the best of my knowledge it was Wilbur Primos and my old friend Ronnie "Cuz" Strickland who made the first quality turkey hunting video, called "The Truth About Spring Turkey Hunting." It opened the floodgates. Competing turkey call and camo manufacturers started cranking out exciting, action-packed videos and TV shows. In these on- screen hunts, they (to steal the words Primos stole ahead of me) "called too much and called too loud."

The video hunts were exciting and fast-paced, with gobblers and hunters competing to see who could make the most noise. Film-makers soon learned the dead air and long waits that comprise the typical turkey hunt don't make good TV, so they wisely deleted all that stuff. The 45-minute approach of a gobbler in real time translated into 35 seconds on tape, and while we viewers were aware of that fact, these extremely truncated television hunts nevertheless reinforced our run-and-gun hunting mentality. *See?* We told ourselves and each other. *This is the way the pros do it, so it must be right.*

My legs were much younger in those days, and climbing mountains and walking miles through rough country wasn't a problem. My modus operandi was simple, direct and mindless. Day One: 1. Cover as much ground as possible. 2. Stop every couple hundred yards and call like a maniac in an attempt to make a turkey gobble. 3. If nothing happens, force-march another 300 yards and do it again. 4. Repeat until you can no longer put one foot in front of the other. Day Two: Ditto.

It wasn't at all uncommon for me to cover six or seven miles on a morning turkey hunt. More, if I could get on one long ridge and not have to cross too many hollows. And yes, I did get a lot of turkeys to gobble, but my success rate on those turkeys was singularly unimpressive. My problem was simple yet profound: I didn't know what to do after I made the turkey gobble.

But I struck a lot of 'em, sure enough, and I'd always sit down and give it my best effort. When it worked it was usually pretty spectacular, with the turkey – sometimes multiple turkeys – charging my position like Gall and Crazy Horse charged Custer. I still managed to screw up most of even those super-hot gobblers by committing some random greenhorn faux pas, moving at the wrong time or whatever, but unfortunately I tagged a few of them, too.

Those infrequent but exciting successes kept me running and gunning for a good many years, and that's why I used "unfortunately" in the preceding paragraph. Every time I managed to kill one of these hormone-addled sophomores (they were almost always usually inexperienced two-year-olds,) it reinforced my faith in those low-percentage hunting tactics. Never mind all the failures. I killed this one, didn't I?

As time went on and the popularity of turkey hunting started catching up to turkey numbers, we run-and-gunners started noticing a change in turkey behavior. By the 1990s, those dozen-gobbler mornings weren't so common any more, and it got harder and harder to strike turkeys with our go-for-broke hunting style. And those we did strike were increasingly more reluctant to approach the aggressive calling. Things had changed.

I didn't, though. Old habits die hard, and I carried on as before, wearing out boots and turkey calls by over-using both. And when one of those increasingly infrequent two-year-olds did come in blowing and stomping and let me kill him in spite of myself, it made up for a lot of turkey-less mornings. And it also reinforced my bad habits.

However, sometimes good fortune comes in disguise. When I fell off a ledge in April 1994 and tore up my right knee, it slowed me down considerably. It didn't stop me, understand; it was turkey season, and after all it was only a screwed-up knee. So I wrapped it tight and played hurt for the rest of the season, gimping through the woods like Quasimodo in search of a bell rope.

Since I was covering much less territory, I figured lower-key calling would be appropriate as well. Somehow it just seemed logical, so I tried it. And I quickly noticed an increase in the number of gobblers I was making contact with. There was also a definite improvement in my kill percentage. By the time that season was finished, I was a fervent disciple of a new religion.

Nobody has ever accused me of half-assing any of my obsessions, and that held true with this new approach. During the season of 1995, even with a healed knee under me, my rate of progress through the woods made snails look speedy. Where I once covered a half-dozen miles in a morning, I was now traveling a mile or less. Sometimes much less. Moss started growing on the north side of my seldom-used box call. Wrens nested in the pockets of my turkey vest.

Okay, I'm overdrawing it some. But I really had dialed it back, no fooling, and the result was I beat myself. That season was pretty much a bust, and I worked fewer gobblers – and tagged fewer – than I had in several seasons. I'd throttled back too much; I'd turned a poor tactic into a good one and then turned it bad again. I wasn't covering enough ground to locate many gobblers, and I was being too hesitant and wimpy with the few I did find. It was pretty obvious I'd overdone things – or underdone them, depending on how you look at it. There was a happy medium in there somewhere, if only I could find it.

I've been looking for it ever since. My knee is okay now but other parts of me are going south, and it seems like every day something new starts hurting. I easily outpace all but the peppiest snails nowadays, but I'm no longer what you'd call a run-and-gun hunter. I guess you'd call my hunting style laid-back, or maybe wait-and-see. Something like that. I cover ground but I don't hurry; I call aggressively sometimes but not always; I can wait, if necessary, with the patience of Job, but I can also (usually) walk away from an obstinate turkey and go look for another one.

And I kill some turkeys these days. Not as many as you, maybe, but I still tag one every once in a while. Enough over the years, at any rate, to have dampened that desperate hunger for the kill that dominated my early turkey hunting. It hasn't, though, lessened my desire to hear them gobble, to work them close, to converse with them in their own language on their own turf, to bend them to my will. That desire is still as strong as ever, and if that need to get inside their heads ever weakens inside mine, that's when I'll quit.

Don't get me wrong here. The adrenalin rush is still very much there. The sound of a nearby gobble still raises the hair at the back of my neck, and when a turkey approaches my heart still races and my breath comes short. Maybe not quite the way it happened early on, but bad enough. Usually, when I killed a gobbler in those early years, I had to go behind a tree and lose my breakfast. Nowadays, it only happens on every third or fourth bird.

Ironically, it may be this dimming of the burning need to kill them that helps me kill more of them these days. Since the kill isn't as important now as it was then, I'm a little calmer and more collected in the presence of the adversary, and this gives me an edge. Maybe.

It's something to think about, anyway, on those hunts when nothing is happening and my mind starts to drift. I'm more than likely into my last decade as a turkey hunter, and sometimes, toward the end of a particularly grueling season, I think back down the years to that seminal moment when

I killed that first gobbler and my life's path took that irreversible swerve. In these moments, I wonder if things might have worked out better had I gone fishing that long-ago April morning instead of caving in to my buddy's nagging and going turkey hunting.

Unquestionably, my life would have been simpler. Less money spent, more spring fishing, maybe a marriage saved somewhere along the way.

But better? Nah.

Chapter 38

Showdown in a Country Ditch

By Larry Dablemont

This is a true story from several years ago, involving an 82-year-old landowner and two conservation agents: It was close to the end of the spring turkey season, and an elderly hunter in camouflaged clothing was crossing a gravel road with a shotgun, heading toward a small house across the road. It was nearly two p.m. and a new pick-up with a conservation department insignia on it was traveling the country road.

It stopped beside the old man who was struggling up the bank and two young agents stepped out. One of them asked if he had been hunting turkeys. He turned toward them from halfway up the side of the ditch and nodded. They asked if he had a tag and he nodded again, taking a landowner's permit out of a shirt pocket and handing it down to them.

The agent handed it back and asked if the land was his. "Forty acres over there," he nodded toward the land he had come from, "and 'bout 20 or so over here behind my house."

"We need to see your shells." The second agent said, to be sure you don't have ammunition with number 2 shot."

"Sure," the old man said, taking a shell from his shirt pocket and tossing it to him. "But what kind of idiot would hunt gobblers with number 2 shot?"

"Well, mister your biggest problem is you are hunting after hours if your shotgun is loaded," said the first agent. "Mind if we check it?"

"Yessir," the man's face began to flush. "I mind...'cause I ain't a gonna give it to you or nobody else, because it's mine and this is my land and I don't give my gun to anybody. Back in World War II I lost four of my buddies because they surrendered their rifles to some Nazis who captured a truck they was in and the sons-a-bitches shot 'em."

The agents went on to explain that if it was loaded they would have to give him a citation because all turkey hunting ended at 1 p.m. He bristled at that. "It sure as hell is loaded," he said, "and I ain't been huntin' turkeys since before noon. I shoot armadillos and snakes and wild hogs and copperheads if I come across 'em, and I can't do it with an empty shotgun.

"I might want to shoot a couple of crows or maybe the possum that has been in my chicken pen eatin' eggs," he said. "So since I am a law-abidin' citizen with the right to carry this shotgun, I intend to do so."

The agent went on to explain that the law said no turkey hunter could carry a loaded shotgun after 1 p.m. and because of that they would have to write him a citation.

"Write it then," the old man said, "then throw it in the ditch or take it with you cause I ain't signin' it and I ain't takin' it and I'll be glad to go to court to tell a judge what a pair of a..holes you fellers are, drivin' along the road tryin' to make a livin' without doin' no work. Course you can't get out in the woods an' find poachers, cause you might get mud on them fancy uniforms!

"It's the way of you new game wardens," he went on. "Back last winter when I called you cause they was spotlighters drivin' this road, you wa'nt interested. Couldn't get nobody out here on a cold night. Right now I know where there's an old boy in overalls with an ol' single barrel shotgun with a stock held together with bailin' wire, tryin' to get him a turkey over a pile of corn, but he ain't in no danger cause you boys ain't about to get out amongst the ticks and walk that far."

One of the agents remarked that if he kept talking that way they would have to take him in.

The old man backed up the bank a step or two and grasped his shotgun at his chest, his face red with anger and dark eyes squinted with determination. "You try that fellers and all three of us'll be stayin' here in this ditch!"

The two agents retreated and drove away, and about an hour later the old man was sitting on his porch with several old dogs beside him when the county sheriff drove up. He came up and sat down on the porch with the old man he had known since he was a boy.

"You about done it now, didn't you, Joe," he said, turning down a cup of coffee he knew would taste awful. "Our two game wardens want you arrested for threatening to shoot them."

"Did no such thing," the old timer said, "Just told 'em if they wanted my gun they had to take it."

"They was in the wrong there," the sheriff said, "and I told 'em that. Told 'em if they ain't got a crime of some sort to investigate not to go around tryin' to take guns from innocent folks on their own doorsteps in my county.

"But I swear they ain't like they use to be," he went on, "I knew the game warden 30 years back, back when they worked alone and had a little common sense. These new young ones thinks they can do anything. They's getting to be a belligerent bunch that pays little attention to the rights of citizens. Had one taser a 76-year-old man in a county up to the north while he was opening his farm gate to go check on his own cattle. He wouldn't show the agent his driver's license. But hell, a conservation agent ain't even supposed to carry a taser."

It was quiet for a moment as the old man slurped coffee and rocked in his chair on the porch. Finally he spoke "Reckon I'm a goin' ta hafta go in town and hire me one o' them crooked lawyers?"

"Might been you'd a had to, Joe," the sheriff said. "They had plans to make an example out of you. But they decided to drop the whole thing once I told them that there was a television camera crew comin' with that woman reporter to get a news story about it all. Don't tell folks what a liar I have gotten to be."

The old man grinned, and wiped off his forehead with a handkerchief. "Sheriff, it's been awhile since I voted," he said with a smile. "But this year yore a gonna get one more vote than you normally get!"

Chapter 39

Legacy

By Jim Spencer

Picture them:

The father. Young, strong, hot and dirty after a long, sweaty day of work on the railroad, smiling self-consciously as he pedals homeward on the brand-new English racing bike.

The mother. Pretty, smiling, perspiring delicately from her labors over the stove, her bulging apron hinting at another form of labor soon to commence; co-conspirator in this plot and trying to keep the boy away from the windows until Daddy gets home.

The boy. Six and a bit, full of life as a chipmunk, pacing impatiently from room to room and sneaking glances through the curtains between pseudo-scoldings from his mother. Where was Daddy, anyway? He should have been home 20 minutes ago. Had he forgotten his promise?

Then the knock on the door. The boy is in his room, fidgeting. Mama was making him nervous, acting so strange.

"Get the door for me, will you, Honey?" his mother calls down the hallway. Her voice is carefully casual.

The boy runs to the door, flings it open. The mother peers around the door frame, feeling as deliciously naughty as a child hiding behind the living room curtains and waiting for Santa.

The father stands in the yard, proudly but still a little self-consciously. His long legs fork the gleaming bicycle. He grins at the boy, who stares wide-eyed at the spectacle of his father aboard a bike. The mother watches from the kitchen, unaware she is holding her breath.

No one says anything.

Finally: "Well, Son, what do you think?" "Gosh, Dad! Where'd you get that?" "Bought it at the Western Auto store." "Is it for me?"

"Yep."

"Neat. Put it around back and let's go dove hunting like you promised."

• • •

The boy, 10 now, is still not quite old enough for his own gun, but he is even more crazy about hunting. He wheedles his father at every opportunity to take him out "just for a little while, Dad." The father always does his best to oblige.

On this particular October afternoon, they are seated against a big tree trunk in the middle of a hickory grove. It is unseasonably warm, above 80, and the squirrels are lethargic in the heat. Very little is going on in the woodlot.

A few late cicadas screech in the treetops. Flies buzz monotonously.

The boy nods sleepily.

The limb bounces just once, but once is enough. Awake and alert now, the boy intently studies the tree. Was it a bird?

No, there he is! Big, fat, red as an Irish setter, the squirrel dances out on the limb, snatches a hickory nut, tightropes back to a comfortable fork and settles in to eat. The sound of determined gnawing soon drifts to the boy's ears.

"Dad!" The stage-whisper could be heard a block away. "I see one!"

"Ssssh. Not so loud. Where?"

The boy points, the father shoots. The squirrel falls dead, a victim of teamwork.

The boy excitedly makes the retrieve. He carries the big squirrel in both hands, holding it like a sleeping pet. He plops down beside his father, noisily, proudly. The father hands him the spent shotgun hull.

The boy strokes the squirrel and sniffs thoughtfully at the pungent, pleasing aroma of freshly-burned gunpowder emanating from the red paper hull. Then he stuffs the shell in his pocket. He touches his father on the knee.

"I'll find 'em, Dad," he says, man to man. "You shoot 'em."

• • •

The shiny new black hip boots sport gaudy red dots at the knees. They are stiff and uncomfortable, and even in the warm restaurant they feel clammy and damp. But they are the boy's first badge of membership in the duck hunting fraternity, and he wears them with pride.

The boy, now a gangling 12-year-old, has had his own gun for two years. He has accounted for more than a dozen squirrels and two or three unfortunate cottontails. Now he feels he is ready for nobler quarry, so he has asked his father to take him duck hunting. The father feels the boy needs another year or two before he's ready for the rigors of flooded timber duck hunting, but the boy is so eager he has reluctantly agreed.

The little café is crowded with fellow hip-booters who fill the room with noise, cigarette smoke and tall tales. Beside himself with excitement and anticipation, the boy is not hungry. His eyes dart here and there as he picks at his eggs.

"Eat your breakfast, Son," the father says. You're going to need it to help keep you warm. This is going to be a lot tougher than squirrel hunting."

The boy does as he is told and cleans his plate, but it is wasted effort.

Outside the restaurant, he upchucks into the gutter. Nerves.

"You okay, Son? Want to go back home?" "Yes sir. I mean no sir. I'm fine. Sorry."

Later, at the edge of the backwater, the father, the boy and the father's hunting buddy look doubtfully at the wreck of a boat they must use to cross the deep bayou just ahead.

"I don't know, Bob," the father says. "I don't like the looks of it."

The boat is ancient, hand-made from cypress planks, and, to put it kindly, has seen better days. A foot-long section of board is missing from the center of the bow, and in order to keep the hole above water level, all three hunters are obliged to huddle together in the stern. This sinks the stern alarmingly low in the water, leaving only an inch or two of freeboard.

"I don't think we ought to try it."

"Aw, please, Dad," the boy says. "We can make it okay. It's not far, is it?"

They take a trial run in the shallows. Although the stern rides dreadfully low, the old boat is so heavy it is surprisingly stable. They decide to do it. It's not far, after all.

They are across the deepest part when it happens. The boy, crouched between the two men, is the first to notice the water coming over the transom.

"Mr. Bob, we're taking on a little water," he says. As if waiting for its cue, the boat sinks beneath them. It makes an audible sucking sound as it goes down.

"Get the guns!" Bob yells, making a dive for his Browning.

"Get the guns, hell!" the father shouts back. He snatches the boy by the waist and stands up in the boat, rising unreasonably to his toes as the icy water rushes up around him.

The old hulk settles to the bottom waist-deep, and the father has never been more relieved than when the water halts its upward journey on his body. He can stand being wet and cold. Swimming his son to safety while wearing heavy hunting clothes he cannot.

The men step out of the boat and it rises sluggishly back to the surface.

They pull it to shallow water, tie it to a tree, and empty their boots. "It's cold out here, Daddy," the boy said.

"I know it is, Son," the father said. "Maybe if we wade back through the woods a little, we'll warm up." But the exercise doesn't help, and the ducks aren't flying anyway. The boy is becoming hypothermic and the men aren't in much better shape, so they decide to call it a day.

And the only way out is back across the deep bayou in that deathtrap of a boat. They remove their hip boots in case they have to swim. The father watches as they cross the deep water, making sure he knows where the nearest tree is at all times. In the middle of the bayou, 50 feet from the nearest snag, the boy looks at his father. "Daddy, I'm scared."

"Me, too, Son," the father answers with a tight-lipped smile. "Me, too."

But they make it safely across this time, and by the time they've walked the half-mile to the car, they are beginning to warm up a little. Not much, but a little.

"Dad?" The boy is huddled over the car's heater as they drive back to town.

"Hmmm?"

"I don't think I want to go duck hunting any more until I'm older."

That afternoon, while the boy slept, the father went back with an axe and chopped the old boat into kindling.

• • •

At 15, the boy knew it all. Just ask him. He had mastered squirrels and now ducks, and youthful reflexes and excellent hand-eye coordination compensated wonderfully for lack of experience on more difficult targets such as doves, quail and rabbits. But he had yet to kill his first deer, and his juvenile patience was beginning to unravel. This was his third season of deer hunting, and so far he had seen no antlers.

The morning was misty-dewy, the way many fall mornings are in the South. The quiet was heavy, almost oppressive, and yet it wasn't quiet at all. A squirrel ran up and down a cypress trunk over there, happy as a squirrel to be alive on a morning like this. His toenails made little scratchy sounds on the bark. Over here, a nuthatch was showing off, hanging upside down on an oak limb and pecking industriously at something in a crevice. There was another squirrel in that cane thicket out front. The boy could hear it scuffling through the leaves.

The boy was too surprised to be excited when the six-point buck stepped out of the cane and looked directly at him. He shot it as if it was a quail, gun to his shoulder and *bang*! That quick. The buck went over backwards, dead right there, and the boy sat with his gun trained on the animal to make sure it wasn't getting up. Then he walked over and sat beside his trophy to wait for his father. His knees, he noticed, were only a little bit wobbly.

Later, when the father came by to get the boy, it was hard to tell who was more pleased. The father helped the boy field-dress the buck, then painted his son's face with blood. The boy wore the blood the rest of that day and would have slept with it if his father hadn't drawn the line. No Comanche warrior ever wore war paint with more pride.

Back at camp, they found a spike buck and a truly monstrous ten-pointer already hanging from the game pole. The boy oohed and ahhed over the big one, but his father had eyes for nothing but the six-pointer.

The boy didn't learn until many years later that his father had been the hunter who killed the big buck.

• • •

Two years of college were now behind the boy. The asinine general requirements – college algebra, English, Western civ, sociology, speech – had been laid by. There had even been time for a couple early electives. One of those early electives had largely to do with topographical map reading.

There were four of them in the boat that day: the father, the boy, and a friend of each. The weather was as cold as it had been on that first duck hunt a decade ago, but the boat was much better this time. Broad of beam and high of gunwale, it was made of heavy aluminum and covered with hand-painted camouflage. A 25-horsepower outboard hung from the transom.

They had been out all day. They'd killed some ducks and missed some, too. They'd stood in the thigh-deep water and when they got chilly, they'd built a stick fire on a floating log and held an impromptu weenie roast. They'd talked and laughed and poked gentle fun at one another, and they had sat quietly and enjoyed the day and each other's company. It had been a fine, fine day.

But now it was getting late, and they were thoroughly lost. The water under the boat was too deep to wade, and the brush was so thick running a compass course was impossible – even if they'd had a compass to consult. Unbelievably, none of the four experienced hunters in the boat had brought one. A heavy cloud cover had moved in at midafternoon, so even dead reckoning by the sun was out of the question. The only navigational aid they had was a 7-1/2-minute topographical map from the U.S. Geological Service.

Funny thing about a map, though: to use it, you must first know where you are. An interesting paradox, but maddening when you are lost.

It was after 4 p.m. and daylight was beginning to fade when, after two hours of fruitless putt-putting through the flooded forest, they broke out into a small, winding bayou.

"Shut it off for a minute, Dad."

The outboard died obediently. The boy unfolded the map. The father lifted the gas tank.

"Almost empty."

"It's cold out here, Dad," the boy said. "And getting colder," said the boy's friend.

"The weather report said snow late this afternoon through tomorrow," said the father's friend.

The boy smoothed the map on the metal boat seat and studied it. He looked up and down the narrow bayou, then back at the map. He shook his head in frustration.

"Where are we, Son?"

"Dad, I can't tell for sure. We're either here or here or here." He jabbed at the map three times. "See how the bayou breaks left and then left again? That's what it's doing here, and those three spots are the only places the map shows this bayou doing that. No way to tell which one we're at until we move."

"How can we tell then?"

"Well, see how the bayou lines out straight for a quarter-mile on the map here? If it does that when we go around the bend, then we're right here." The boy tapped the map. "If it curves back to the left pretty quick, we're either here or here." Tap. Tap. "And if we're either of those two places, we won't have enough gas to get back to the boat ramp."

So they started the outboard and went around the bend and the bayou lined out straight and they were home free. They ran out of gas anyway, but they were so close to the landing it didn't matter. They paddled the last 200 yards, laughing and joking in the twilight.

In the coffee shop the next morning, a casual listener might have thought he was hearing about a modern-day Daniel Boone as the father told a slightly embellished version of the incident. His son was the best woodsman in the state. That boy could find his way back from the dark side of the moon during a total eclipse. There was no way to get him lost.

No siree.

The boy sat across the table, his ears burning with embarrassment and pride. The pride didn't stem from the fact that he'd known how to find his way out of the flooded bottoms. Anybody with a few hours of instruction could have done that.

He was proud simply because his father was proud of him.

• • •

The campfire crackled merrily, gobbling up the dry wood the boy, now grown, kept piling on it. It wasn't really cold enough for a fire, but that thought never entered his head. When it got dark in a hunting camp, you built a fire.

"Don't heap so much wood on there, Son," the father said. "It's getting too warm over here."

The boy grinned through the smoke. "It's cold out here, Dad," he said. "If you're hot, move farther back." Another chunk of wood as thick as a man's thigh thudded into the flames, sending a geyser of sparks skyward. The Father grinned back and took the boy's advice. They didn't say anything else for quite a while, each lost in the private thoughts that surface unbidden and flutter around like moths whenever one gazed into a campfire. The father watched the boy across the fire. Twice he started to speak. Both times he checked himself.

"What is it, Daddy?" The boy's voice was more forceful than he'd intended.

The sudden question caught the father by surprise. "Sssh. Not so loud. I didn't know you were watching me."

"What is it?" the boy asked, softer this time.

The father hesitated. "It's hard for me."

The boy waited silently, eyes on his father. He poked absently at the fire with a stick.

"I went to the doctor last week," the father said. "I haven't been feeling good. He took some X-rays and had some blood work done."

The boy quit poking at the fire.

"I've got advanced pancreatic cancer, Son. The doc said I've got maybe three months."

The boy was quiet for a long time. Then he got up, threw his poking stick into the fire, walked around behind his father and put his arms around him. For some reason – he had no idea why – he hadn't hugged his father in a long time.

"What do I say, Daddy?" the boy asked softly, when he felt he could trust his voice.

The father patted his arm. "You just said it, Son."

• • •

The car crunched to a stop on the pea-gravel. The father stepped out, carefully testing the soggy grass to make sure it wasn't too mushy underneath. The boy stuck his tousled head out of the passenger window.

"It's cold out here, Daddy!" he said in a chirpy voice.

"I know it is, Son. Come on."

They walked across the cemetery, the boy's small hand folded inside his father's big one as they waved carefully between the row of tombstones. The boy tried to skip, but the ground was too soft and he gave it up as a bad effort. The father was looking, looking...

Yes, there it was. The stone was modest, dignified. It looked like a hundred other markers in the cemetery until you came close and really looked at it.

That's when you noticed the little niche carved into the center of the stone, and the small, neat engravings of a duck on one side of the hole and a squirrel on the other. A couple family members had argued that ducks and squirrels had no place on a tombstone. They were wrong.

"Who's buried here, Daddy? Hey, look, a duck!"

"Sssh. Not so loud. Where?"

"See him right there? There's a squirrel, too! Who's buried here?"

"This is your Grandpa, Son. He used to take me hunting a lot."

The boy was running his small fingers over the outline of the duck when something in the niche caught his eye. He reached in and brought out a frayed paper shotgun hull, bleached nearly white by time and the elements. Only a faint pink cast remained to show the shell had once been red.

"Look, Daddy, a bullet! Can I keep it?"

The father smiled. "Not that one, Son." He took the hull from his son, sniffed at it. No gunpowder smell was there, but the father's mind supplied it. He looked at it for a moment, then replaced it in its niche. "It belongs to Grandpa. He gave it to me a long time ago, and when he died I gave it back to him. I'll give you one someday."

"Good! Can we go hunting today? Then you can give me one."

"I don't see why not. Now say 'bye to Grandpa and let's go back to

Grandma's. Your mother should be there by now."

"Can Grandpa hear me?"

"I wouldn't be a bit surprised."

"Okay. 'Bye, Grandpa! I had a nice time." The boy scampered back toward the car, dodging tombstones like a rabbit. The father watched him go. Then he looked back at the tombstone, and he didn't feel foolish at all when he started talking to it.

"He's a pretty good boy, Dad. I know you'd like him. I'll keep you posted on how he's coming along, but I think he's going to do just fine. After all, you taught me how to raise him."

• • •

The boy was already in the car when the father arrived.

"Aunt Jemima, what took you so long?" the boy yelled out the window, then dissolved into a fit of giggles at his own vast wit.

The father got in the car and started the engine. "I got something in my eye, Son."

He sat there a minute, looking out the window in the direction of the tombstone with the duck and the squirrel on it. No, you couldn't quite see it from here.

"Let's go, Daddy!" the boy yelled. "I want to go hunting."

"Sssh. Not so loud."

The father wiped his eyes one more time to make sure that whatever had gotten into them was gone. He grinned at the boy, and the boy grinned back. Then he put the car in gear and they rolled down the drive and out the gate and away.

Chapter 40

The Angel and Zeke Jones

By Larry Dablemont

I wish you folks could have known Zeke Jones. His name 'Zeke' was short for Ezekyal Somolon Jones. Zeke's folks weren't nearly as educated as he had become, and they spelled both his first names wrong on the paperwork so he was stuck with them. They did get Jones right though. At least that's what my grandma told me, and she knew things like that. No one in my dad's pool hall where I worked after school knew him by anything but Zeke.

He was what they call ex-centric. But I think he might have been real educated because of the way he talked. He only came into the pool hall on rare occasions, but he always made an impact. He was a spiritual man, sort of. He spent about a half hour once giving me the details of how it was indeed possible that Noah was swallowed by that whale and how he thought it may have come about. I thought about telling him I didn't think it was Noah who got ate by the whale, it was either Joshua or Jonah. But I couldn't remember which so I didn't say anything.

One cold winter night when we were all sitting there on the front bench...me and ol' Jim and ol' Bill and Jess Wolf and Saldy Reardon... Zeke got to carrying on about how he had been visited by an angel back during the squirrel season. I don't know what got us into that, but I think some young fellow had been talking about how his wife was just an angel and he was so happy with her. Ol' Bill said sort of quiet-like how the guy hadn't been married long or he wouldn't be talking that way.

And that's when Zeke told us about seeing a real angel when he was hunting way back in the woods over on the other side of the Big Piney. She had descended before him out of the heavens, with long golden hair and wings that sparkled and shined like ivory. He said she was the most beautiful woman he had ever seen but even so, it near about scared him to death.

My dad had told me many times that while he knew I would never be able to just sit there in the pool hall while I was working and keep quiet, seein' as how I was the way I was, he insisted that I keep my mouth shut in case of arguments over politics or religion.

But no one else said a word, so I couldn't help but ask Zeke if the angel had actually talked to him.

"For a long spell, son," Zeke said. "I come to find out she was part of a sort of survey, where angels were sent out by God to talk with selected men of greater intellectual capacity, and I was one of the chosen ones."

Bill snorted about that. "I reckon maybe God tol' some angels to go out yonder an' find some drunk squirrel hunters an' axt 'em if they thought it ought to be legal to hunt squirrels with dogs," he grinned in his skeptical manner, "or maybe to get some good squirrel recipes."

"It wasn't so far from that...oh ye of little faith," Zeke went on. "She said that the great Creator was interested in finding out if more commandments should be added to the first ten, and He placed great value in the opinion of a man with a greater understanding of the historical aspect of the Bible and the flaws of society in general."

Saldy Reardon was rolling a cigarette, something he did often, and he leaned over to Norman Salyer, who was sort of napping a little, as he often did there on the front bench. "What'd he say?" Saldy asked. Norman just sort of shrugged his shoulders and lapsed back into relaxation.

"I figger we have enough rules in the Bible," ol' Jim said with a shake of his head. "I am pretty sure it says somewheres 'thou shalt not lie'!" Everyone snickered at that, knowing full well that if old Zeke wasn't guilty of anything else in his whole life, lying wasn't one of the things he wasn't guilty of.

My dad had told me a time or two that I would have to get a quite a bit older before I would fully understand what was and wasn't lying. He said that lots of times it sounded like he was lying to my mother when he really wasn't guilty of anything other than trying to keep the peace. The Bible does say 'blessed are the peacekeepers', and while he was home with Mom, I think that was his favorite verse.

Lying to a woman is likely not a sin, the way I seen it then. You can't tell a woman she's ugly if she is, but don't think she is. And if some lady asks you what you think of her new dress you have to say it looks really nice, even if it looks like it might have been made out of an army tent and slept in by a hibernatin' bear. I remember telling girls in school how pretty their hair was, just to get them to help me with my homework.

The reason I think it might be okay to lie to a woman is knowing that God Himself told Eve she was fully equal to Adam, knowing full well she didn't have as many ribs as Adam did. Every Sunday school teacher I ever had was a woman and every one of them said that men and women were equal. They overlooked the fact that me and my cousin, Butch McNew, could beat girls several years older than us at arm-rasslin'.

Most every man there in the pool hall knew that women weren't equal to men at hardly nothin', but every one of them were hesitant to say so. It isn't the truth that makes women happy, it is lyin' to them. And ol' Bill said once that that is the very reason that lyin' ain't always a sin, because God wanted men to make women happy and that was the way to do it.

But Zeke Jones said the beautiful angel that visited him in long white satin clothing and gold speckled white wings was interested in whether or not he felt there should be a commandment concerning gambling.

Should one be added saying, "Thou shalt not gamble?" the angel asked him.

Zeke said he told her right out that he was against it, because most of his old friends on the front bench of our pool hall played nickel and dime poker on Friday nights at old Bill Hoyt's place, and adding another commandment to the ones they broke on a regular basis would certainly place them on very shaky ground, despite all the good points they had.

"I told her that if there was indeed a survey of good men from a country sort of background they'd be ten-to-one against any such additions to the Ten Commandments." Zeke said. "Well, the angel said ten-to-one was awful good odds, and she'd bet that good men everywhere would overwhelmingly approve of a dictate against adding the activities of reprobates."

You see, that's what I meant about Zeke, he said things that used words you never heard before...'a dictate against reprobates'?

Ol' Jim Splechter tried to act like he knew what Zeke was talking about. "I bet she wuz right 'bout that. Good men ought to stand up agin' repper-baits. An' I'm agin' usin' goggle-eyes fer baits on a trotline too by golly!"

Zeke paid him no mind. "Well, that beautiful golden-haired blue-eyed angel was wearing a gleaming gold bracelet, just sort of hovering there above the ground to keep her sandals out of the dirt, and I was just marveled by it. In turn she had been eyeing my ol' '97 Winchester pump-gun and she just up and told me she would bet her bracelet against my shotgun that when the tally was in, the anti-gambling amendment would be added and poor ol' Bill and Jess and Jim and Virgil would have to be judged as the sinners they were."

It was then he hauled out the bracelet, shiny and gold and heavenly looking, and several of the Front Bench Regulars gathered around to look at it. "Well, she was an honest angel," Zeke said, "and when she lost the bet, she brought this to me on my next squirrel hunt. I would like to keep it, but I am needing the money and I suppose I would pass it on to someone with a wife or daughter if I could get what it's worth."

Rupert Sims, who had two different girlfriends, was excited. It was plain to see it was either pure gold or something similar, and he had to know what it would take to buy it. Zeke thought about it awhile and then said that while it had been appraised at 200 dollars he had decided to sell it for 100. "But," he said, "I have decided to let someone have it for 50 dollars tonight if it is a transfer involving cash."

You know, Zeke never did sell that bracelet. Rupert wanted it something terrible but he only had nine dollars on him with some change. Zeke got into a bit of a heated argument with ol' Bill Stalder when Bill said that he'd bet his shotgun against that bracelet that Zeke would go to Hell before any of the rest of 'em did just for bringing the spiritual aspect of life into a pool hall, while there were two fellows playing snooker on the front table for a cold soda pop and peanuts.

My dad came in about then and broke it up and Zeke went home with his bracelet. A week or so later I asked my Grandpa McNew, the most church-goin'est and good man I had ever knew, if he thought it was a sin to gamble.

Grandpa thought about it a moment and said he'd bet a dollar that it was indeed a sin. Then he laughed heartily at his joke. And I never did find out for sure if gambling is a sin. I hope not, 'cause I took some awful chances when I was a kid.

Duck Hunting for Supper
A small flock of ducks, all together,
Left the north in the teeth of bad weather
They flew south past me,
And I shot at two or three
But they flew off without losing a feather.
So tonight I'll go home in my truck
Empty handed because of bad luck,
To chili and crackers,
'Cause I missed all them quackers
But I'd much rather be eatin' duck.

Chapter 41

The Great Turkey Conspiracy

By Jim Spencer

C all him Bill. It's not his name, but it'll do. As a baby during the Roaring Twenties, he fell victim to a raging, dangerously high fever. Bill survived, but the fever left him...well, not quite right.

In some ways, Bill had the intellectual powers of a Harvard graduate. He never forgot a name or a face or a detail of any long-ago conversation, and you sure didn't want to play dominoes against him. But in other ways, he remained childlike and innocent. Bill died in 1991, when his 70-year-old heart got tired and quit. He was a friend of mine. This is his story.

A country boy, Bill grew up in a hunting-oriented family in the Arkansas Ozarks. Although his limited physical coordination kept him from becoming a proficient wing shot, he nevertheless got pretty good at hitting squirrels. Over the years, he tagged a buck or two as well.

Inevitably, as turkeys were re-introduced to his home area and the flocks began to grow, Bill got interested in turkey hunting. "Interested," though, is too mild a word. "Obsessed" is closer. Bill joined the National Wild Turkey Federation and read each issue of Turkey Call from cover to cover. He attended local calling contests and hunting seminars. He talked turkey, to the point of exhaustion, with anybody who would listen or who couldn't make an escape.

This next thing is difficult to explain without sounding snotty and superior, but I don't mean it that way. Please don't read it wrong. The thing is, though, turkey hunting is a game of strategy and finesse, and Bill's level of mental development and sophistication just wasn't up to the task. In the matter of hunting these grand birds, my old friend was in over his head.

And so, after watching Bill become more and more frustrated at his inability to call in and kill a gobbler, a mutual friend decided to help a little. Call him Tom.

Tom tried to do it the straightforward, honest way at first. He solicited the help of another mutual friend, a famous Missouri turkey hunter whose name you'd recognize if I mentioned it.

The Famous Turkey Hunter tried hard to get Bill in front of a turkey, or vice versa. But Bill had other health problems, too, and he wasn't able to walk very far or very fast. That greatly increased the degree of difficulty in an already difficult undertaking, and the FTH couldn't quite pull it off. They managed to locate a hot bird one morning that was close to a road on gentle terrain, and it looked like Bill was finally going to kill his first gobbler. But the closer the turkey came, gobbling at every step, the more Bill trembled and shook. Finally, just as the bird was about to show itself, Bill got so rattled he dropped his shotgun on the rocks at his feet.

End of gobbling. End of turkey hunt.

End of Bill, too, nearly. "I thought he was going to die on me right there," the FTH told me later. "He was trembling and breathing hard and grabbing his chest. I asked him, 'Bill, are you okay?' and he said yes, he thought so, but he felt the same way the time he had a heart attack."

Back in camp, the FTH told Tom he didn't think the legitimate approach was going to work, and they might kill Bill if they kept trying. So they drafted two more friends – Dick and Harry – and the Great Turkey Conspiracy was born.

Early the next spring, the Famous Turkey Hunter bought a good-looking bronze domestic gobbler with a thick, bushy beard. A week before the opening of Missouri's season, he put the gobbler in a ramshackle shed on a hunting property he had under lease, leaving it with plenty of feed and water.

On the third morning of turkey season, Tom brought Bill to the lease at daylight and comfortably installed him in a portable roof-and-wall blind at the edge of a field, just a couple hundred yards from the shed housing the domestic gobbler. Tom put a decoy in front of the blind and closed all the openings except the one overlooking the decoy. Then he got in the blind with Bill.

When all was ready, Tom gave a loud series of yelps. Dick, standing at the shed, heard the pre-arranged signal and went into action. He went into the shed, caught the gobbler and headed for the blind, the bird riding peacefully under his arm. He'd been getting this same ride every day for a week. Once Dick was in position, slightly behind and a few yards to the right of the blind, he softly yelped back at Tom.

Meanwhile, Harry was setting up a video camera just to the left of the blind. When he was ready, he yelped, too.

Inside the stuffy blind, Bill and Tom peered out the front window at the decoy. "Tom, I think I hear one!" Bill whispered excitedly.

"Me, too," Tom said. "Maybe you better call a little." And so Bill sent out three ragged yelps on his box call, thereby unwittingly giving Dick the signal to release the gobbler.

They had rehearsed this part with the gobbler, too, using a small pile of corn at the decoy to train him to walk to the proper place and stop. It being a turkey "hunt" and all, and baiting of course being illegal, the corn pile was missing this morning. Still, the gobbler played his part perfectly, as befitted the star of the show. He walked along the edge of the woods toward the decoy and stopped where the corn as supposed to be – at point-blank range, squarely in front of the blind.

The gobbler didn't have much time to puzzle over the absence of his little corn pile. Eight yards away, the muzzle of Bill's old double-barrel wavered, then steadied. *Kaboom!*

On the video, you can see the gobbler flinch as the tennis ball-sized warm of sixes goes whizzing by his head. He takes a few nervous steps away from the noise. *Kaboom!* again. A flaw in the plan was becoming obvious: they hadn't allowed enough range for adequate pattern development, and Bill's nervousness and hoochie-koochie gun barrel weren't getting the job done.

On the audio, you can hear muffled curses and clanks as Tom and Bill struggle to reload the shotgun in the close quarters of the blind. By the time they succeed, the gobbler is 25 yards away, finally far enough for Bill's pattern to develop. Three's the charm, and this time the bird goes down. Despite an attack of uncontrollable giggling, Harry managed to capture the event on film.

It's a priceless piece of footage, especially the recap featuring a grinning, still-shaking Bill, who, despite his own excitement, still has the courtliness and generosity to offer the use of his blind to Harry, who hadn't yet tagged a turkey that season. I have a copy of that video, and you don't have enough money to buy it.

• • •

Some will say it was a dirty, dishonest trick. Others will fault the fact that an unsuspecting barnyard gobbler was summarily executed. Some will say it was probably illegal. All those things may be true, but before you pitch your tent in any of those camps, consider this:

Until the day he died (which wasn't too many springs later,) the spurs, beard and fan of Bill's first and only gobbler hung in a place of honor in his simple little house. If you asked – or even if you didn't – Bill was always happy to tell you the long, involved story of how he dueled for hours with this magnificent bird before skillfully and single-handedly bringing him to the gun. Bill's innocent, childlike mind, you see, had taken the event far beyond its facts. The old man sincerely believed he had called that gobbler in all by himself, overcoming immense difficulties all along the way.

As you sat and listened to Bill's story, as I did many times, you were invariably struck by the awe and reverence in the eyes and voice of this generous, good-hearted man-child. His face came alive with excitement and pleasure, and his chest swelled with the curious mixture of pride and regret a turkey hunter feels when recalling a job well done, a kill well made, a bird fairly taken.

That feeling is what bonds turkey hunters one to another. It's a thing we all share, if we're worthy of being called turkey hunters; impossible to explain to an outsider, unnecessary to explain to each other.

It's a feeling that came to Bill only once in his lifetime. But, as you nodded your head and exclaimed at the appropriate places during his story, as you watched his faded old eyes flash, as you saw the smile play around the corners of his mouth, you realized once was going to be enough. Bill had the feeling captured. It was never going to escape.

Yep, the critics are right, but only up to a point. It wasn't an honest thing to do, and though the statute of limitations has long since run out, it was probably illegal as well. Any way you look at it, the whole elaborate scheme was a complicated, premeditated, unmitigated lie, and lying is a sin.

Still, I suspect there are some sins that will earn you a ticket to Heaven.

Chapter 42

Two Gobblers

By Larry Dablemont

I started guiding turkey hunters in the early 1980's, an offshoot of growing up guiding fishermen on the river. An outdoor writer has to learn to supplement his income when he is raising a family, and I found out there was a lot of money to be made taking turkey hunters on two or three day trips, camping somewhere in the mountains of Arkansas and showing them an experience like they had never had.

The hunters I took were wealthy, most of them lawyers or doctors, men who made a lot of money and didn't have enough time to experience the outdoors on their own. In those days when I lived in Arkansas, I made much of my income guiding those kinds of outdoorsmen on float-fishing trips, fall duck hunting trips or turkey hunting trips in the spring. They paid well, and a few were a pain in the neck. But most were great people.

One of those was an Oklahoma neurosurgeon, Dr. David Fell, and he was a super guy. He was a real joy to hunt with because even though he had never killed a gobbler, and didn't seem to be that concerned if he didn't get one. Truly, he enjoyed being outdoors. He joined me in Texas County in Missouri and we floated the Big Piney River where I had grown up, fishing for bass and goggle-eye that April afternoon. The next morning at dawn, we were out in the deep woods and several gobblers were sounding off around us.

One in particular was gobbling constantly, but slow to move. Within an hour, a mature gobbler came by us within easy range, but he never gobbled at all. Dr. Fell was so consumed with the one we were hearing that he didn't even see the other. In two hours, that noisy gobbler had moved from 200 yards away to about 75 yards, but though we could hear him, we couldn't see him in the underbrush. I kept hearing another hunter on another ridge, trying to call the gobbler we were working. He was using a diaphragm call, and he was too loud, way too anxious with it...doing too much calling. Still, I think the gobbler might have been quicker to come to my call without the competition.

Finally the old tom was within 40 yards, strutting in full view, and Dr. Fell dropped him. He was elated. Within minutes, the other hunter showed up to admire the fallen gobbler. He was about 15 years old, the eldest son of one of my old school mates. They lived on a small tract of land nearby.

Dr. Fell headed back to Oklahoma late in the afternoon. I would spend the night with my folks at Houston, and hunt a little the next morning. But I kept thinking about that kid, so about dark I drove out to his home and gave him one of my calls. I showed him how to use it and told him to quit using that diaphragm. "Save it for turkey calling contests," I told him with a laugh. He looked puzzled.

I started to leave, but I just couldn't. I knew he hadn't ever killed a gobbler in the spring, though he said he had killed a couple of young turkeys in the fall, illegally. So I asked him if he'd like to go with me in the morning. His face brightened like the sun had come back up.

The next morning about 30 minutes after we set up on a wooded ridge-top, I called in a nice gobbler just with my mouth, and the boy killed it. Oh yes, it would have been mine had I not brought him along. And maybe, if you are a young turkey hunter, you may not understand this, but if you are a grizzled old veteran turkey hunter, you will...If I had killed either of those two gobblers in those two spring mornings, I wouldn't have been nearly as happy as I was, driving back to Arkansas without one.

I had another hunter to take to the Ouachita Mountains in a day or so, and I got paid well for a gobbler he killed just a few miles from the Fourche la Fave River. Still, the kid who never paid me a dime for that morning so many years ago gave me just as much as anyone ever did. I remember him lugging that big gobbler toward the porch of that old farmhouse, and some of his brothers and sisters waiting there for the school bus, jumping up and down with excitement. I can still see him, turning toward me with a grin as wide as that gobbler's beard was long, and saying "Thanks Mister Dablemont!"

He's a grown man now...I don't know where. But I hope he takes some kid turkey hunting on occasion. And I'll bet my best turkey call that he does.

Chapter 43

An Aging Schoolboy Trappers's dream

By Jim Spencer

We were lost somewhere in the never-never land between 13 and 14, Buck and I, when we hatched our plan to run a river-bottom trapline.

We'd already trapped together two whole seasons, an eternity when you're 13 going on 14. But it was schoolboy stuff, running a dozen traps apiece by flashlight and bicycle before classes. Our catch consisted mostly of skunks, rabbits and possums, but every so often, on a red-letter day, one or the other of us would catch a coon. One unforgettable morning, Buck even caught a mink.

We lived trapping. Breathed it, too. This was a romantic enterprise, following in the footsteps of John Colter, Jedediah Smith, Jim Bridger and even ol' Hugh Glass hisself, who nearly got et by griz and lived to tell the tale. Heady stuff for a couple of ragamuffin kids in the early 1960s. We were trappers, by gosh, separated from our beaver-trapping, buckskin-wearing heroes only by geography and by time – back then, a mere 140 years.

Besides, a possum sold for 35 cents, a "star" skunk (nearly all black) brought $1.25 to $1.75, and a big coon was worth nearly four dollars. And a mink! Why, a mink would fetch the astronomical sum of seven or eight bucks. Maybe even ten. That the skunks almost always left traces (sometimes considerably more than traces) of their presence on our clothing was of little import. Life was simpler back then.

Buck and I split our trapline profits down the middle, and a typical week's wages might amount to four or five dollars each. More, if we caught a coon. That was a king's ransom in 1962, more than enough for a movie, popcorn and coke – 55 cents total – on both Saturday and Sunday, with plenty left over for sodas, candy bars and frivolities during the week. Life was cheaper back then, too.

We could even have afforded to take a date, if (a) we'd been interested in girls, and (b) any girl would have consented to go to a Saturday matinee with a boy who smelled faintly like a skunk and had mud under his fingernails.

But the girls didn't have to think up excuses, because we were oblivious to their charms. We were totally absorbed in trapping, and that absorption spilled over into the ten non-trapping months as well.

So, sometime during that annual eternity that separates trapping seasons, we hatched our plan. In that dim, distant future when we finally graduated from high school, we'd move to the White River bottoms and run an extensive trapline both upriver and down, using as a base of operations my parents' ramshackle cabin at the tiny riverbank settlement of Crockett's Bluff.

We spent that summer laying elaborate plans. We read and re-read our shared, dog-eared copy of *The Schoolboy Trapper.* We pored over the pages of the F.C. Taylor and O.L. Butcher trapping supply catalogs, our mouths watering at all the traps, lures and other trapline-related equipment. We made a list of the gear we'd need for our expedition, laboring over it hours at a time, adding and subtracting (but mostly adding) stuff as we thought of it. Thinking back on that list (if memory serves, it was six pages long), I figure it would have been sufficient to feed and equip a 20-man safari to Mozambique. My parents' tiny cabin would never have held it all.

That dream lasted for the better part of two years. Then, gradually, it began to unravel.

Buck discovered girls and then I did, or maybe vice versa. Either way, we slowly arrived at the reluctant conclusion that a jingle in our pockets failed to make us attractive enough to the local ladies to make them overcome their aversion to eau de skunk and grimy fingernails. Accordingly, we began to make adjustments.

Then the bottom dropped out of the fur market, and those four-dollar coons were suddenly bringing a buck-fifty. Possums and skunks were nearly worthless. Mink held their value, but since we weren't good enough to catch them with anything more than *good-gosh-would-you-look-at-that! frequency*, it didn't matter. Finally, my parents sold the ramshackle old cabin at Crockett's Bluff, depriving us of our future trapline headquarters and killing our noble plan. Even at 14 or 15, we weren't addle-pated enough to think we could run a winter trapline from a tent. We weren't real mountain men and we knew it.

We made one last stab at trapping the next winter, trying to avoid skunks and concentrating, mostly unsuccessfully, on mink. I think we caught five.

The summer we turned 16, Buck and I fell out over something. I disremember now what it was, but it dissolved our partnership. I got an after-school job at the local bowling alley, and Buck started sacking

groceries. As far as I know, neither of us set a trap that year.

But an unexpected thing happened. I discovered, during that winter's sabbatical from the trapline, that I missed it terribly. Most small-town schoolboys in that day and time trapped a little in their early teens but grew out of it by the time they graduated from high school. It was obvious from my one-year layoff I wasn't with the majority. The next fall, the fall of my senior year, I quit my low-paying bowling alley job and hit the trapline again, this time with an old Plymouth for transportation in place of the bicycle. With more range, I found better trapping locations than I'd been limited to with the bike, and I caught enough fur that year to pay expenses, make up for the wages from my former job, and squire my girlfriend around in what passed for style in our little home town.

More than that, that season proved to me a trapline could pay its way. I've never taken a trapline sabbatical since, and I've always put as much time into my efforts as I could spare without absolutely wrecking the fabric of my life. More than half a century later, I still haven't outgrown it. I'm still as addicted as those two 13-year-old kids who rode their bicycles to check traps before school. Some years I barely cover expenses, some years I scratch out a decent profit. But every year I'm Out There, because the thrill has never left.

That longline in the river bottoms

never came to pass. College got in the way, and then the responsibilities of job and family. But sometimes, when I'm getting my traps ready in the fall, or when I wake up in the middle of a winter night, I think about that grand scheme Buck and I had so long ago, and how enjoyable it would have been to carry it out.

Still today, every time I find myself in the neighborhood, I drive down the gravel road that ends at Crockett's Bluff. It wasn't much of a town in the 1960s, and it's shrunk even more today. But the cabin is still there, now abandoned, moldering away, sinking slowly into the red clay on which it sits.

And I sit in my truck, and look at it, and dream.

Chapter 44

Armour and the Panther

By Larry Dablemont

Charlie Watson had seen him...he had been out there in the dark with him one terrifying winter night on the river only a few months before. The panther had pulled several of Charlie's traps out of the river above Mineral Springs, tore the muskrats all to pieces without eating them, and then stalked him all the way back to his old pickup.

"I jest barely made it," he told me, "and when I was a drivin' off, he jumped on top of my old pick-up and screamed like a banshee. There's scratches there, what he made, tryin' to get at me, you can see that for yourself boy. I ain't never goin' back down there, my trappin' days is over!"

Charlie Watson was about 60 years old, and he looked a little like a turtle. He'd sit on the front bench of my dad's pool hall, wearing that baseball cap, overalls and a long sleeved shirt buttoned to the neck, about half dozing at times when he was bored with the snooker game on the front table, his arms folded and his head forward, making his neck look longer than it was.

But he wasn't a story teller. Charlie was a little bit odd, but he wasn't one of the bullshooters who came in and told big yarns and knowed full well nobody believed 'em. He was just an old bachelor farmer. He and his brother lived on a few acres north of town where there wasn't enough income, so they took to trapping that winter to bring in some extra money. Charlie wasn't the trapper my grandpa was, but he knew how to catch muskrats and a few coons. Then the doggone panther had found his trapline and put an end to it, rather decisively.

It all had quite an impact on me. Every time someone would get Charlie to telling that story he'd get all serious and his voice would get quiet and low and the hair would stand up on the back of his neck and mine too. I knew that stretch of the river well...how many times I had floated down to Mineral Springs late in the evening after a day of fishing, when the sun had already set and the screech owls were wailing as I waited for Dad to arrive in the old pick-up. It was just a miracle I hadn't wound up like those muskrats in Charlie Watson's traps. I thought quite a bit about that panther that summer, since I did quite a bit of squirrel hunting in the fall of 1961, down in the Tweed Bottoms which led to the McKinney Eddy only a few miles above Mineral Springs. I wasn't sure if my dad's old '97 Winchester pump gun, loaded with number 6 low-brass squirrel shells, would stop a mountain lion, or a black panther or whatever it was folks talked about hearing and seeing along the Piney.

Some folks said it was all just in the imagination of old ladies and men who liked to stretch the truth. But they had said the same thing in 1926 when my grandfather was young, and he found a black panther sitting in his boat one misty pre-dawn morning. Grandpa said the big cat was eating a couple of beaver carcasses he had skinned, and he said when it charged out of the boat and ran past him it took his breath away, near about scaring him to death. He was so excited he went back to town and told everyone what he had seen, and nearly got laughed out of the county. For weeks, folks would ask him if he had seen any panthers in his boat lately, and he got so mad about it he just started staying away from people.

Then a fellow named Matt Todd was out running his dogs one winter night and they treed that black panther. Todd shot it, and brought it to town to be photographed and it was in the paper the next week. It vindicated my grandpa, and his neighbors and town people didn't laugh anymore. But the cat was a black leopard, and it was starving to death from its appearance. Come to find out, some woman traveling through the Ozarks in the summer had owned a pet black leopard and it had gotten loose from her and escaped into the woods up around Rolla.

So, I knew there was a possibility that a black panther or a regular mountain lion could be living on the Piney, maybe even two of 'em. It made squirrel hunting seem a little risky.

Armour was a big hefty Doberman Pinscher, and I was a 13-year-old kid. He was my first dog, and I took him everywhere, or sometimes, he took me, depending on which end of the leash had the momentum. Charlie Watson, the old timer at the pool hall, had told me all about the panther on the Big Piney which had followed him as he ran his traplines. As Armour and I headed for the woods that late fall afternoon to hunt squirrels, I couldn't help but think about what I would do if I encountered a real live mountain lion.

The afternoon still had a couple of hours left in it, and with Dad's old '97 Winchester pump-gun and a hodgepodge pocketful of shells, I figured on getting two or three squirrels in the Tweed Bottoms which led down to the Piney. Filled with oaks and hickories, there were big rocks there, one flat-topped boulder the size of a pick-up bed or bigger.

That was a favored spot of me and old Armour. Covered with moss and lichen, it was fairly soft for a rock, and we'd climb up there and watch for squirrels in the trees around us. Well, I did anyway. Armour usually went to sleep, stretched out on that rock quivering and shaking as he dreamed of chasing field mice. But that afternoon was still and warm and the woods were bathed in deep shadows. I couldn't stay awake. I lay back for awhile thinking I'd just nap a little while the squirrels got over their nervousness and started to stir.

Somehow, I fell into a deep sleep, and woke up with only about thirty minutes of light left, the warmth of the afternoon giving way to an evening chill. And my companion had snuck away and left me. Old Armour was gone. At first I figured he had maybe lit out for home, but I couldn't figure him doing that. he never had before. Then as I climbed down from the rock, I thought I heard a yelp from the woods off to the west, on a gently rising ridge. I whistled for him, then listened. There was nothing but quiet. And so, about half worried, I called out his name twice. "Here Armour, here Armour, come here boy!"

At first there was nothing, and then I heard it, a deep bark up on that ridge, then a yelp, then another and then a bloodcurdling yodel, filled with pain. In the flash of realization that something was up there big enough to hurt that big old Doberman, I thought of Charlie Watson's warning about the panther, and I knew down inside it was no big story. Armour had found that vicious cat, and he was lying up there dead or dying and I couldn't do a thing about it because I had nothing but squirrel loads for defense.

Suddenly, that pump shotgun seemed awfully small and inadequate. I remembered a story in Outdoor Life magazine about how a hunter had been attacked by a bear in the great frozen north and all he had was a shotgun. He had taken out several shot-shells and ringed them with a knife right where the paper cartridge met the brass base, weakening the lower two thirds of the shell so that when it fired, it took the whole end of the shell rather than opening up to release the individual shot load. The result was something like a slug, rather than a pattern of lead, and it had killed the bear and saved his life. I had the choice of trying that, but losing valuable time in the doing of it. If that mountain lion took his time coming for me, and I was there in the dark, what good would such a defense be. You can't shoot what you can't see.

My other option was to run like the devil and try to get home before dark, hoping the mountain lion was content to stay there and eat old Armour and not want to eat me. I made my decision rather quickly. I'd run like hell and do lots of praying, hoping the Good Lord would forgive me for enjoying scaring old Tubby Lucas into the pond, letting him think old Armour was a killer dog ready to attack at my command. I had behaved myself for weeks and hadn't ever really been slightly inclined toward bullying anyone, and now I'd gotten off track just once and I had to face this kind of punishment!

The ridge across the creek and to the east was fairly high, and the path up the side of it fairly steep. It was a path I had made, and used often in coming down into the Big Piney bottoms, and the Tweed Creek that led down to the McKinney hole. I could follow it in the deep dusk, as light faded. If I made it to the top, there was a hundred yards of woodlands, then a grown up field of brome sedge and sumac and cedar, then the fence to cross next to the golf course. From that fence I was only a half mile from home. If I got there, I had a chance.

No kid ever traveled faster, and I knew my dad would wince if he saw me running up that hill with a loaded gun. He had taught me never to do such a thing. But then, Dad never figured I'd be out there running for my life, about to be ate by a mountain lion, not a mile from my own house.

Adrenaline is a powerful thing, and I found myself halfway up that hillside in just the blink of an eyelash. It may be that in all of my life up to that time I had never traveled so much territory in so little time. My heart was pounding, and I was sweating, despite the dropping temperatures. Darkness was coming fast, and I paused only for a second to listen. I heard, distinctly and clearly, a heavy body coming across the creek below me, and downstream. There was the clink of flat rocks hitting together, and I was filled with panic. I knew he was much too close, I'd never make it. The big cat was trying to gain the ridge top ahead of me, circle around to cut me off and make his kill. If I failed to beat him to that fence, I was doomed.

I don't know if a 13-year-old kid, just an average one, can outmaneuver a full grown mountain lion in the woods. But I was set upon by a burst of determination. I'd give it an above average try, put my back to a big white oak and give that mountain lion three rounds of number 6 field load Western Auto shotshells. He'd make a good meal out of me, but he'd do it with some teeth missing and both ears blowed plumb off.

And then I was there, in the last hint of light on top of that ridge, too doggone dark to see much of anything, listening to that killer panther crashing through the brush only 50 or 60 yards away, coming at me like a runaway garbage truck. I brought my shotgun partway to my shoulder and squeezed off a panicked shot – way too quickly, firing high over the approaching cat, trying hard to make out his tawny form.

Pumping a new shell in too quickly, the ejecting hull caught in the mechanism, and as I stepped toward a tree for protection I tripped on something and went to my knees. It is hard to describe the stark terror of a 13-year-old boy who knows he won't ever know what it is like to be all the things which went through my mind, like what it might be like to pass through the digestive tract of a mountain lion, deposited here and there on the Big Piney watershed. There wasn't time to promise God I'd try to treat my sisters better if I had another chance, that I'd find ol' Tubby and tell him I was sorry me and Armour had run him into the golf course water trap. There wasn't time to try to make a deal. God had decided I was no-account and to give this mountain lion a good meal out of my carcass and I knew it was over.

Suddenly there he was, in the darkness, and lo and behold he wasn't tawny at all! He was black! Holy mackerel, this was a black panther and he smelled like a skunk, even at 20 yards away and closing. I swung the barrel of the shotgun at him, lost my grip and fell to the ground. Quickly the black panther was on me, taking my breath with the sharp acrid stench of skunk, licking my face with a big wet tongue, just like old Armour used to do.

I may have passed out, I don't know. I only remember that when I came to my senses I was throwing rocks at that darn Doberman, trying to keep him away from me so my eyes would quit watering. He must have ate that darn skunk...or maybe there were two of them and he only ate one. He stood out there in the darkness, whining, wondering why his best buddy had tried to outrun him, then tried to shoot him, and now was trying to get him to take another route home. I was weak and shaking, and I was about to cry, half sick from relief and the nausea brought on by concentrated skunk juice. But I was alive, and I couldn't believe it.

I had a bath in tomato juice and lemon juice that night. Didn't seem to do any good. Armour slept in the shed next to the smokehouse, and he'd bark every now and then, and whimper and whine and wonder why, since he had never seen a skunk, he could be blamed for the consequences of trying to retrieve it.

In a month, the whole thing became of less significance, since the odor of everything, including skunk, will diminish with time. Dad didn't do what he said he was going to do to either one of us and eventually, Armour and I had the run of things again. At first I remember being nicer to my sisters and treating old Tubby Lucas friendlier than I ever had. But the truth be known, by Christmas I remember telling him that the next time me and old Armour caught him out away from school I'd have my dog rip his ears off and make him look like a volleyball with a belt around it. Tubby and I just never could get along.

I never went back to the Tweed Bottoms with the same carefree feelings I had before that night of the panther who wasn't there. You grow up a little when you get older. In my case, not much, but you do grow up a little and you know that life is filled with unseen dangers and worries and problems, sort of like what you can't see in the night. You get a little less carefree, you know he might be out there lurking somewhere, waiting to cross your path. And then again, it might just be your dog!

Charlie Watson saw the panther again and again, and he fought with that big cat 'til the day he died. Some folks think he was imagining things, but I don't. wasn't his imagination that tore up the muskrats in his traps along the Piney, and it wasn't his imagination that put those scratches in the top of his old pick-up. It's just that, if you are going to believe in panthers, you've got to be out there amongst 'em, like me and Charlie was.

Sometimes even today, I miss old Charlie and Old Armour and the Tweed Bottoms. But not real often!

Chapter 45

A Turkey Runs Through it

By Jim Spencer

Who knows how I'd have turned out if it hadn't been for the turkeys. If not for them, I probably could have made myself into something. I might have actually become somebody – a doctor, maybe, or a successful businessman.

They've always been out there, though. The turkeys, I mean, skulking around the edge of my thoughts the way they skulk around in the spring woods, just out of sight and/or gun range, pinning me down, keeping me from becoming a productive member of society. Instead, for better or worse, I became a turkey hunter.

This insanity hit me relatively late in life. A child of the '50s and '60s, I came of age during a time when both deer and turkey populations were low, even nonexistent, across most of the country. Therefore, small game got my attention. Rabbits, ducks, doves, squirrels and quail were standard quarry for the bunch of hooligans I used to run with, and we hunted them relentlessly. Deer and turkeys were as far off our radar screen as the kudu, Cape buffalo and leopards we used to read about in Robert Ruark's books.

I was satisfied with the situation. At least, I thought I was. But then came that fateful day in 1978 when a friend bullied me into going turkey hunting with him.

Actually, It wasn't too bad at first. I hunted turkeys off and on for the next few years, without really becoming addicted. I didn't know enough about it, you see, to make the excitement happen. I spent four or five days each season blundering around in the woods, not knowing what the hell I was doing but enjoying myself anyway. I got in conversations with a few turkeys, but if I told you I actually worked those birds I'd be stretching the point. Certainly I never came close to killing any of them, and in those first couple of years I didn't feel the burning desire to keep on pushing day after day. In other words, I was a typical low-impact turkey hunter, as likely to go fishing as turkey hunting on a sunny April Saturday.

But somewhere during that third or fourth spring, things began to change. I killed a bird called up for me by a more experienced hunter, thereby proving to myself that turkey hunting could indeed be more than a theoretical exercise. Then I began to kill a turkey every once in a while on my own, usually a suicidal two-year-old that came in despite the bonehead things I was doing that should have run him off.

Meanwhile, small game hunting was starting to take a back seat to turkeys. I still hunted squirrels and ducks – still do, in fact – but turkeys began to assert themselves more and more on both my psyche and on my free time. I started taking a few days of vacation each year to chase turkeys, rather than just hunting on weekends. I started making a short trip each spring to hunt turkeys out-of-state. I found myself leaving the fishing rods in the rack until after turkey season closed.

In short, turkeys got inside me. The snowball was rolling, and what had been a casual activity gradually morphed into an addiction. The addiction in turn morphed into an obsession, and somewhere along about 1985, I became a full-fledged, unapologetic turkey bum.

Let me tell you just how bad this thing has me by the throat. Over the past four springs, I hunted 171 days, and according to my records I spent 1059 hours hunting. Seventeen states and a foreign country were mixed up in it, from Florida to South Dakota, from Vermont to Chihuahua, Mexico. I put an average of 11,550 miles on my truck each of those four springs. I could also tell you how much money I spent during the process, too, but it's too painful to write it down so I won't do that. I could also tell you how many hours it took me to bag each gobbler I took during those four years, but since that number is also painful, I won't do that either.

Thank God I'm not alone in all of this. The 1980s were the prime years of turkey resurgence across the country, and many of us fell over the edge, helpless as lemmings hearing the call of the sea. I was among the more acutely afflicted lemmings, it's true, but I still had plenty of company in this loony bin.

There are still plenty of us, though some of us are getting pretty long in the tooth. "Birds of a feather flock together," they say, and that seems to be as true with turkey hunters as it is with turkeys. If you doubt it, go to Nashville next February for the National Wild Turkey Federation's annual convention.

This convention is as strong a showing of like-mindedness as you'll find in the world today, and we who are of that mindset come together every winter to feed off each other's addiction and get ourselves pumped for the coming season. As if any of us need pumping.

That's one of the many anomalies that beset turkey bums. We love getting together during the off-season, or around the campfire after a day in the woods, and telling each other our war stories. "Misery loves company" is another thing they say, and I suppose that's as good an explanation as any. But our flocking instinct has its limits, and when it comes to actually getting out there and fighting the turkey wars, most of us prefer to do it alone.

Sure, in this age of television hunting shows and hunting DVDs, it's become fashionable to hunt in pairs, threesomes and even foursomes, with two or three hunters accompanied by a cameraman setting forth to do battle with a wary turkey gobbler. Like most of the other folks who do what I do for a living, I've taken part in some of that group-hunting in front of a camera. If I'm lucky, I'll do some more of it before I'm done.

Likewise, there's something to be said for hunting with a trusted and familiar partner. Two experienced hunters who know each other's habits and tactics can pull tricks on turkeys a single hunter simply can't pull off. My hunting partner is my wife Jill. We've had each other's back on numerous occasions over the years, and we've killed quite a few birds hunting together that I doubt either of us would have killed alone.

Furthermore, it's a solemn responsibility for experienced turkey hunters to pay it forward by introducing others to the sport. As I've already confessed, another hunter helped me get over the hump by calling in my first gobbler for me. Then, as we stood over that flopping gobbler, he told me to go forth and do it like it's supposed to be done: solo. Actually, what he said was: "All right, sumbitch, you're on you own." But it boils down to the same thing.

I've since played the part of grizzled mentor for a handful of other beginners. There are few things more satisfying than watching a new turkey hunter shake and tremble as his or her first longbeard approaches the gun. And after those kills, I've told every one of those hunters pretty much what my mentor told me: Get out there by yourself and start figuring things out.

Because in the end, turkey hunting is at its finest when done alone, one hunter in the woods all by himself, with nothing to rely on but his own wits. Whether you kill him or not is unimportant; it's the contest that really matters, and the contest is most satisfying when it's one on one.

On second thought, I said that wrong. Whether you kill the turkey or not is an important thing. It's just not the most important thing. I'm not trying to Pollyanna this, so don't get me wrong – I like to kill turkeys as well as anybody. But if the kill was the only thing I enjoyed about it, I promise you I wouldn't hunt 40 to 50 days every spring. The possibility of the kill needs to be there, or else the whole thing falls apart; hunting with a camera isn't hunting. But the trigger pull itself is like the period at the end of the sentence – it's the thing that marks the end of the really important stuff.

Stuff like getting up in the meanest, darkest, smallest hours of the night, and drinking coffee in your truck as you drive through the blackness toward your hunting spot. Stuff like being in the woods alone, far from that truck, before the first hint of dawn colors the eastern sky. Stuff like waiting for the morning's first gobble, and planning a hunt strategy both before and after you hear it. Stuff like working a bird and having him gobble a hundred times as he comes to the gun.

Stuff like that.

It doesn't always go according to script, though, and we all know it. Sometimes the light doesn't come to the eastern horizon so fast, because it's obscured by rain clouds. Sometimes the bird doesn't gobble at all. Sometimes he gobbles but refuses to come to the call, no matter what you do.

Those hunts are enjoyable, too. If they weren't, most of us would quit hunting, because the off days outnumber the days when everything goes right. It's what's called a rule of thumb: For every easy day that comes along, you can rest assured there'll be a few tough ones to make up for it. Turkey bums must continually pay installments on their dues in this manner; it's one of the few certainties in this masochistic sport.

All of this teaches you things. Stoicism, for instance.

Humility, too. Some days, you can hunt as well as you know how, and blow sweet notes on your calls until your mouth is sore, and all you'll get from it is a headache. Some days, you can walk the ridges for hours on end, and your only reward will be fresh air and sore feet.

And then some days – and these are the cruellest of all – everything will seem to be going right, up until that instant of the trigger pull. And that's when the gobbler will duck his head, or you will raise yours, or gremlins will transplant a sapling in front of your gun barrel, or some other mysterious thing will happen, and the turkey will run away unharmed. And you will curse, and beat your fists on the ground, and swear you will never, ever go turkey hunting again, because you will have momentarily forgotten that it truly isn't the kill that's important.

But after a while perspective will begin to reassert itself, and you will pull yourself back together, retrieve your hat from wherever you've thrown it, and get on with the hunt. You will never forget the ones you miss – at least, I haven't been able to forget any of mine – but they will eventually become sources of, if not exactly amusement, at least good war stories.

And the seasons roll on. Sometimes, toward the tail end of yet another grinding spring, when I'm frazzled and sore-footed and red-eyed from chronic sleep deprivation, I find myself wondering: Am I actually happy to have discovered turkey hunting in my 31st year, like I said I was? Or would I have been better off if I'd never gotten this monkey on my back in the first place?

Certainly, I'd be richer. Certainly, I'd have gotten more sleep, and worn out fewer boots. Certainly, I'd have done a lot more spring fishing.

But just as certainly, I'd have missed an awful lot of good times. In the end, it's only money and sleep and boot leather, and a fish is after all just a fish, whereas a turkey is a force of nature.

So my life is what it has become, and a turkey runs through it. There are those who have told me I've misspent the past 40-odd springs, but I disagree. Like I said, I probably could have been somebody, but I suspect "being somebody" is overrated.

I'll settle for being a turkey bum.

Chapter 46

Grandpa and the Ghoul

By Larry Dablemont

G randpa sat in his recliner with his two granddaughters on the couch beside him. The movie was over, the TV was turned off and bedtime was approaching.

Grandma was finishing up in the kitchen, where she had shed a tear or two thinking about how her little granddaughters had grown up. They were eight now, cousins of the same age. And for the first time, on the weekend visit to their grandparents home, they had decided they were too old to sleep with Grandma...that had set her back a bit. Tonight, they would sleep in the big bed upstairs, the guest bedroom with the featherbed and the window that looked out over the garden and the rickety old barn beyond. Tonight, they would be grown-up girls, and that was the reason Grandma was a little sad.

But the girls had questions to ask after watching that scary movie, and one question was, "Grandpa, have you ever been scared really, really bad?" The old man thought about it a bit and replied, "I reckon the scaredest I ever was, was that time I was playin' dominoes with a good-lookin' young lady in the community center an' your grandma walked in!"

"Albert!" came the grandmother's terse warning from the nearby kitchen.

The old-timer chuckled and then continued, "Well, let's see now, the scaredest I ever been..."

He took off his old cap and looked at the ceiling as the little girls gathered closer to his recliner. He squinched up his leathery old face as if he were thinking very hard and then he went on. "I reckon the scaredest I ever have been was 20 or 30 years ago whilst I was catfishin' all by m'self down on Mad Holler Creek right where she flows into the river. I had my trotlines set and baited and was fixin' to crawl into my old lean-to and cover up with some quilts an' sleep an hour or so. The campfire was burnin' down low an' the moon was dark. It was so still you'd think there wan't a livin' thing in the whole durned world. Almost spooky it was, no whippoorwills nor crickets nor hoot-owls, not even a frog a-croakin'."

The old man paused a moment and then said, "Well sir, I'll show you girls how it was...turn off them lamps in the corner so it's good an' dark in here."

With eyes wide, they complied with his wishes and except for the light from the kitchen, it was dark in the old farmhouse.

"Well sir, I just throwed another stick or two on the old campfire and it throwed up a high trail of sparks to the sky and blazed up enough to where I could just barely see out into the crick where my old boat was a settin'."

It was still for a moment as the old man paused to give his story a greater impact on the two little girls. And when he spoke again his voice was lowered, steady and slow and gripped with a frightened tone.

"It was about then that I heard it," he said finally, "out in the water. It was sort of a slurpin' sound like you get when you pull your foot out'n the mud. I looked and I thought in that faint light I could see somethin' standin' there with long heavy arms, on the other side of my boat."

He had his granddaughters's attention all right. With open mouths and wide eyes they knelt beside his recliner clinging to every word.

But the old man didn't rush it. He knew about story-telling and with him it was an art. He fidgeted with his cap and reckoned out loud that he shouldn't go on. He said that even growed-up girls like those two young cousins didn't need to know everything about wicked evil entities that wander in the dark.

But the girls wouldn't hear of it, and they bade him continue, assuring him that nothing of the sort could bother them.

And, so he did. "I saw my old boat just move off into the darkness beyond the light, then off down the creek toward the river until it was gone," he said.

"I thought about goin' out to get it, but there in the campfire's dim light I saw 'im standing in the knee-deep water and it only came up to his ankles. At the time he was so big I couldn't see his face well, but he weren't actually a man an' he weren't actually a animal. He was tall and wide an' his arms were so long they hung close to the water. They was only two or three fingers at the end of each hand and hair hung down around his body like long strands of thick moss, all green and grungy."

Now the old man's voice changed. He wiped his forehead with an old handkerchief and you could hear the downright fear in his voice.

"Well, whatever the thing was, it was plain he was comin' towards me... somethin' tall as them fruit trees out by the old privy, and then the fire flared up a bit an' I got to see his face. It was just god-awful to look on, all twisted and gray, with one eye that looked somethin' like a marble in a bird's nest, and the other one just hangin' out, all bloody an' oozin'."

The old man looked down at his granddaughters clinging to his knees and said he should probably stop there as he didn't want their mothers to think badly of him and he didn't want word to spread that he was a crazy old lunatic.

But the trembling girls would have no part of that. "Grandpa," one asked fearfully, "How did you get away?"

"It's not an easy thing to think back on," the grandfather said. "I've never thought of myself as a cowardly sort, so I stands up and I grabbed a boat paddle and I says, 'Who are you an' what do you want?' He just drags himself on up a little closer," the old man said, clinging tightly to that bandana as if under a great deal of stress.

"I could see it plain by then and hear it a-groanin' an gurglin' down deep inside. Its nose wasn't human, it looked more like a big pig's nose than anything else, and it had a sort of lizardy mouth. Its mouth was open to where I could see most of its teeth was broke out and snaggeldy. It seemed there was a crooked one or two, but a couple were long and sharp like a dog's tooth. By then I could see blood runnin' out of one corner of his mouth. Then I could see why. In one of his deformed hands hung a big old cottonmouth snake, writhin' and curlin'. And I could see that the snake had no head. That monster had just bit off its head an' was chewin' on it." "Girls, I reckon my legs ain't brave enough to hang around an' watch the rest of me get et up by a monster," the old man said.

"I ran," he said, shaking his head in mock shame. "I ran up that hillside behind the camp through the cedars and the buckbrush all the way back here and I locked up the house behind me and never told a soul about whatever it was I saw. And to this day you'll notice I always lock up this old house at night."

The two girls had their lamps turned back on and were huddled together on the couch under a blanket.

"I thank the good Lord that the thing was so slow, 'cause I could hear it a-screamin' and scrapin' along on that gravel bar behind me, all upset that I had got away."

That's when Grandma showed up with milk and cookies and the granddaughters began to relate some of what they had heard in excited voices.

"Grandpa said it was the scaredest he ever was," one of them said.

The aging grandmother shook her head and proclaimed that she had been listening to some of the nonsense as she cleaned the kitchen. "Don't pay no attention to your old grandpa," she cautioned, "he's scared of lots of things, about half the time...the older he gets."

"Now wait a minute girls," the old man objected, ignoring his wife, "I didn't say that was the scaredest I ever been. No sir, I was scared worser than that last winter when your grandma had the whoopin' cough an' I had to sleep in that old bed upstairs."

It was quiet for a moment as they ate cookies, but one of them had to ask. "What was so scary about that, Grandpa?"

"Well, there was some snow then if you'll 'member and I heard somethin' scratchin' on the winder in the middle of the night and sort of a-groanin' and gruntin' and I woke up and looked out to see what was goin' on."

"An' right there on the other side of the winder was the face of that horrible critter lookin' back at me, not any farther away than I am from you-uns'. I guess he had got cold. Well, I ain't been back upstairs since it happened."

That night, as they had done since they were babies, the two little girls slept downstairs in the same bed with Grandma. When Grandpa climbed into his bed in the other room, he just chuckled a little bit to hisself, and closed the curtain!

Chapter 47

The Romance of the Road

By Jim Spencer

"Drivin' my life away, lookin' for a better way," sang Eddie Rabbit a long time ago. Those words fit my psyche like a crawdad fits its hole. I love to travel in the spring of the year, when the Earth is renewing itself, searching out new places to hunt turkeys, always "lookin' for a better way." If my destination lies a thousand miles from my driveway, so much the better.

Yeah, I know, that's weird. My home state of Arkansas contains 52,000 square miles, more or less. Within that 52,000 square miles are an estimated 200,000 turkeys. As much time as I've spent chasing gobblers right here in my home state, I still haven't seen a hundredth of the available turkey territory.

It torments me to know that I'm going to die without having enough time and money to alter that percentage very much. You'd think, with that much of the turkey range in my home state still unseen, I'd be more inclined to stick around and see more of it.

And I love doing just that. We have both the Ozarks and the Ouachitas, two of the best-known mountain ranges among turkey-hunting circles, not to mention a wealth of good turkey hunting in both the Gulf Coastal Plain in the southern part of the state and the Delta in the east. I like not only exploring new territory in the Arkansas turkey woods, but also revisiting old, familiar places. There are several favorite spots to which I return every year, and next spring will be no different.

It's just that…well…there's a lot of good turkey hunting in other states, too. And if I've only seen a hundredth of what's available right here at home, how tiny is the fraction I've seen elsewhere?

It's not just the turkey hunting opportunities in other states that regularly draws me onto the road. That's usually my excuse, of course, since I am what I am. But in addition, a big part of the appeal of the road – for me, at least – is simply the road itself. The pure, adrenaline-rush adventure of just being Out There.

"Windshield wipers slappin' out a tempo, keepin' perfect rhythm with the song on the radio," sang old Eddie. The 'song on the radio' can be as varied as the places I'm going, but in order to fit the mood, it must have a hard, driving beat. The artists, too, must have a certain...I don't know. For lack of something better, call it a "go-to-hell" attitude. Bob Marley, Sheryl Crow, Waylon Jennings, Ray Wylie Hubbard, The White Buffalo, Steve Earle, Toby Keith, Vonda Shepard, Warren Zevon, Hank Jr., Frank Foster, Jason Boland. That kind of people. Those folks provide appropriate music for the beginning of a trip. Yeah, Eddie Rabbit, too. Toward the end of a journey, when the truck is full of that scratchy, edgy sadness that comes on when it's almost over but there's still a hard two-day drive staring you in the face, it'll be time for Enya, John Coltrane, George Winston, Linda Ronstadt. But not at the beginning. Not on the way Out.

On the way Out, the trip is still perfect. It won't stay that way, of course, but for now, nothing has gone wrong. The rain hasn't fallen in buckets on Opening Day, the turkeys haven't dummied up, the gobbler I've traveled halfway across the country to kill hasn't ring-around-the-rosied me and gone his merry way. So far, everything is going according to plan.

There are sights from journeys past I carry with me always, and I can summon them with no effort. Some involve people and/or turkeys: the old Navajo woman selling the prettiest jewelry you ever saw along a hot roadside in northern Arizona, with desert sage in front of her and a Merriam's turkey gobbling himself hoarse on the ponderosa pine hillside at her back; the seven Rio-Eastern hybrid gobblers that strutted a half-mile across a field to me in Kansas; the three Osceolas that duked it out less than 20 yards in front of me in a palmetto thicket near Yeehaw Junction down in Florida; the kid who hauled the huge, triple-bearded gobbler into the rural Missouri check station, wearing a grin a foot wide; the grumpy black bear that ran off the only gobbler I called in during eight hard days of hunting in the mountains of West Virginia.

But most of these burned-in, on-the-road memories involve geography: the surprising first glimpse of the Great Salt Lake basin as you drop out of the Wasatch Range heading west toward Salt Lake City; the vast sweep of sawgrass flats as you roar along Alligator Alley through the Everglades; the molten-lava color of the northern New Mexico mesas as you weave through them on U.S. 84 between Santa Fe and Chama; the breath-taking drive up the California coastline on Wonderful One between Big Sur and Monterey; the lush, green softness of the Natchez Trace; the arid harshness of the cactus/mesquite landscape between Corpus Christi and Brownsville; the hostile, above-timberline, snow-flurries-in-August moonscape of Beartooth Pass in northwest Wyoming.

There's plenty of memorable geography here in Arkansas, too, of course. I've already mentioned the Ozarks and Ouachitas, and it's not my intent here to minimize the beauty of those places. But all that is close to home, and though the destinations are every bit as nice, the trips don't afford the same sense of raw adventure.

That's why I'll be heading farther afield than is really necessary this spring and every spring for as long as I'm able, chasing gobblers in distant places, making footprints where I've never made them before. I'll be prowling the river bottoms and mountains of Arkansas quite a bit, too, but every now and then, I simply have to jump in my old truck and head somewhere, for no other reason than those places are Out There.

"Hey, waitress, pour me another cup of coffee, pop it down, jack me up, shoot me out, flyin' down the highway; lookin' for the morning."

Always, always, lookin' for the morning.

Chapter 48

An Engine Ain't an Injun

By Larry Dablemont

My pickup had a flat tire and the jack was broke. I started trying to thumb a ride. A fellow picked me up and we exchanged pleasantries. He asked me what I did and I told him I was an outdoor writer.

He chuckled and said, "Well, most riding is done outside!"

"No," I said, "I actually I write some inside too, but I like to write outside when I can."

"Do you generally ride outside all by yourself?" he asked. "Always" I told him, "I don't like to be distracted. I write alone!" "I saw a Randolph Scott movie by that name," he said.

I started wonderin' if this guy wasn't a little squirrely. "By the way, what do you do?" I asked.

"I work on engines," he told me.

"My great grandmother was an Injun in Canada," I said. "Ever been there?" He looked at me as if he thought I was a little squirrely.

"No, he said, "but an engine is an engine." He said. "I fix 'em whenever they need fixin' and I enjoy it."

That kind of irked me. "There are lots of good Injuns," I said, "not all of them need fixin.'"

"Well I won't argue that," he said, "but I love fixin' the ones that don't work. Sometimes it takes time but when I get through with one it works. I like workin' on the old ones."

"When an Injun won't work it is because the government makes it so they don't have to." I said. "Alcohol has a lot to do with it."

"Alcohol can ruin an engine," he said.

"Some Injuns stay away from alcohol," I said, "and they work as hard as any."

"That's fine with me," he said, "but I get paid to fix the old ones that won't work, alcohol or not. And I get paid well for it. I have a lot of expensive tools and I fix 'em right. I never have to work on any engine twice 'cause I fix 'em right the first time."

That was about all I could take. I told him to stop and let me out.

"Someday when you stand before judgement I hope you are confronted by all the Injuns you have 'fixed'." I told him.

"You are nutty as a fruitcake," he said. "I think you are going to wind up doing a lot more outdoor walking than riding."

As he drove away, I told myself that I had to forgive people like him rather than wish he'd run off in the ditch. Most likely one of his ancestors had been scalped.

Another fellow pulled up and stopped and I told him I just needed a ride into town. Rolling down the road, he asked what I did for a living.

"I am an outdoor writer," I told him, "how about you? "I am an optometrist," he said.

"Oh," I answered, "I am something of an optimist myself."

SAD LIMERICKS

There was a young man named Bruce,
Who set forth to shoot him a goose
But in the swamp, with a thud,
He fell in deep mud,
And struggled all day to get loose.
That same strange hunter named Bruce,
Decided he'd call up a moose
He called like a cow,
And I guess that's why now,
He's sitting so high in that spruce.
There once was a nice country lass
Who wanted to catch a big bass
She went down to the river,
With some froze chicken liver
And didn't catch anything but catfish.

L. A. D.

Chapter 49

Maybe They'll be there in the Morning

By Jim Spencer

It was gloomy and dark outside the ramshackle beer joint, and sheets of rain blew noisily against the windows. The waitress had just brought me my cheeseburger and I was thinking about a second PBR when Steve and John walked in. They were muddy from stem to stern.

"Bad news," Steve said by way of greeting. "There aren't any ducks using our field."

Familiar words, those, and not at all surprising. However, I hadn't driven more than 300 miles through increasingly bad weather to be put off by such a trivial thing as a negative scouting report. The incurable optimism that permits me to be a duck hunter came bubbling to the surface.

"The rain's supposed to blow out of here tonight," I said. "Maybe they'll be there in the morning."

"Maybe so," agreed John, who is also a duck hunter and therefore an optimist himself.

Sure enough, they weren't.

Sloshing 600 yards through knee-deep water and ankle-deep mud matted with floating rice stubble is likely to get your wind. This is even more likely if you're wearing chest waders and too many clothes and you're carrying the accoutrements of a serious duck hunter: a shotgun, a box of 3-inch shells, three duck callers (minimum,) two garlic bologna sandwiches, a half-dozen boiled eggs, a set of cardboard salt-and-pepper shakers in a plastic bag, a coffee thermos, a bottle of water, a roll of toilet paper in another plastic bag, a pair of binoculars, a couple candy bars, a package of frankfurters and a shoulder bag full of camera equipment. It's even more likely if you're about 30 pounds above your fighting weight.

Consequently, I was sweating like a September teal hunter by the time I reached the outer fringe of the decoys. Steve and John had outpaced me by a good margin and were already standing below ground level in the pit blind. In the near-darkness with nothing but their heads and shoulders above ground, they looked weird, as if somebody had planted them.

"Hey, Aunt Jemima, what took you so long?" asked one of the heads. "He does favor Aunt Jemima a little, doesn't he?" agreed the other head. "Or at least he would, if he'd lose some weight." The heads laughed idiotically. It doesn't take much to amuse a duck hunter.

I was too beat to reply. I kicked a little muddy water at them, fell into the pit and plunked down on the warped two-by-twelve that served as a seat.

Made of heavy-gauge steel and angle iron, this pit was 20 feet long and more than three wide. It would hold six hunters with ease, eight in a pinch. With only three of us in it, we could have stretched out on the floor and taken a nap, if it hadn't been for the five inches of rainwater down there. The pit had two straw-covered plywood lids mounted on rollers, and with the lids closed the hunters inside the pit disappeared from the face of the earth. There was enough space between the lids and pit walls that you could scrooch your neck sideways and see what was going on out over the decoys. It was warm and out of the wind and even cozy, sort of, if you discounted that water in the bottom.

It was a pretty good pit. All it needed was ducks.

"This is a pretty good pit," I said. "I just wish it had ducks."

"It did have," said John, scratching his back on an angle-iron brace. "I saw them leave when we walked in here."

"Yeah, I saw 'em too, all six of 'em. Big deal."

"Six would be a pretty good start," Steve said. "Look, here comes a bunch."

It was still well before shooting time, so we made no effort to hide. The small bunch of ducks – probably the ones we'd flushed and either gadwalls or widgeons, it was still too dark to tell – swooped in, saw us standing in the pit and changed their minds about landing. A dozen wings whistled as they clawed for altitude directly above us.

We swung our guns at them, practicing.

"I could have killed a couple of those," I said.

Steve looked at me sideways. "Sure. That's what they all say."

Time passed slowly, painfully, the way it does in those last few minutes before legal shooting time. Wedges of ducks – mostly mallards, mostly high – traded back and forth.

Light grew slowly in the east, as if someone below the horizon was turning a rheostat. I leaned against the side of the pit and watched the ducks against the dawn. Something I'd read a long time ago came back to me.

"'The early morning sun has gold in its mouth,'" I said, just to hear myself say it.

"Huh? Who said that?" John wanted to know.

"Some dead guy. Thoreau, maybe, or Ben Franklin. Franklin, I think."

"Big deal. Leave him out of this." There is no culture in a duck blind.

Two green-winged teal zipped into the spread and splashed down noisily, with a great deal of self-importance, the way teal do. Caught off guard, we froze.

"Is it shooting time yet?" Steve whispered.

I sneaked a furtive glance at my watch. "Yeah."

The ducks sat there preening and waggling their little butts. Our guns were loaded, but they were on top of the pit lid, pointing the wrong way. We looked circumspectly at the teal. They stopped preening and stared suspiciously back at us. One stood on his tail and flapped ferociously, making much more noise than you'd expect from a bird the size of a Christmas orange.

"This is what's known as a Mexican stand-off," observed John.

His voice broke the spell. The little ducks took of for Yucatan and we scrambled for our guns. We needn't have bothered. By the time we were ready to shoot they were 25 yards out of range.

"So maybe we ought to close the lid," Steve suggested.

We did, and the next bunch of teal kamikazed the decoys south of the pit while we peered out over the decoys to the north. I heard the series of splashes and took a peek through the crack over my shoulder.

"We got company," I said.

We shoved the lids back and came up shooting. Our performance was better this time; three of the little speedsters stayed behind as the rest of the flock left.

I stayed in the pit and burned film while Steve and John made the retrieves. One of the birds was only wing-tipped, and they hadn't carried their guns. A long, splashy chase ensued, punctuated by their heartfelt curses and my gleeful shouts of useless advice, such as: "Run faster!" and "Take longer steps!" Nobody fell down, though, a small miracle in itself, and they eventually brought the little duck to bay. It was all very entertaining.

At least, I thought so. Steve and John evidently had a different perspective.

"Don't think you're going to hide behind that damn camera all day while the work's going on," Steve puffed as he laid the midget ducks on the lid of the pit.

"Get in here and shut up," I said. "We got ducks in the breeze."

We did, too, another gyrating, swirling swarm of green-wings that soon made fools of us. They came in low and hard, flying as if their tails were on fire. Just as we stood to take them, they broke ranks and went out over us like a dozen miniature Blue Angels performing a starburst. Three gun barrels waved frantically. We shot, but we did it with the same attitude I used to have when I swung at full-count fast balls many years ago: more from a sense of duty than from any realistic hope of hitting anything. I knew when I pulled the trigger I was five feet behind my duck.

Once they were out of range the flock regrouped, lost altitude and skimmed away to the south. They were barely clearing the tops of the foot-high levees.

"Arrogant little bastards," John said mildly, watching them disappear. He stuck his empty hull into the bib pocket of his waders, then spit in the direction of the departed ducks. "They got no respect at all."

Other bunches of teal went bumble-beeing around the field, but they all fought shy of the decoys. They were fun to watch, though.

"Seems like they'd get dizzy," Steve said after one particularly erratic bunch jittered by a hundred yards out.

The sun was up now, weak and watery behind the horizon haze. Gradually the flocks of teal went somewhere else. After a while we rolled the lids back and stood up. The high ducks were still trading back and forth, participating in the mysterious commerce of waterfowl that has puzzled us ground-bound humans for centuries.

"Why do you suppose they fly so high?" John asked. "Look at that bunch, would you?" He pointed at a nearly invisible wedge of specks swimming through the bluebird sky. "Gimme the binoculars. Mallards," he said after a bit. "They look cold. I'll bet it's 30 below zero up there."

Once we heard some specklebellies, but even with the binoculars we were unable to locate them. "Funny how far goose talk carries on a cold day," Steve said.

A muskrat swam contentedly through the decoys, occasionally nuzzling one in a friendly, curious sort of way. He dived prudently when a marsh hawk made a half-hearted swoop at him. The hawk saw us and veered away to the other side of the flooded field. He hovered nearly motionless over a levee, scanning the narrow strip of land for stranded field mice.

A bunch of shovelers came and went. Mallard snobs that we are, we let them fly away unmolested. "Boy, those things are grotesque," John said.

At nine o'clock we ate my lunch. It was as good a meal as I've ever eaten. My hunting partners seemed to agree. "These are pretty good groceries," Steve mumbled through a mouthful of boiled egg. "We might invite you back."

A lone pintail drake picked that time to come zinging in low. Steve saw him coming and stopped eating long enough to grab his shotgun and dump the duck. It was very nicely done:

The sprig came hell-for-leather across the flooded field. Steve waited, egg crumbs clinging to his lips. At just the right moment he rose and shouldered his gun in one smooth, swift motion. The duck saw the movement and flared straight up, but it was an exercise in futility. The load of bismuth threes caught him square in the seat of his spiky pants, and when he came down he nearly fell in the pit.

"Hey, boy," Steve said to me. "Fetch." He gestured duckward with a cold frankfurter, broke his over-under and blew the smoke out of the top barrel. "I wish I could do that more often," he said around a mouthful of cold weenie.

I fetched. Before I could return to the pit, Steve and John were crawling out.

"We might as well go," John said. "Even the high ducks have quit flying now." It was true. The turquoise sky was empty as an inverted punchbowl.

We stood there beside the pit for a while, watching the marsh hawk and soaking up the pale winter sunlight. More goose talk floated out of the sky, fragile as wind-blown soap bubbles. Again we couldn't find them. We grinned inanely at each other; it had been a fine day.

"Maybe they'll be there in the morning," John said as we drove back to town.

"Maybe so," I said.

Sure enough, they weren't.

Chapter 50

Norman and the Noon Flight

By Larry Dablemont

A duck hunter should steer clear of the city! Harley Brown made one trip when he was 18 years old to work on a construction site. He only stayed three months, but he married and brought home with him the first city girl he met. She took to the rural life really well and two years later, when her younger sister came to the country to visit, Harley's cousin Rupert took a shine to her. Enough so that he went to the city a time or two himself, and before long he was in the same fix Harley was...married.

Just like that, the two cousins were brothers-in-law. They got good jobs down at the local factory, advanced rapidly, and started raising families. Before they were 30, they had become stalwarts in the small community where they had grown up.

You could generally find both of them mowing the lawn on Saturday morning or in the back pew at church on Sunday morning except for a few weekends in November and December.

Harley and Rupert had that one problem... they hunted ducks, almost to the point of obsession, and it got worse every year. Yet somehow the two marriages seemed to hold up pretty well until that hunt just before Christmas, several years back. That was the time the two wives put their collective foot down.

"It ain't like we can't go," Rupert said as the two worked on a group of goose decoys in Harley's basement. "We just have to work around our in-laws a little bit. After all they'll just be here 'til the day after Christmas. Shucks, I know fellers who have to live around their wives' folks all the time!"

Harley shook his head. "I'm tellin' you this, I'd as soon take Debbie's mother out there as that little brother of hers."

The "little brother" was Norman, now 18 years old, a computer whiz, a mathematical wizard, a college freshman with the kind of intellect that would make him a great college professor someday. But Norman would never make a duck hunter. He didn't know a mallard from a merganser. "Last time I saw Norman he was talking about a high potanoose or something like that," Rupert said, shaking his head. "Wonder why he wants to go duck huntin'?"

"Cause he jus' loves to be a pain in the hindquarters." Harley paused to look up from his work. "Do you know that when we went up there last summer he spent all afternoon tryin' to convince me that my job could be done better by a computer?"

"You know the geese have moved in now," Harley said, changing the subject. "I think if I can get these old decoys in shape we might get a goose or two. Doggone, it's gonna be some hunt with Norman in that blind with a loaded gun."

"Yeah," Rupert agreed. "I remember last year when I set a can on top of a fence post to see if he could hit it. Danged if he didn't blow the top strand of wire right off the post. Course you know who hadda fix it."

Harley gave up what he was doing and leaned on his workbench, half seated on a stool. "Well, no matter. If we're going to keep peace in the family we're gonna have to take Norman duck hunting over the Christmas holidays. But we'll make the most of it. Whatever I do or say, when we get him out in the blind, just go along with me."

The in-laws came to the country a few days before Christmas, and both wives commented about how wonderful it was that their husbands would work so hard to show little brother Norman such a good time on his first hunting trip. They dug out an old parka, a pair of hip waders two sizes too big, and, of course, the old single-shot break open, 12-gauge hammer gun that kicked like a mule.

The day before Christmas Eve was a duck day if there ever was one, a front coming down from the north and flights of mallards riding the wind. The three brothers-in-law had breakfast well before the first light, then drove to the lake, where they loaded the boat and motored to their blind overlooking a shallow marshy pocket.

Norman was excused from setting decoys since he had a hole in one boot just above the knee, but he stood beside the blind in the predawn darkness and offered advice concerning the placement of decoys according to what he saw as proper geometric design.

When the boat was hidden and gear packed inside the cramped duck blind, Norman was given the honorary spot in the middle. He broke down the old single shot, loaded it, and began calculating the amount of energy behind each pellet, and the speed of a wild duck in feet per second. Norman had done some studying, and he brought figures to that little blind that would choke a cormorant.

Harley listened for awhile, then reminded Norman that it is wise to be very quiet in a duck blind. It was good advice, because only minutes after shooting hours, a small group of mallards winged in to cautiously circle the decoys.

Harley and Rupert began to call, and chances are good that those mallards would have eventually settled in the pocket between the decoys. But Norman, complete with his knowledge of flight speed, energy and shot load velocity, got a case of buck fever. The ducks looked close to him, and he thought he heard somebody else getting up to shoot. So Norman let 'em have it at about 80 yards.

That's when it came to Harley that a man with a single-shot gun and no concept of its range is capable of (a) shooting 15 or 20 dollars worth of shells with no chance of success and (b) scaring away every duck that comes within hearing distance.

That's when he began formulating the plan that would save the day. A small group of coots feeding in the grasses nearby helped somewhat. Harley remembered that the state duck stamp he bought for Norman was still in his billfold, not attached to the license which Norman had pinned to his wader strap, much like a trout fisherman would.

Harley reached over and looked hard at the license.

"I'm danged," he said in astonishment. "Norman, you've went and lost your state duck stamp. I told you to put that license in your pocket."

Norman was shaken; he had visions of a jail sentence dancing in his head, should some game warden happen along. But Harley had the answer. He said it really wouldn't be a big problem. Norman could still legally shoot the black and white ducks. He'd just have to pass up the green-heads. Rupert threw in his two cents worth, commenting on how often he had known of the game warden hiding across the lake, watching their blinds with binoculars.

So it was agreed that Norman would shoot only the black and white ducks which flew or swam by the blind and hold his fire when the green-headed ducks flew in. By mid-morning, Norman had forgotten his misfortune. He was tickled pink to be ahead of Rupert and Harley with four coots that had made the mistake of swimming within range. The two experienced hunters, meanwhile, had only five greenheads between them, but they winked at one another and slapped old Norman on the back every time he smoked another coot.

Tar Baby, the little black Labrador, was a bit puzzled by it all, but she retrieved the prize each and every time, be it black and white or not.

As the flights slowed, Harley and Rupert waded out to adjust some decoys, to make sure there was plenty of open water for Norman to shoot through. Harley moved his half dozen Canada goose decoys much closer; the last thing he wanted was a stray load from Norman finding one of those hard-to-come-by goose blocks.

Well out of hearing from the blind, Harley speculated that it was about time to leave the duck blind to Norman and Tar Baby and take a trip to town for lunch.

"How we gonna do that?" Rupert asked.

"Just leave it to me," Harley whispered, "and go along with whatever I say."

Thirty minutes later, the skies were still empty, and Harley reckoned it would be good for two of the three to motor back and get some sandwiches. The only problem, he pointed out, was that sometimes the noon flight was just outstanding in that area.

"The noon flight?" Norman took the bait.

"Sometimes they come through here by the hundreds right about noon," Rupert pitched in, "moving out to eat I guess. Seems like ducks really get hungry about noon."

"The best part of it is those black and white ducks are the ones that are the thickest during the noon flight," Harley said.

So they decided they'd all flip coins to see who the lucky one would be. Harley's coin was a head, and so was Norman's, but Rupert's flip came up tails. Harley said that meant Rupert was out, and he and Norman flipped again. This time Norman had a tail. Harley dropped his nickel in the mud, so he pulled out another and said they'd need to flip again. Norman came up with a head, and Harley groaned without revealing his coin.

"You're a lucky son-of-a-gun, I'll say that," Harley said, faking the disgust, "but fair's fair, and I guess Rupert and I have had our share of noon flights."

Minutes later, Tar Baby sat in the blind watching her owner motor slowly away, wondering what was happening.

Norman, clutching the old single-shot cannon, waved at the boat as it puttered away. He grinned at the black Lab beside him and patted her head. "Heck, girl, I'm not so lucky," he said. "I cheated on that last flip!" It was half past one at the Old Duck Hunters Tavern. Harley and Rupert had finished a couple of beers and cheeseburgers and played two games of pool. They stopped every now and then to slap each other on the back and laugh to themselves about the prospect of old Norman out there shooting at coots.

Then finally they got to worrying a little about their greenhorn brother-in-law. After all, it was gettin' colder, and he was probably gettin' pretty hungry. Besides that, there would probably be a few ducks starting to fly soon. So they picked up a cold sandwich, a bag of potato chips and a Nehi peach soda, Norman's favorite drink, and headed for the marsh.

At first, Harley and Rupert got a start as they neared the blind. Norman was standing out on the mud beside Tar Baby with one boot missing, nearly jumping up and down with excitement. It was obvious Norman was happy about something.

When they cut the motor, he excitedly began to babble about getting two with one shot – big ones, lots bigger than the others, he said.

Harley and Rupert couldn't help but grin at one another. They'd never imagined this kid getting so excited about busting coots on the water. But Norman went on: he had shot these big black and white rascals flying ... lost one boot helping Tar Baby chase one down. He had them both in the blind because he wasn't sure he had the right stamp for 'em, but, after all, they were black and white.

That was about the time Harley started wondering, and he was almost to the blind when he realized that Norman was talking about all the hollering these ducks had done.

His jaw fell to his chest as he looked down into the blind. There beside Norman's four coots were two big Canada Honkers.

That night Tar Baby lay snoring on the carpet as Harley slouched in his old easy chair, while their wives mother and father added last minute decorations to the Christmas tree. Christmas music was playing on the radio, and in the kitchen, the two hunters' wives and in-laws sat listening again to Norman's account of his exciting afternoon on the marsh, as they wrapped presents from the final day of Christmas shopping.

Norman told again how he had fallen asleep in the blind, and how Tar Baby had jumped up on his lap to awaken him. He related in exciting detail how he looked up out of the blind to see 15 or 20 big birds settling into the close-set decoys, hollering in a high pitched voice. Then he told them how he had struggled to stand, and what a tremendous sight it was there before him as the flock rose in flight. Norman said he tried to aim, but some straw had caught on the barrel, so he closed his eyes and just shot at the whole group. That's when he paused to savor the moment. "It's been a tremendous day," the bright-eyed Norman was saying, "Rupert got two, Harley got three..."

Half asleep, in the other room, Harley leaned his head on his elbow and mumbled to himself, as he listened to a choir singing 'Jingle Bells'.

"Yeah, Norman, yeah. I got three and Rupert got two...and you got six!"

Chapter 51

C.A.R.P – an Idea Whose Time May Never Come

By Jim Spencer

The idea was born, as many weird notions are, around a campfire in a fishing camp. Beer was present. It may have been a contributing factor.

We were college students on spring break, bass fishing down on Toledo Bend, camping on a pretty, peaceful pine ridge that tailed off into the lake just yards from our tents. The cool students, the frat rats and sorority coeds and those with a jingle in their pockets, went to Panama City or Islamorada or other "with-it" destinations where sand, sun and surf collide with babes, bikinis and beer. But we were too poor for that stuff and, I suppose, too uncool besides. We were, after all, forestry and wildlife students from LSU.

So we went fishing.

It was warm, and the bass were in the shallows. We were working on them pretty good. Also in the shallows were hordes of German carp, flouncing and flopping and thrashing in the brushpiles and along the shoreline in the ecstasy and frenzy of mating. It was inevitable that sometime during our week-long trip, campfire conversation would turn to carp.

Ray Scott's Bass Anglers Sportsman Society was in its early stages, and somebody in our group got the bright idea we ought to start a Carp Anglers Sportsman Society, patterned loosely after the organization and rulebook of B.A.S.S. I got drafted to keep up with the rules as we thought them up. Somebody found a pencil and a notebook, and we started brainstorming.

The first obvious obstacle was the acronym. We wanted to call ourselves the Carp Anglers Sportsman Society, C.A.S.S. for short, because, like I said, we were copy-catting B.A.S.S. and figured there'd be some value to having our names sound somewhat alike. Trouble was, an ugly, morbidly obese folk singer of the times was also named Cass. So we tried to come up with something else, and were absolutely flummoxed when it came to thinking up a name that made any sense whose initials would give us the desired C.A.R.P. logo. The closest we came was Carp Rodders and Polers, but in those days you couldn't get away with an acronym like that.

We finally gave up, stuck with the original name of Carp Anglers Sportsman Society, and used C.A.R.P. as the acronym anyway.

Technically, it didn't fit, but someone pointed out that this was a carp fishing club we were talking about, and nobody in our target membership audience would probably bother to think about it much. We decided it was probably good enough. C.A.R.P. it would be.

Next we needed a motto. Ray Scott's snooty new bass club didn't have one that we knew of, and that would give us something to lord it over him with. But all the mottoes we seemed to come up with were even less suitable for publication than the acronym for Carp Rodders and Polers. Finally somebody who'd had a year of high-school Latin suggested "Carpe carpio," which meant, he thought, "Seize the carp."

I, on the other hand, a victim of two years of high school Latin, informed the Philistines surrounding me that the suggested motto's tense was wrong, that it should instead be "Carpe carpium." But I got overruled, on the same reasoning by which we'd decided on the Carp Anglers Sportsman Society/ C.A.R.P. conundrum – that an ungrammatical motto was probably better for carp fishermen, anyway. Thinking about it in that light, I had to agree.

From then on the decision-making got easier. Or maybe we just got drunker. Could have been either. We drew up a list of potential sponsors. Carp bait-makers like Post Toasties, Sun-Maid Raisins, Skippy Peanut Butter, Wonder Bread and Bisquick all made the short list, as did equipment companies like Warn Winches (special custom carp reels,) Brunswick (pool cue carp rods,) and Wireco Cable Company (carp fishing line.) Clothing manufacturers included folks like Carharrt and Red Ball. For the official C.A.R.P. boat, we decided on two 1948 Plymouth hoods welded together. Forrest Wood should thank his lucky stars we never could find two of 'em. If we had, a Ranger boat would probably look a lot different today.

We found it impossible to narrow the field to just one official C.A.R.P. propulsion system, so we settled on two: a cracked wooden sculling paddle, or a push pole 8 to 12 feet long. The pole could be cottonwood, sycamore, willow or persimmon, but the bark had to remain attached. Graphite wasn't in the picture yet, but we decided no fiberglass poles would be legal.

Allowable types of fishing tackle, we decided, would be pretty much anything goes, except no dynamite or rotenone would be allowed unless the contestants planning to use it brought enough for everybody. Then we got down to the nitty-gritty. C.A.R.P. tournament rules:

- The tournament entry fee would be a case of beer and either a tube of Slim Jims or a pound of jerky, payable directly to the tournament directors (us.)

- The tournament limit would be all the carp that could be crammed into a 55-gallon drum.
- Points would be deducted for live fish brought to weigh-in.
- The minimum length limit was left undecided, except we unanimously felt that any carp small enough to be used for trotline bait was definitely too small for the weigh-in. However, anyone caught releasing undersize fish would be disqualified and banned from all future tournaments.
- Archery tackle would be legal in C.A.R.P. tournaments, but prohibited within 200 yards of any marina. Tourists the shape of Mama Cass often feed carp at these places, and we figured sticking an arrow through some Yankee vacationer's cellulite would be bad PR.
- During a tournament, no angler could fish more than 20 hooks at one time.
- No one who had ever owned a rod/reel combo valued at over $50 would be allowed to enter a C.A.R.P. event. All entrants must submit to polygraphs to enforce this rule.
- Fishing outfits valued at more than $30 (rod, reel and line combined) could not be used in a C.A.R.P. event.
- Chumming with more than 100 pounds of corn or other organic matter at any one spot would be illegal; however, there would be no limit on the number of chumming spots an angler created and baited.
- In addition to standard prizes for total poundage and biggest fish, C.A.R.P. tournaments would also have prize categories for the carp with the biggest scales, the carp with the biggest lips, the carp with the biggest eyes, and the carp with the reddest fins.

We went on bass fishing that week, refining the C.A.R.P. charter every night, but of course once we got back to classes it all got put on the back burner and we eventually forgot about it. The only reason I remember all this stuff now is because I found that old spiral notebook in a box of old college books the other day.

There's some sort of half-baked fly-fishing carp tournament out West nowadays, I understand, but it'll never get off the ground. I mean, c'mon. Fly tackle? For carp?

Our idea, though, might have grown wings, if only we hadn't gotten sidetracked by all those other pesky things: getting an education, making a living, having a life. Compared with a whole family of reality shows based on Gilligan's Island, C.A.R.P. sounds pretty reasonable.

Author's note: If you're interested in charter C.A.R.P. membership, send me $150 in small, unmarked bills. And some Slim Jims. And some beer.

Chapter 52

A Two-Dollar Gift

By Larry Dablemont

Grandpa McNew and my dad bought the pool hall on Main Street in 1959. I was nearing 12 years old at the time, and immediately Dad let me start working there, racking balls and collecting money, when he and Grandpa were out for awhile.

There were a host of old men and middle-aged men who came in regularly to talk hunting and fishing, and the outdoors was all I thought about. It was the greatest place in the world for a boy like me.

Ten or twelve of those old men became my best friends, men with little education and great wisdom.

One who influenced my life a great deal was old Saldy Reardon. Dad had a day-job in a factory at the time, and Grandpa would open the pool hall at 7:00 a.m. and work until noon. Saldy would take over at mid-day and work until I got there at 4:00.

Dad said Saldy was as fine a man as he ever knew and he would trust him with every penny the pool hall made in a week, which usually wasn't enough for anyone to run off with anyway. And he was my friend so it hurt sometimes to see him like he was late on a Saturday night when he had been drinking heavily, I guess when the loneliness was too much to bear. Everyone talked about how great an athlete he had once been. Dad said that when he himself was just a boy and all the Ozark towns had baseball teams, Saldy was the greatest pitcher anyone had ever seen. There were times on a Sunday afternoon when Saldy would walk miles to a country ballpark and pitch a double-header.

The other team just felt good if they got a few hits, no one expected to beat him.

He was young then and had a wife everyone knew as Pinky. Pinky was young and beautiful and so adored by Saldy that he couldn't go on after she died. In his mid-thirties at the time, Saldy fell apart, and turned to alcohol to forget. He never found anyone else, he never pitched again, never held a steady job, he just drank and drank and drank.

I didn't know anything about all that 'til I got older. I'd just come in after school and Saldy would say, "Where the heck you been, Squirt?" like he was mad because I was always a little late from stopping by the drug store for another outdoor magazine. He always said he didn't figure I'd ever grow enough to amount to much. But he always smiled, and messed up my hair and I knew it was all in jest.

Saldy carried the only two-dollar bill I had ever seen, and one evening when the place was nearly empty he showed it to me and said someone real important to him had given it to him a long time ago, so he couldn't sell it to me like I wanted him to, not even for two dollars and a quarter as I had offered. But on Christmas Eve that year Saldy handed me an envelope and said, "Don't open this 'til Christmas, Squirt." At home that night I read the card inside and found that faded old two-dollar bill. I could not have imagined a greater gift.

As much as I admired Saldy, he taught me in reverse how not to live. I saw him as I grew older, staggering along the dim-lit street near a local tavern, or lying on a street bench wet with urine and waiting for the local police to find him and take him in.

There were tears in his eyes when I went away to college and he told me he was wrong, I had grown a little. And then he said to me, "Don't do like me, Squirt, don't take up with a bottle. It's the devil's partner and you can get tied to it like I've been all these years. It pulls you under and you can't fight it off."

I've enjoyed living life to the fullest without ever needing the alcohol that took Saldy. He died within the year, in mid-November of 1965. I doubt if he knew that he made an important positive impact on a young life. Today when I see some young kids tipping a bottle or bragging about how drunk they got the night before, I wish they could have been fortunate enough to see into the future as I could, as a boy, when I watched Saldy fight that demon and lose.

Somebody told me years later that a two-dollar bill was bad luck. I guess Saldy would have maybe agreed. It never brought him much luck. But me, heck I was the luckiest kid in the world. I had friends... friends like Saldy Reardon.

As sad as the story is, Saldy had a friend too, and we both knew about Him. On that Christmas Eve long ago we were about to celebrate the birth of someone who came to earth and made all lives count for something. And it is because of Christmas that there is hope for the least and the lowest of us. Saldy didn't really lose the battle. Liquor eventually lost its hold on him and he slipped from its grasp into forgiving hands.

Chapter 53

Red-Tailed Cats of the Amazon

By Jim Spencer

T he braided line twitched, telegraphing the savage strikes as the school of piranha tore chunks from their dead relative at the end of my line. Half a two-pound piranha seems like a big bait, but 30 seconds of attention from its cousins will reduce it to tatters. I was about to reel in and rebait with the other half when the clicker on my big reel made a couple hesitant ticks, then a few more. By the time picked up the rod, line was melting off the spool at an impressive clip.

We were just south of the Equator, fishing for pirarara, red-tailed catfish, in the Rio Unini, a blackwater tributary in the northern reaches of the Amazon River Basin. The Unini is mid-sized, and its surroundings looked familiar to this Arkansas river rat: sand bars, blackwater swamps, low bluff banks, oxbow lakes, sloughs and chutes connecting various waterways. Replace the mahogany, rosewood, rubber tree and other exotics with oak, ash, cypress and sycamore, and the Unini could pass itself off as the lower White River in eastern Arkansas.

But there the similarity ends. The Unini, like the other rivers of the Basin, teems with fish the like of which Arkansas waters have never seen. In addition to the piranha and the pirarara (which can weigh 100 pounds and commonly reaches 50 pounds and more,) there are literally hundreds of other bizarre species here. A sampling: several species of freshwater stingray, some as big as a kitchen table and weighing more than 100 pounds; a thing called a piracuru that can reach 500 pounds and looks like a cross between Satchmo Armstrong, a tarpon and a torpedo; a snake-eel-skipjack-looking amalgam known as arawana that has a trap- door mouth and makes its living by spitting water at fruits, birds, insects and other edibles and knocking them into the water; who knows how many species of fruit-eating and nut-eating piranha known collectively as pacu; and a fierce little grinnel look-alike that rarely weighs more than five or six pounds but can bite a hole in a steel plate and will wriggle across the bottom of your boat to bite you on the foot.

And, of course, there are the several species of peacock bass that all us gringos go down there to fish for. But it had rained almost 40 inches (yes, you read that right) in the five days before we arrived, and the rivers were high and off-color. So we decided to spend our first day on a quest for big catfish, to give the river some time to settle.

Speaking of big catfish, I neglected to mention the real heavyweight of the Amazon basin – the piraiba. This guy is a streamlined, shark- like monster that grows to more than nine feet and 650 pounds and is credited with eating people alive. Actually, no one knows how big piraiba get, since the biggest ones are simply too strong to be caught, with rod and reel, nets or anything else short of a Japanese whaler.

Anyway...my heavy monofilament line was whizzing off the reel and the clicker was chattering like a cicada on a summer afternoon. Earlier in the day, my fishing buddy had landed two pirarara that weighed 30 and 40 pounds, respectively. Just little fellows. I had visions of a human-sized beastie at the end of my line when I finally flipped the lever that engaged the reel.

We were using circle hooks big enough to fit around a coffee mug, and the correct technique with a circle hook is to refrain from yanking on the rod. Instead, you're supposed to let the fish set the hook by simply holding on until the line comes tight. If you yank on the rod, the angle between the barb and the fish's jaw gets out of whack and the hook pulls out of the critter's mouth. I'm an experienced circle-hook trout and bass fisherman, and though the size of the fish was different now, the principle was the same.

So even though I knew I was doing it right, as I watched the line come tight not hauling back on that rod was the hardest thing I'd ever done. I held that opinion until the line actually did come tight. That was when I decided

that keeping this damned fish from pulling me off the sandbar and into the river was even harder.

He wanted to go downriver, and since there didn't seem to be anything I could do to prevent it, I let him. For three or four minutes we gave and took, me doing most of the giving and the fish most of the taking. I was beginning to get the upper hand, I thought, when everything went limp. I reeled in and found the fish had either broken or chewed through my 130-lb. braided line. Since we were fishing steel leaders, my guess is he broke it.

Later in the day, my fishing partner connected with and landed a third pirarara, this one weighing 50 pounds. It came in making the chuffing, snorting, belching noises typical of the species, the same noises the two smaller fish had made earlier that day. Meanwhile, I lost another big fish to another break-off.

At sundown, at our final stop for the day, I had one last run-away. When I flipped the big reel into gear and set my feet against the sudden strain of the tightening line, the fish dragged me more than 10 feet across the sandbar, my feet making parallel skid marks in the wet sand. I sat down. Now my feet and my butt were cutting three ruts, and I was still headed riverward. Everybody was laughing – my fishing buddy, the trip outfitter, the native guide. Everybody, that is, but me.

I was about three feet from the edge of the Rio Unini when I informed the outfitter that when my toes touched the water I was going to give the fish that $500 Penn rod and reel combo. Suddenly he lost his sense of humor. Shouting a paragraph full of pidgin Portuguese to the guide, he grabbed me by my left arm. The guide grabbed me by the right.

This was a big, big fish, but he couldn't drag a quarter-ton of humans into the river. When the line snapped it made a muffled sound underwater that telegraphed itself up the line: *kuchunk!* I got shakily to my feet.

Behind the sand bar, in a thick stand of tall palms, a pair of blue-backed parrots started screaming and squawking, telling each other and all the rest of the world that this slice of the jungle belonged solely to them. A pair of freshwater porpoises surfaced and shot noisy blasts of air through their blow-holes. Somewhere back of beyond, deep in the rain forest across the river, a troop of howler monkeys started their resonant, other-worldly whooping. I slowly reeled the line in, and Bill clapped me on the shoulder and handed me a canteen.

"You ready to go eat some catfish?" he asked with a grin. I was. We did. And it was delicious.

Chapter 53

The Value of a Quarter

By Larrt Dablemont

Dad and I closed up the pool hall one spring night, noting that we had only accumulated a total of 16 dollars as a result of the entire day's business. Dad said in order to keep the pool hall going we should average about 20 dollars a day, including the soda pop profit.

I was 13 or 14 then, and with all the pool playing and snooker shooting I had done since he bought the place a couple years before, I was getting pretty good at it. So when I would take over running the place after school, allowing Grandpa McNew to conclude his day, I began to start looking for easy marks.

If I could get someone to play me a game of snooker and I won, then he had to pay 20 cents for the game. If I could get him to bet a soda pop on it, I would end up making 30 cents for the moneybag in 20 minutes. Dad didn't allow gambling, but he okayed playing a game for a soda pop if no one got into a fight about it.

Of course, if I lost a game, there was that 10-cent soda I had to pay for out of the moneybag and 20 minutes wasted that I could have been using to do homework. And that is the reason that my grades never were very good. As much as I wanted to get that homework done, shooting pool and snooker had to be done. It was a case of survival. Not many kids worried more about making money for the family than their homework. It goes to show what a special attitude I had at that age!

Spring and summer were rough times for the pool hall because everyone wanted to be outside. Sometimes even the front bench regulars weren't there when I came in after school in the spring. If there wasn't a soul in there, I couldn't get anyone to play snooker. If we had a rainy day, that really funneled men into the pool hall, and in the winter when weather was bad we did a good business. There were Saturdays in the winter, or rainy days in the spring, when we might take in around 40 bucks. Those were great times, cause Dad would always be so happy. If we made that much on Saturday, Dad always sang a little louder in church on Sunday. I never cared much for going to church on Sunday morning because it took away time Dad and I got to spend on the river. But when ducks were flying in at the beginning of winter, or the goggle-eye were biting in early April, Dad wasn't one to waste a Sunday on church-going. He just insisted we made it a strong option rather than a stone-engraved necessity. He strongly believed that if you wanted to catch more fish and bag more ducks, you needed to be in church when there wasn't anything else you needed to do.

Today of course, there are few 14-year-old kids worrying about family finances, but I really stressed over those hard times when Dad was worried about paying the pool hall's electric bill. I offered my ideas on saving money. One was the elimination of my regular hair-cuts. About every three weeks Dad would come to the pool hall before Main Street businesses closed and send me across the street to the barber shop, in a day when Mr. Holder, the barber, thought that if there was any hair within 3 inches of your ear, it ought to be whacked off. If I had had the nerve to be rebellious, I would have had a fit about that.

I'd go back to the pool hall and the old men would all have some kind of smart aleck remark about how much lower my ears were growing all of a sudden, or how good I smelled or whether or not my cap would fit any more.

So I told Dad that I figured he was spending about 20 dollars a year on my haircuts, and that was one whole good day's profit in the pool hall, and an absolute waste of money. He thought I was on to something there, and proposed perhaps having Uncle Roy cut my hair. Uncle Roy had three sons and if he had taken all three of them to a barber shop, the annual outlay on haircuts for him would have been about 60 dollars. His sons, Butch, Dave and Darb, always looked a little scalped, like me and most boys back then, so none of the three relished a haircut delivered on the back porch by their dad. I wonder to this day if I would have had more success with girls if I had ever had hair long enough to see if it curled or not.

Eventually I convinced Mr. Holder, who liked to play golf, that if he would cut my hair free, I would keep him well supplied with almost new golf balls I found scouring the weeds around the golf course, which sat up above the McKinney Hole on the river, only a little ways from our home. Other golfer-pool players, like Shorty Evans, found out about that and I began to make some pretty good money finding lost golf balls. I got a quarter for the good ones, and any that had bad scuffs or cuts on them were worth a nickel or a dime. When you combine that with the money I made in the summer guiding fishermen on the Piney River, you can understand how I could sometimes accumulate a pretty good sockful of money in my secret hiding place.

It wasn't that I didn't trust Dad, but you can see how a man hard-pressed to raise a family in that time might be tempted to borrow a little if he knew where I kept that sock. I never did think it was fair – that float trip arrangement. I paddled the old wooden johnboat all day for three or four dollars and Dad got three dollars for renting the boat! But when you consider the way things were when Dad was a kid, I guess I had a pretty good thing going.

One of the old timers at the pool hall said that when he was a kid, his dad gave him a nickel to go without supper, then snuck in and stole it out of his overalls pocket while he was asleep, and wouldn't let him have any breakfast because he had lost the nickel!

He didn't seem to have any lasting effect from that kind of childhood, as he was fairly rotund and happy. But you could make an argument that he suffered psychologically, since he showed up at every church picnic and ate some or all of everything. He would dang near empty our penny peanut machine every time he came in and would put a handful of peanuts in his soda pop. You could argue he was trying to hide them from someone going back to his boyhood and those stolen nickels.

As I think about it today, I come to the realization that what was wrong with me and Dad and those old timers back in those days was the rarity of quarters. I am absolutely sure that for every quarter there was when I was 14 there are a million today. And there is the answer to our problems as a country...let's just make more quarters, and fewer 20-dollar bills. But it might also be good to go back to a time when you could trade used golf balls for a haircut. It worked really well once, in a time when my grandpa traded a pig for a 1949 Chevrolet pickup, then traded a bushel of potatoes and a dozen eggs to have some neighbor fix it so it would run.

Maybe that kind of thing wouldn't work today in the city, but I have a boat motor I would trade for a good bird dog! And I have a lawn mower too that I would trade for about anything. Do you realize the futility of mowing a lawn when you live out in the country? Mowing a patch of weeds like the ones that make up my lawn might kill a baby rabbit or two, or mash some whippoorwill eggs or ruin a patch of wild flowers about to bloom. And what good will it do you? The whole thing grows back in a couple of weeks just like it was.

I know I had something I was wanting to tell you in this story that was really important but now I can't remember what it was. If I remember it, I will write about it later. Meanwhile I will leave those of you who constantly praise my poetry with this verse I wrote a night or so ago... Keep in mind that as a poet I do not write under my regular name. My poetry is oft published under Lawrence Arthur Dableaumonte as I have noticed that poets ascribe to poetic names, like Harry David Thoreau or Elizabeth Barnett Browning. I call this poem, "Inevitability":

I am glad to see the spring come,
I hope it lasts awhile.
The hatching birds and flowers,
always makes me smile.
The breeze is warm, the fish will bite,
and wildlife will be lively.
But then before you turn around,
summer will arrively.
And there'll be snakes and ticks and
heat that hangs on like the plague.
'Cause spring's a fleeting young beauty,
and summer's a mean old hag.

Chapter 55

The Benchwarmer

By Jim Spencer

The gobble was faint and distant, out there on the ragged edge of fantasy. It came from the deep recesses of the hollow below us, and there was no possibility of going after him that day.

The weather was going sour in a hurry, and what with the wind, the distance and my long-abused eardrums, I wasn't sure whether I'd heard it or imagined it. But when I cut my eyes around to look at Jill, forming the question with my eyebrows, she nodded and pointed down into the hollow. It was a turkey, all right, but he was a long, long way below us. It was late afternoon, and we didn't have enough daylight left to try for him.

We'd driven that morning from the central Ouachitas to the southern Ozarks. We'd each taken a Ouachita Mountain bird earlier in the week and, flushed with success, we hoped to fill our two remaining Arkansas tags with Ozark gobblers before leaving for a Kansas hunt in three days. Now, less than an hour after walking into the Ozark hardwoods, we had a turkey to hunt the next morning.

He didn't gobble much, this bird for tomorrow, and he was so far away it was impossible to tell for sure what he was gobbling at. He didn't answer any of my calls, but once in a while we'd hear him, many benches below us, gobbling at something – or, just as likely, at nothing. He gobbled about 15 times between 7 p.m. and 8 p.m. With the onset of dusk, he shut up.

Rain tonight, said the weatherman, and for once he was right. Back in town, we munched pizza and pored over a topographical map while watching curtains of it blow across the motel parking lot. We determined from the maps that the gobbler had been fairly close to the bottom of the hollow, and we figured we could get into his neighborhood the next morning by coming in from the bottom rather than dropping off the top. Given the slippery footing, we felt it would be a lot easier to make a 1-1/2 mile level hike and climb a short way up from the bottom than to descend a long way from the top – and then have to climb back out of there to boot.

I'd hunted the hollow before, but not for ten years. Perhaps that explains why we got a trifle lost the next morning. But we'd allowed extra time for contingencies like that, so it worked out all right. We were only a few minutes late when we located the proper offshoot going north from the main hollow and climbed three benches out of the bottom to get away from the noise of the rain-swollen creek.

He was one bench below us when he started gobbling – not a bad position to be in with a mountain turkey. But we felt we could get in a better position without bumping him, so we backed off a couple hundred yards and dropped down onto the bench with him. Then we crept closer, looking for a good set-up spot.

It was a strategic, classic strut zone. He'd set up shop on the toe of the bench, between the main hollow running east and west and the side hollow that branched off north. The finger ridge between the two hollows had an eastern exposure, and the bench was almost perfectly flat. The gobbler had a football field-sized stage on which to show off for the ladies, clear of undergrowth and dappled with early-morning sunlight. It was easy to see why he was reluctant to leave it.

He'd worked his way to the eastern edge of the strutting area during the time it took us to move, gobbling often enough so we could keep track of him, and there was just enough slope to hide us from him as we sneaked into the western edge of the flat and made our set. Jill was out in front to do the honors, and when we were both ready I made a few soft yelps on the Lohman box. The turkey gobbled back immediately, aggressively and hard. He sounded mad, eager and lonesome, and Jill snugged her gun closer to her shoulder. *All right*, I thought, and laid the call in the leaves.

Ten minutes later, he gobbled again, farther around the toe of the bench. He was drifting away. We quickly moved 60 yards forward and set up in the middle of the strutting arena. He gobbled back hard, again, at the next soft yelps, and the next time, he sounded like he was right where we were when we'd first heard him – on the next bench up.

We backed off west again and climbed the bench to get level with him, but meanwhile he was coming off the bench to get level with us. When we called, so did he, each from the other's former position. It was shaping up to be one of those hunts.

This sort of thing went on for 90 minutes. By the end of it, Jill had named him The Benchwarmer, with an expletive. But whether the turkey had a name or not, we weren't any closer to killing him than we'd been the previous afternoon. After another hour or so of jockeying for position by both parties, everybody found themselves in pretty much their original positions – roughly 125 yards apart, on either side of his primary strutting area.

But this time, he came to the call. Sort of. I first saw him at 70 yards, intermittently walking and strutting. He went behind a tree at 60 yards and Jill moved her gun barrel in his direction. *All right,* I thought, for the second time that morning.

For considerably more than the second time that morning, I was wrong. We never saw him or heard him again. Twenty long minutes later, after a fussy hen came in from behind us and went away cutting and yelping without drawing a response, it finally sank in that the game was over.

During our whispered post-hen recap, Jill told me she'd seen the gobbler spook and run away about 30 seconds after it had gone behind the tree and she'd moved her gun. She offered the opinion that I'd boogered the bird by making noise with my waterproof cushion. I offered the counter-opinion that she'd done it by moving at the wrong time.

Whatever the truth of it, the result was a spooked gobbler. We slipped out of there and hunted a different area that afternoon, telling ourselves and The Benchwarmer that, like Schwarzenegger, we'd be back.

Rain again that night, and The Benchwarmer didn't say anything at first light the next morning. The old-timers say a wet turkey won't gobble, and though that's sometimes false, it was true enough on this drippy morning. When we finally raised him at 7 a.m., he was right where he was supposed to be – on the toe of the ridge between the hollows, where the early sun could get in there and dry his plumage.

By 8 o'clock he was gobbling a lot, but once again he was playing hard-to-get, moving up and down from bench to bench, coming tantalizingly close but never showing himself. After a frustrating hour of it, I left Jill in a good position in the middle of his strutting arena and fell back, in an attempt to pull him by her. I figured that if he wouldn't come to the call but would move around here and there while gobbling back at it, we'd stand a better chance of the shooter wasn't in the same place with the caller.

It was a good plan. I can't help it if it didn't work. He eventually tired of the game, shut up and went away. Benchwarmer 2, hunters 0. We took the afternoon off and watched HBO.

No rain that night, for a change, but it didn't make The Benchwarmer any more vocal at first light. But when he showed up on his big, sunlit stage the third morning (again at 7 o'clock,) we were waiting for him. He approached all a-gobble, a bird on a mission. But as soon as he came in sight at 50 yards, he stuck his head up, putted and ran down over the lip of the bench.

Gritting my teeth against the frustration of the moment, I slipped forward and sat down beside Jill. "What?" I whispered. "What?" She shrugged her shoulders. Who knows, when it comes to turkeys?

Ten minutes later, my frustration was lessening and my normally sweet disposition resurfaced. I asked Jill if she was ready to go look for another gobbler.

"In a minute," she said. "Call one more time from here first." "Won't do any good," I said, but I dug out the box call and stroked out a string of short, choppy yelps anyway. The Benchwarmer gobbled back immediately, 150 yards up the slope and back slightly to the east.

Back to work. Repeating the strategy of the day before (I was out of fresh ideas,) I dropped back and attempted to pull the gobbler past Jill as she guarded the middle of the strut zone. I'd move to A; he'd move to B. I'd move to C; he'd move to A. I'd move to B; he'd move to C, via A and D. Meanwhile, Jill sat at X and saw the bird twice, but at too great a range each time.

After more than an hour of this, I quit calling and let The Benchwarmer simmer down, then eased back to Jill's outpost. We sat silently for 20 minutes, listening to the woods and enjoying the perfect morning weather. During that 20 minutes, our turkey never made a peep. Then I pulled out a crow call, and when he answered it he was 200 yards away and two benches straight uphill – in different territory from where we'd worked him for the past three days.

"Well, let's go," I said. "He still wants to play."

"No, you go," she said. "I'll stay here in case he starts that chessboard stuff again."

I took rounders to the west and climbed to what I thought would be his approximate level, then eased along a narrow bench to the east. It culminated in a little rocky hump that rose 30 or 40 feet above everything around it, the type of land formation we call a "tater knob" here in the Ozarks. I slipped up the west side of the knob, stopped just short of the top and yelped softly on a slate...and The Benchwarmer nearly blew my hat off my head.

I dove for cover and barely had time to get my gun on my knee when he popped into sight, half-strutting and half-looking for the hen that had been juking all over his mountain for three days. He was killable when I first saw him, but I thought I'd wait and watch the show for a while.

That is, that's what I thought until I suddenly remembered how this turkey had acted the last two times I'd had a look at him. He was still trying to decide whether to strut or run when I saved him the angst of decision-making by sending a hot swarm of 5s through the greening forest.

Standing on his neck moments later, I hooted, the way I always do after a kill when I'm not too wound up to remember it. Jill answered me from two benches down. At the sound of her higher-pitched hoot, a gobbler answered from the east side of the north hollow. In three days of hunting this spot, it was the first time we'd heard another turkey.

The Benchwarmer's replacement, maybe, come next spring?

Chapter 56

The Legend of Hobart Johnson

By Larry Dablemont

In 1968, there was a wild gobbler that roosted on the side of Gates Mountain, up above Mustard Creek, so smart and so wily that no hunter could fool him. He'd fly down into the bottoms across the creek and court a small flock of hens in April, and a handful of turkey hunters chased him through most of the season, convinced that the wise old monarch was invincible. Over the years, he had become a creature of legendary proportions, whether he existed or not. Turkey hunters needed him. He was something to talk about, to try for, to exalt as the unattainable quarry.

He was so smart that he spent the night roosting in giant oak trees on a slope so steep that any would-be roost-shooters couldn't get to him in the dark without risking skinned elbows and a damaged tailbone at the very least, and a broken limb at the worst. Old Ground-Raker, as they called him, was too heavy to fly up onto a roost, he had to walk up that hillside to a point above the trees and pitch off to settle on one of the limbs beneath him. One hunter who caught a glimpse of him, strutting before a submissive group of hens in a little persimmon grove, swore he'd weigh thirty pounds and had a beard a foot and a half long. He went on about how the sun shined off his spurs like they were polished daggers.

They'd gather at Benson's Country Store up at the crossroads, and set on the porch and talk turkey every spring, and go on about how Old Ground-Raker had made a fool of some greenhorn hunter, or how some old veteran had come within a whisker of bagging him. Every now and then some lucky Nimrod would come by to check a wild gobbler, and they'd sit there and listen to his story most all afternoon. Then the talk would get back around to how this feller or that one intended to go down into the Mustard Creek bottoms in the morning and try to call up Old Ground-Raker one more time.

But it all came down to the same conclusion...the old tom was too smart, too wary, too old, and too wild. Nobody could fool him, none but the absolute best could afford to waste time on the old gobbler when dumber ones were growing in number, jakes and two-year-olds that might come running to a call in the hands of just an average turkey caller.

You could learn a little about turkey calling there on the porch of the little country store. At times, about mid-day in April, there would be 15 or 20 hunters and farmers gathered there, drinking coffee or soda pop and eating baloney and cheese sandwiches, lined up and waiting for old lady Benson to get one lunch made so she could fix up another. And there'd be this hunter and that one showing how he used his call, and how this worked and that didn't...how he finally fooled a gobbler with this technique or that. If some poor soul, during the early morning, had spooked one or missed one or just come close, and confessed it, there'd be two or three others to tell him what he shoulda done, and what he ought to try next time.

But no one ever had much advice about fooling Old Ground-Raker, the gobbler which had become legendary in that little area of the Ozarks. Some hunters speculated he was one of the first gobblers stocked in the area, as much as 12 or 15 years before. Some scoffed at the idea of a turkey that old, but others believed it. He'd only succumb to old age they claimed, no bobcat nor great horned owl nor camouflaged hunter would ever be the match of the old veteran gobbler.

Hobart Johnson and Joe Farley were two old veterans who kept trying, year after year, coming up with more failures and more excuses than anyone cared to give serious consideration. They were competitors, two cousins who had been at war since childhood days, and each considering themselves the best outdoorsman in the county. They seldom agreed on anything, and each tried constantly to outdo the other. Joe had always had the upper hand when it came to trapping or fishing or shooting a good game of pool. Poor old Hobart, who was no doubt the windiest of the pair, seemed to always be the unluckiest as well.

But it was Hobart Johnson who went out on the last day of the turkey season in 1968 and fooled Old Ground-Raker...called him in and lowered the boom on him..."uncapped his head," so he later bragged. There on the wall of Benson's Country Store was the black and white photo to prove it, with Hobart grinning from ear to ear, and spread out in front of him a wild gobbler with an eighteen-inch beard and spurs two inches long. Oddly enough, Hobart took the gobbler way up the highway north to the county seat to check it at Mincie's cafe and sporting goods store, and no one at Benson's crossroads hangout for country folks ever got to see it. A local newspaperman had taken a picture of it, there in the back of Hobart's pick-up, and the bragging hunter had wagged that picture around ever since.

Hobart rode his cousin Joe pretty hard about it. Claimed he had went out there and called that old gobbler away from his harem of hens, drew him in like he was on a string. He said he only went after him because he had heard Joe had tried for years to bag that old gobbler. And Hobart claimed it proved beyond a doubt that he was the champion turkey caller in the whole county, and maybe all of southern Missouri. He went around every turkey season for years to come with his chest thrown out, showing that picture of the tom he insisted was Old Ground Raker.

Along about 1975 I stopped by old Joe Farley's little cabin which sat up on the hillside overlooking the river bottom, just before turkey season. We sat out on his screened-in porch, enjoying the afternoon warmth, welcome at the end of a cold winter and a the early spring which had begun cool and rainy.

"I saw your cousin Hobart down at the service station," I told him. "He said to ask you if you wanted him to come out here and call-up a turkey for you."

I was surprised to see Joe smile a little..."That durned old blowhard," he said shaking his head, "most every gobbler he ever called within range hadn't left the roost yet...most every one he ever killed was well before first light."

"But he did get Old Ground-Raker," I reminded him.

"Like thunder he did," Joe snorted. "There never was no Old Ground-Raker...you could hear two or three gobblers on that hillside most years, and they were just regular old toms like you'd find anywheres else. Cousin Hobart and some of his wife's family kept that story goin'...makin' smoke where they never was no fire."

He reached over beside his old wooden rocking chair for his pipe and tobacco, and asked me if I knew anyone who ever saw that old turkey after Hobart killed it. I thought about it, and allowed as how I hadn't. Then Joe filled his pipe deliberately, lit it and leaned back to tell me the story.

At the country school where they were boys, some 50-odd years before, Hobart and Joe had been close, and the adversary of one was the adversary of the other. The competition was always good natured, but Joe was a little better at most things boys did than Hobart was. Hobart would lose all his marbles in the weekly marble games, strike out more than anyone else when they played softball, and never could whittle out a whistle that worked.

"We got along awful good 'til Effie McElroy come along," Joe recollected. "We went to school in town when we got to high school age, and there she was. Both of us took a shine to her, and naturally, she took up with me on accounta I was a whole lot more of a man than Hobart even at that age."

I grinned a little, and Joe saw it. "Well now, I was," he went on, "I was better lookin' and made better grades and had a way with the girls and ol' Hobart bumbled and stumbled around and couldn't talk to one less'n there was a rock to kick while he was doin' it."

I gathered quickly that a great deal of competition developed for the hand of Effie McElroy, and Hobart lost. Apparently he took it personal. "It was the best thing I ever did for ol' Hobart," Joe said, "Effie didn't amount to a thing. We got engaged and she took off with a fiddle player. It broke my heart and I never really recovered from it. I guess that's why I never married."

I stopped grinning. Joe was quiet for a moment, looking off across the river bottom to the pine studded ridge in the distance, shrouded with a blue haze. I guess it hit me that after all the years, Joe was still thinking of her, still wishing it had all worked.

"Aw, I had plenty of girlfriends when I was young, but I just never could come to trust another one," Joe regained his composure and went on. "I never figured any one of 'em would have been worth givin' up my freedom, and I never could trust a woman again. 'Course, Hobart met his wife, Lottie June, and married her and they're still together today with all those kids, and happy. An' mind you still is today...maybe skinnier, and a bit more shy."

I didn't say anything...Lottie June Johnson had been my Sunday School teacher up at the Blue Meadow Baptist Church when I was young. I just thought she was a wonderful lady, always felt sorry for her, marrying old Hobart. Some of her kids turned out just like him, making her plight even worse.

Joe seemed to sense what I was thinking. "Oh now, I ain't sayin' she ain't a true prize for cousin Hobart," he said, puffing on his pipe. "She was the best he'd ever get, but he's still fool enough to remember I took Effie away from him an' not realize it was the best thing I ever done for 'im. He'd a had a miserable life with that woman!"

"But that's only part of the story," Joe grasped the arms of the old wooden rocker and bit down on the stem of his pipe. "From that time on, every time there was a big bass caught, it was me caught it. Ever time he bragged on gettin' a big buck during deer season, I got one bigger. Why shucks, that big set of antlers hangin' up in Elmore's Plymouth dealership, that's the buck I killed in the fall of 1959, not a half mile from Hobart's house."

I let out a low whistle, just to give proper respect. "That was one big buck all right," I said. "Folks were talkin' about that buck for a long time."

"Shore they was, an' that jus' made matters worse," Joe shook his head and sighed. "...an' then I caught that 50-pound flathead catfish late the next summer, after old Hobart and his boys were after him for months, talkin' up how big he was an how they was gonna get 'im. Hobart got so doggone mad he wouldn't buy a paper for nigh onto a year, just because they put me an' that fish on the front page."

"I'm beginning to see what you mean," I nodded, "the Old Ground- Raker was Hobart's only real moment in the spotlight."

"The Old Ground-Raker was only a big spoof," Joe snorted, "he was a fragment of everbody's imagination."

"Figment, I think you mean," I corrected him. Joe paid little attention.

"They ain't no turkeys so smart they can't be called in," he went on. "They ain't none so fat they bend the limb they roost on, unless they're half tame. And there never was no 18-inch beards and two inch spurs.

"Hobart and his brother-in-law made that beard out of bindin' twine strands, put 'em together heavy and strong and painted it up to look just like a beard, then cut off that turkey's beard and cut a little place in the skin, and stuck the made-up beard in there and sewed it up. Then they ground off the old spurs, and glued on a pair of locust thorns to the stubs, and painted and patched and polished 'til they looked halfway real. Then they just went up to the newspaper office, got that nimwit editor to take a picture. Well shoot, that editor ain't never been out of town on foot, he don't know what is real and what ain't. He'd a took a pitcher of a banty rooster and figgered it was a prairie chicken if 'n that's what somebody said it was."

I sat there with my mouth open. "You've got to be joking me," was all I could say.

"No sir," Joe got up and walked over to the edge of the porch and stared down at the river. "I knowed somethin' wasn't right, all the time, and then somebody said they'd got the lowdown about it from Hobart's brother-in-law once when they was over to the Roundhouse Tavern and he had too many beers. Well that's how come nobody ever actual saw that gobbler, just the pitcher, an' you can't tell what is and what ain't from a pitcher."

"So you let old Hobart have his minute in the sun," I said. "I say you are a bigger man for it."

Joe turned and faced me and spoke in a softer tone. "Aw, I came purt near to spillin' the beans, once up at the pool hall when old Hobart was a blowin' about what a turkey hunter he is. But I guess I just saw him in a different light that night...knowin' how it hurt him that Effie McElroy had picked me, and that maybe Lottie June woulda picked me too if 'n she coulda. Seemed like it was silly to be arguin' over who was the best at this or who was the best at that as old as we're gettin'. I just let it go."

"You seemed to be getting on better than I remembered in years past, when I was young," I said.

Joe looked at the floor and finished the story. "Well, the reason for that is, a year back, just before turkey season when Hobart was up at the feed mill with a couple of his boys, a pair of young knotheads from over at Hattiesville was up there showin' off their turkey callin' and hurrahin' old Hobart about that turkey, sayin' they heard it was a fake and all. Several farmers were around and some of his neighbors, and Hobart was all flustered, trying to hold up his end of the argument and not doin' too good. Reckon it hit a soft spot in me, and I lit into 'em. I said, 'you two is too green to know the difference between a struttin' tom turkey and a black oak stump, an' besides that, you was still messin' your diapers when me and ol' Hobart here hunted the Ground-Raker."

Joe tapped the burned tobacco out of his pipe and continued. "I saw they was taken aback a little, slowed down some on their jawin'...so I went on. 'I seen that old tom, many times over the years, a giant of a gobbler with a beard so long it dragged the ground even when he held his head high, and you could see those spurs flashin' ever time he took a step, hear 'em clackin' ag'in one another when it was still. Early on a spring mornin' he'd make the hills echo across that valley, shakin' the mornin' dew off the hickory buds and the dogwood blossoms with his thunderin' gobbles. An' more than one of us who fancied ourselves the kind of turkey hunters you boys would like to be, more than one of us gave it our best, only to see him lead his harem off the other direction, too wise, and too wary to be fooled.

"'He was the boss tom, the Old Ground Raker,' I told 'em, an' they stood there and listened. 'But Hobart here', I says, 'maybe "I wondered why you and Hobart he just got lucky and then maybe he didn't...maybe he was just a little better at it than the rest of us. And some has seen the picture, and some has their doubts, but me, I seen the old tom hisself, layin' there dead in the back of Hobart's pick-up, and in truth, I never saw the like of it."

I was quiet for a minute, and Joe continued..." I didn't lie about it, exactly," he said, "I never actual saw the like of it, and that's what I said. Anyhows, it shut them boys up, and everbody kinda patted ol' Hobart on the back and he stuck his chest out again. Later at the pool hall, he come by and kinda quiet like said he had some yaller suckers spotted and wanted to know if 'n I'd come by some time and go grabbin' 'em with 'im."

"Did you go?" I asked.

"Shore did!" Joe said, seating himself in his old rocking chair again and gazing out across the valley. "An' will again this spring I reckon... grabbin' yeller suckers and arguin' over who was the best rifle shot 40 years ago. But I'll not leave before I tell him again how lucky he is to have his boys, and Lottie June, and how I wish I could have got that old Ground Raker turkey before he did."

I didn't say anything, and it was quiet for a moment. Joe asked if I'd drink a cup of coffee, and I said I would. We got up to go into his kitchen, and with his back toward me, filling the blackened coffee pot, he added something that'll stay with me forever.

"Wish I had known when I was younger how good it felt to let ol' Hobart be the best ever' now and then," he said.

Back out on the porch, we drank our coffee, and down the river aways, a gobbler sounded off, answered by another. Joe looked at me and a smile broke across that wrinkled, weathered face. "One of Old Ground-Raker's descendants," he said with a wink. "Ain't no use in goin' after that one...why he's too smart to leave tracks...ain't got no shadow...got a beard he trips over when he walks!"

I nodded, and sipped my coffee. "I've heard about gobblers like that."

Chapter 57

Dues

By Jim Spencer

Who knows how I might have turned out if it hadn't been for the ducks? I'm an above average guy, intelligence-wise; no brain surgeon, certainly, but no lamebrain either. I could probably have made myself into something. I could probably have been somebody.

They've always been there, though. The ducks, I mean, hovering on the outer edge of my thoughts the way they hover over the outer edge of the decoys in those final, agonizing seconds when things can still go either way.

And because I'm a sucker for that kind of suspense, I became a duck bum. No matter what, I get after them every chance I get – waiting, watching, wanting to see which way they go.

See, I grew up in Stuttgart. And when you grow up in Stuttgart, you are bombarded from pre-puberty to post-senility with so much duck propaganda you really have only two choices: (a) you ignore the whole subculture and take up some non-related activity like golf, or (b) you embrace it with all the fervor and ecstasy of a Christian throwing himself to the lions.

When I was about ten, still too young to know what I was doing or realize the long-term consequences of my actions, I chose (b). I've been paying for it ever since.

The payment varies from trip to trip, as any duck bum knows, in both species and intensity. Some hunts are less expensive, so to speak, than others.

But for every easy day that comes along, you can bet your last box of 3-inch magnums there'll be an extra-tough one to compensate for it. There ain't no free lunch in duck hunting. Duck bums must continue to pay their dues. It's one of the few certainties in this masochistic sport.

• • •

Money, of course, is one way we pay dues. Duck hunting is expensive, and getting more so each year, even when you do it as economically as possible. Have you priced a pair of neoprene waders lately? Or a box of nontoxic duck loads? Or a boat, or a motor, or a dozen decoys?

But money really isn't what's at issue. The real dues involve other things. Things such as getting up, like Biblical wives, while it is yet night. While other, saner folk are still sleeping, duck bums stumble bleary-eyed around the kitchen, trying to figure out why the timer on the damned coffee-maker didn't work.

There's always something missing from the small mountain of hunting gear, too, some small but indispensable item that will make or break a duck hunt. Finding the item invariably involves a lot of banging and bumping and opening and shutting of drawers and squeaky closet doors, so that by the time the brave hunter sallies forth, he leaves in his wake a sleepless house. A house to which he must eventually return, thus necessitating payment of even more dues.

And that's just the non-hunting part of this dues-paying business. There's also the long drive to the hunting spot, followed by the pre-dawn ride in an open boat in sub-freezing temperatures. There's untangling and deploying from several dozen to a hundred or more decoys, with fingers as clumsy as blocks of wood. There's standing around in knee-deep to waist-deep water that's within a few degrees of being ice cubes, feeling your extremities slowly disassociate themselves from your body. There's the shipping of that same frigid water either over or through those expensive neoprene waders.

• • •

Falling down and getting wet is a distressingly common way of paying dues. I'm not the falling-downest hunter in the world, thank goodness. Off the top of my head I can think of maybe three people in my life who were more prone-prone than me. One of them was 12 years old. Another had a prosthetic leg. The third guy was just plain clumsy.

No, not clumsy. That's unfair. Jimmy was just haphazard, that's all, and he had an uncanny talent for finding underwater surprises like beaver runs, stump holes, tie vines, cypress knees and sunken logs. His propensity for duck hunt swimming may have been enhanced by the fact that as he grew older his latitude gained on his longitude, making him progressively more top-heavy. Apparently, he never learned to compensate.

Whatever the reasons, I liked hunting with him because I didn't end up being the goat all the time. Some of the time, I admit, but not all the time.

Jimmy was highly imaginative in his falling. We hunted in flooded timber, mostly, and flooded timber is full of submerged stumbling blocks. I've seen him use a wide variety of these obstacles as the launch pad for his underwater forays.

Most of his performances (the hundred or so I witnessed, anyway) were ho-hum affairs. He would walk along, stumble, shout, fall, flail the water. Then he'd get up, cursing and shivering, streaming water like a muskrat.

But a couple or three times every season he'd turn in a brilliant performance, a 9.9 on any judge's scorecard. One such fall stands apart from the rest, a pure slice of tragicomedy in the best I Love Lucy tradition:

We'd been hunting the timber all morning. It had been one of those rare easy trips – mild weather, cooperative ducks, adequate shooting performances on our part. Icing on the cake, we were both still dry. Now we were wading out of the backwater, pushing it a little, trying to get home before the Arkansas-Texas kickoff. The water was calf-deep and we were really churning through it.

You could see it coming five yards before it happened. Jimmy hooked a loop of possum grape vine with one foot, and it started following him. When all the slack was gone, the vine snapped tight as Fred Bear's bowstring. Jimmy went floundering off to port, listing hard, trying desperately to get his legs back under the rest of him.

For a while it looked like he might make it. But just as he was beginning to get vertical again, he shoulder-blocked a six-inch persimmon tree. He was still moving pretty fast, and the solid tree trunk spun him like a top. He sort of screwed himself into the water, amid an ignominious flurry of water droplets, leaves and floating overcup oak acorns. He still had enough momentum to roll over a time or two, thereby ensuring complete body coverage.

Since I'm telling this for money I feel compelled to add that I fell on my face only a few minutes later, but when I tell it for fun I always leave that part out. A good storyteller knows when to quit, and anyway, my fall didn't hold a candle to his.

But for what has to be the most spectacular fall in duck hunting history, I'll turn you over to my friend Wilbur, who saw it happen long ago on a man-made dead-timber reservoir. The reservoir was only a few years old at the time, and the trees had died but were still standing. Most of them were still pretty stout. Some local brainiac decided to nail a bunch of scrap 2x4s on the trunk of one of those dead trees to make a ladder, then hoist a 55-gallon barrel up there to serve as a one-man duck blind. The idea caught on. Very quickly, the lake took on the look of an eagle rookery, with barrels in treetops every few hundred yards over most of the lake.

You can probably see this coming. Here's Wilbur:

"Most of the drums and trees fell within a few years, and the few that stayed were in trees too rotten to climb. But I was motoring past one of them one day when I noticed a boat tied to the base of the tree. A tall, skinny fellow was climbing up those two-by-fours with a shotgun slung on his back."

Wilbur stopped his boat to watch. The skinny guy made it to the top okay and managed to get in the barrel without incident, though the tree was swaying some. Things seemed to be under control, though, and Wilbur was just about to go on when it happened.

"The guy swung his shotgun back and forth a few times, I guess limbering up for all the ducks he thought he was going to shoot," Wilbur said. "On about the fourth swing, that tree broke in half about a foot below the bottom of the barrel. It was only about 15 yards to the water, but I expect it seemed a lot farther to him."

Luckily the idiot fell into the lake instead of his boat, and Wilbur motored over and fished him out of the eight-foot-deep water. The guy cranked his outboard and left in a hurry, his shotgun still somewhere on the bottom.

"He never even said thanks," Wilbur said.

Not too surprising; I'd have been too embarrassed to say anything, too. Three weeks later, on a hunch, Wilbur went back to the spot with a big industrial magnet. First, he pulled up the 55-gallon barrel. On the second drop, he got the shotgun – a pre-1964 humpback Browning autoloader. The stock and forearm were considerably water-swelled, but he dried it slowly in front of a fan, and after a month or so the swelling almost wholly disappeared. Wilbur still has that gun, and if you recognize yourself as the guy who fell out of the tree, don't bother contacting him. You're too stupid to own a firearm.

• • •

Falling, sad to say, isn't the only way to end up in the drink. Once upon a long time ago, hunting in the woods, I stepped away from my tree to take a look behind me and got clobbered in the solar plexus by a low-flying wood duck traveling at about 40 knots. It was hard to tell which of us was more surprised, but the duck was the uncontested winner. He got away clean. I ended up sitting shoulder deep in the water, gasping desperately for air. Unfortunately, there were witnesses, and I have never lived it down.

Climbing in and out (mostly out) of boats figures heavily in many a tale of getting wet. One time I took a pair of east Tennessee hillbillies to the flooded timber. Neither had ever hunted ducks, except for jump-shooting a few local stock ponds, and they were ready. Too ready. We motored up a narrow bayou and back through the flooded timber before daylight, fighting our way through hellishly thick brush. It was tough going, especially in the dark, and finally I succeeded in jamming the boat so tight between two ironwood bushes it wouldn't come out. While I was reaching for the boat paddle to pry us loose, I heard a splash, followed by as imaginative a paragraph of foul language as I'm ever likely to hear. One of my Volunteer State friends had volunteered, and he'd jumped off the bow – into neck-deep water.

There's more. We hauled Vol out and wrung him out some, and he pulled off his hip boots and poured most of the water back into the woods. Finally, we reached water shallow enough to wade. I got out first, to tie the boat to a tree and lead my guests to the day's shooting hole. Vol once again climbed out of the boat...and this time his boots were still rolled down. You could have heard his scream of disbelief back at the boat landing, three miles away.

• • •

Becoming intimately acquainted with a lot of ice water is not, let me hasten to add, the only way to pay your duck hunting dues. Frustration, humility and one-upmanship also weigh heavily on the balance sheet. And old axiom tells us misery loves company; therefore, duck hunting is usually a shared sport. And it seems that everyone I share it with is either a better caller or a better shot (often both) than I am.

An old friend and I were hunting a small Louisiana backwater many years ago. I'd been bragging to Joe how well I could shoot my new Charles Daly over/under.

You can see this one coming, too.

Three teal came whizzing through our opening, flying as only motivated teal can fly. I saw them first, but before I could get my deadly Daly to my shoulder, Joe killed the bird I had my eye on. I got the gun on the second bird, but Joe killed it before I could shoot. I switched to the third one. Before my finger closed on the trigger, it went down, too. All this in the space of an athlete's heartbeat. I complimented Joe with a sincerity I did not feel – it should be mentioned here he was shooting a 28-gauge – and went back to my tree to sulk.

Minutes later our calling interested a lone greenhead, and after a couple of obligatory fly-bys he cupped and fell in on us like a kamikaze pilot with glory on his mind. The duck was on Joe's side of the hole and I waited for him to shoot, but I guess he was being polite and held off. By the time I stepped out from my tree and engaged the target, said target was within swatting range. The duck saw me, back-pedaled and started getting out of there. Two launches from my deadly Daly later, he was highly motivated but still untouched. Joe dropped him stone dead at 40 yards, and he is very fortunate that my shotgun only held two shells.

• • •

Stalking (read crawling, sneaking, creeping, sliding, slithering) after ducks is another way to crazy up an otherwise sensible day. Especially when you're young and undignified, like I was in my 20s. Nobody does much duck or goose stalking without acquiring an impressive array of scars and contusions, and not all of them are physical. I've given up this form of hunting because of the damage it was doing to my psyche. Also, I have become too, um, dignified.

I remember one especially psyche-scarring stalk. Three of us were rabbit hunting one bluebird day when we happened upon a big flock of mallards feeding in the middle of a large, semi-flooded rice field. (To give you some idea of the vintage of this hunt: the lead loads we were using for rabbits were at that time perfectly legal to use on those ducks.)

It seemed there was no possibility of getting within range of those ducks without crawling. So here we went, slithering through the muck like reptiles, pushing our guns ahead of us, trying simultaneously to keep our barrels free of mud and our bodies below the foot-high level of the rice stubble.

Ill-conceived or not, our plan was working beautifully until that blasted flock of Canada geese lit in the field between us and the ducks. This would have been fine, except that Canadas were forbidden fruit in Arkansas in those days. We were about 100 yards from them, and they were about 30 yards from the ducks.

We crawled into a ragged circle and held a whispered summit conference. The consensus was that we had a lot invested and nothing to lose beyond a few more shirt buttons. So we crawled until we judged we were as close to the geese as we could get, checked our barrels for mud, struggled up and charged across the field like a Kiowa raiding party, a veneer of mud and rice straw substituting for war paint and feathers. We hoped to get within range before the ducks escaped.

Have you ever tried to run through squishy mud, carrying a shotgun, through the middle of a flock of 75 flapping, honking Canada geese? Don't. One big gander got confused and more or less attacked the guy to my right. He panicked and veered into my lane. Our feet got into a wrestling match and down we both went. I don't know how my buddy landed, but I did it barrel first, closely followed by my face. I raised my head out of the goop just in time to see the goose go by four feet away, not as big as a 737 but pretty damn impressive anyway.

The confusion confused the ducks, too, and they blew out of there in every direction. Enough came our way that my two companions killed three apiece, while I sat in the mud and cried.

• • •

All this stuff teaches you things. Stoicism comes to mind.

Humility, too. Some days, you can hunt as well as you know how, blow sweet notes on your calls until your lips will no longer hold the seal, and your only reward will be a headache. Some days, you can shoot half a box of shells at easy targets and never cut a feather. Some days, you can watch empty skies until you're convinced there's not a duck within a hundred miles.

But then there are those other days. You don't get wet. Your nose and toes don't freeze. The ducks work to your calling. You can hit what you're shooting at. Those are the days you know why you subject yourself to this torture, day after day, season after season, why you spend more than you should in your quest, why you neglect both job and family in pursuit of this feathered grail we know as a duck.

Those are the days you know why you're a duck bum.

Chapter 58

Old Joe

By Larry Dablemont

When I was a boy, he wandered round town, an old
guy that most everyone knew.
Old Joe had a shack off the river,
on the hillside beside Catfish Slough.
I went there at times, and sat on his porch,
to listen to stories he told.
My mom never thought I should be there,
so young, while ol' Joe was so old.
But I thought he was somethin', and he was, in my eyes,
for the things he had seen and had done.
The old timer who lived on the river,
the old soldier from World War One.
In town he was laughed at, an old blow-hard they said,
and I know that their jokes hurt him so.
In the grocery store or the pool hall, they'd say,
here comes ol' Windy Joe.
He'd come into town in his hip boots and coat,
drivin' that old pick-up truck.
With the fenders a clangin', his old hound in the back,
with some fish or a sack full of ducks.
And he'd tell everyone how he'd got 'em,
and he'd talk about times long ago.
And they'd all nod and smile and wink as he did,
more big stories from ol' Windy Joe.
There were catfish so big you couldn't boat 'em
and bass half the size of your thigh.
He remembered a buck in the thirties
that had antlers halfway to the sky.
He had hunted for bear in Alaska
and trailed big cats in the west.
He'd had a taste of Canada's lakes,
but he still liked the Ozarks the best.

He limped a little, when the weather was bad,
from wounds he'd received in the war.
'Cause he answered the call of his country;
his heroics had won the Bronze Star.
But no one had seen any medals,
and most figured it was all a big yarn.
Like the time he had seen flying saucers,
in the night over Ben Miller's barn.
But I could see he just wanted some credit,
for a life lived without much acclaim.
He wasn't the liar they thought him to be,
the old man without a last name.
Then one spring, when warm days came early,
three young girls and their teachers set forth,
In canoes on the river with no hint at all,
of a storm moving down from the north.
The sun disappeared as dark clouds moved in,
the rain came down heavy and straight.
The river rose fast and the temperature dropped
and the search party would just have to wait.
In the dark and the fog, there could be no search,
when the new day dawned, they would go.
But in the night, a johnboat set forth,
as downstream in the dark, went Old Joe.
Lights wouldn't work in the darkness,
with fog you could cut with a knife.
But he knew that river by head and by heart,
and to save them, he'd risk his own life.
He found them huddled together,
almost too frozen to save.
But Old Joe had brought food and blankets,
and he knew of a big nearby cave.
He built a warm fire and made coffee,
as a cold wind brought ice from the sky.
But snug in that cave in an old river bluff,
the girls and their teachers were dry.
They feared the worst as the dawn came;
almost no one could believe it was true.
But they still talk today of the rescue,

how the old riverman had come through.
Old Joe became a town hero
he was welcomed whenever he came.
And folks who at one time ignored him,
used Mister in front of his name.
Today there's a place 'neath a pine tree,
behind the church where ol' Joe,
spent his last years as a member,
singing hymns in the very first row.
There a monument stands to a hero,
who was buried there some time ago.
Now grown, I go there to visit
the man they called Ol' Windy Joe.

Don't Mourn for Me

Don't mourn for me when I am gone,
Just milk the cow and carry on.
Don't cry and mope and act all blue
'cause you have too much work to do.
Keep firewood stacked up on the porch,
And a warm fire burning like a torch.
Churn the butter and make the bread,
work on that quilt to line the bed.
Feed the chickens and slop the hogs.
And keep the ticks picked off the dogs.
Don't cry for me, and wish I was here.
Just remember me, I ask you dear.

Have pleasant thoughts when you think of me.
Remember times when we were young and free.
You've still got the kids, and you've got ol' Rover.
And I'll be back when deer season's over.

Chapter 59

Epitaph for a Turkey Hunter

By Jim Spencer

He was one of a kind. Big (not fat, just big,) rawboned, sunburned, leathery, John Thomas Aycock was the epitome of a country boy. Except when he was wearing camouflage hunting clothes, and for the last few weeks as he lay on his deathbed, I'm not sure I ever saw him in anything but blue jeans.

Tommy was the epitome of a turkey hunter, too, and he hunted these big, elusive birds with the focused, single-minded intensity of a Hindu penitent. We met in May, 1981, when he walked into the shop of the business where I worked and spied a gobbler tail fan I had recently boraxed and tacked to a board. I'm glad he saw it, because that tail fan launched a friendship that lasted 40 years.

Tommy was already a 20-year veteran of the turkey wars, while I (as proven by the fact that the tail fan mentioned here was from my very first gobbler) was the rankest of beginners. But that made no difference to Tommy; I was a blooded turkey hunter, and that made us brothers in the fraternity, both of us members of the Tenth Legion before either of us had ever heard of Tom Kelly. In Tommy's direct, to-the-point way of thinking, that made us equals.

What struck me during that first of many, many conversations, was the obvious fact that he was as happy that I, a stranger, had killed a gobbler as he would have been about tagging one himself. Soon enough, I learned this was a hard-wired part of his make-up. He was generous with his joy of living, readily extending it to others.

It took us an hour to swap out his oxygen bottle that day, a job that could normally be accomplished in three minutes. It would have taken longer, but my boss came back to the shop and dragged Tommy out of there by the arm.

We shared many varied experiences over our four decades of friendship, most of them involving outdoor stuff: duck, dove, squirrel and deer hunting; bass, trout, bream and catfishing; trapping for mink, beavers, otters, bobcats and other furbearers. But mostly, we shared turkey hunts, either in each other's company or vicariously through frequent phone calls during turkey season, as we called each other to brag, commiserate or seek advice on a particularly obstinate turkey. I promise you, I picked his brain about more than one obstinate gobbler over the years.

We traveled a lot together, mostly chasing turkeys – in Arkansas, Mississippi, Missouri, Oklahoma and Kansas – and we shared many experiences, both good and bad. Some of our hunts had elements of both. Like this one:

We were in the Devil's Backbone Wilderness Area in southern Missouri. Back then, in the late 1980s when our legs and lungs were younger, it was our favorite place to hunt. We got on a stubborn late-morning bird and finally got him coming. It was Tommy's shot, but as the gobbler closed the distance he slid off to the right, forcing Tommy to shoot left-handed.

If you've ever shot off your wrong shoulder, you know how awkward it feels. That's why Tommy wanted the bird to be standing still for the shot. But the dang turkey kept walking to the right, and Tommy kept corkscrewing farther and farther around his tree, and it was about to become impossible. Panic in his voice, he stage-whispered, "Make him stop!" I clucked sharply on my box call, and in the next half-second, three things happened: The gobbler stopped walking. He ran his head up. And Tommy killed him.

I jumped up and started running to the bird, the way we used to do before souped-up turkey loads and heavier-than-lead shot made it pretty much unnecessary. After a few steps I realized I was running by myself. I stopped, looked back and saw Tommy on all fours, blood pouring out of his nose onto the leaves. He'd had the gun so far to the right his left thumb was on the right side of his nose, and the recoil of the big 12 gauge broke his schnozz as efficiently as a high inside fastball.

"You all right?" I asked.

"Yeah. Go get my turkey." It was a reasonable request; the gobbler was thundering around out there in a tight circle, beating the forest floor with both wings. So I ran a few more steps and turned around again. Tommy was struggling up on one knee, leaning on his shotgun, blood still pouring out of his nose but now onto the front of his shirt.

"You sure you're all right?" "Yes! Go get my damn turkey."

So I went and got his damn turkey, and I've wished a thousand times I'd had a camera that day. By the time we got back to the truck he looked like a gladiator who'd been playing for the losing team. There was human blood all over the front of his clothes and turkey blood all down his back. "It's worth it," he said. "I'll do it all over again if I ever get the chance."

In case you don't recognize it, that's turkey hunting dedication right there. It gripped this man like horsehide grips a baseball.

Another time, we were camping and hunting in the Ouachita Mountains of western Arkansas, not far from Mt. Ida. To call this a poor-boy camp would be an understatement. We had a tent, two sleeping bags, one Coleman lantern, a black skillet, a spatula, a coffee pot, two chipped coffee mugs, an ice chest, a five-gallon water canister, two rickety folding camp chairs and a roll of toilet paper. Our provisions consisted of a loaf of bread, a dozen eggs, a pound of bacon, five pounds of potatoes, a package of bologna, some rat-trap cheese, a salt shaker and a little can of coffee. That was our entire string.

But it was enough. We were tough and poor and still young enough to stand it, and neither of us had enough sense to realize we were roughing it. We were, after all, sleeping smack in the middle of the turkey woods. What more could you want?

First day, nothing. The second morning, we hiked up the ridge behind camp. At the top, Tommy went east and I went west. About 9 a.m. I heard a shot back in his direction, and I figured he'd killed one. Okay, good. Turkey breast and 'taters for supper. After a while I moseyed back that way, and down in a little ravine about where we'd split up I saw a dead turkey. Fresh. A hen.

I figured Tommy had killed it by accident, maybe shooting at a gobbler. It happens. I left her where I found her, and when I got back to camp Tommy jumped me about it.

"Why'd you kill that hen?" He'd seen her laying there, too, and had left her the same as I had.

I denied it and accused him of doing the deed, and he denied it, too. I believed him then and believe him now. Tommy would lie about turkey hunting as quick as the next guy, but we didn't lie to each other about it. The only explanation we could come up with was that some other hunter had got in between us, shot the hen and left her.

Sitting in camp eating dry bologna and cheese sandwiches, we got to thinking about that hen turkey up there going to waste. I have already mentioned we were in a bare-bones camp, broke as the Ten Commandments, and in the end, practicality won out over legality. We went back up the mountain, ran a red-shouldered hawk off the hen and breasted her out on the spot. Then we guiltily snuck the meat back to camp and cooked her for supper that night. All the while we were nervous as first-time bank robbers, certain we were going to get caught any minute. But we didn't, and the statute of limitations has long since run out so I can safely tell you about it.

She was delicious.

Tommy Aycock was more than just a good, dedicated hunter and outdoorsman. He was a master rice and soybean farmer, for one thing, one of the best in Arkansas. He was a family man to beat all family men. He was also the kindest, gentlest, most generous, most thoughtful man I've ever known. He was a gentleman in the truest sense of the word – a gentle man. We were friends 40 years, and I got 40 birthday cards from him. If he'd lived another month, I'd have gotten another one. It shames me to say that I failed to reciprocate, but it never occurred to Tommy to feel slighted by it. He was about giving, not taking.

Tommy was fiercely loyal to his friends, and I guess if he had any enemies he was loyal to them as well. But I honestly couldn't tell you if he had enemies or not. If he did, he never mentioned them to me. Matter of fact, I never heard him say a truly bad thing about anybody.

He was a highly moral man, and – not that I think drinking is immoral, mind you – he never was a drinker. The only alcohol I ever saw him consume was red wine, which he drank for a while when one of his doctors told him an ounce or two of the stuff every night before bedtime would be good for his heart or his red blood cell count or his insomnia or something. There for a year or two he always had a bottle of dago red with him. It was both comical and entertaining to watch him screw up his face and choke down that little glass of nightly wine.

By the same token, it would have been comical to watch him that afternoon in about 2004 or 2005, when we were hunting near where Jill and I live in the north Arkansas Ozarks. Staying in our small guest house, Tommy got a plastic bottle out of the refrigerator to carry on an afternoon hunt. He thought it held water, but instead for some now-forgotten reason it contained gin put there by my wife. It was a warm late-April day and Tommy walked quite a distance to get to his chosen hunting spot, and by the time he got there he'd worked up a thirst. Out came the "water" bottle, and he took a couple healthy chugs before realizing something was dreadfully, horribly wrong.

That evening after we all got back to the house, Tommy told me where my "water" bottle was, and what I could do with it when I found it. He said he blew every turkey out of that section of woods with his coughing and gagging and choking, and he thought he was going to die before he got things back under control.

I thought it was hilarious. Tommy failed to share that opinion. After giving me the cussing of my life (moral he was, anti-profanity he was not,) he accused me of setting a booby trap for him. But I didn't, I swear. Not that

I'm above stuff like that, but I just didn't think of it. Anyway, none of my practical jokes ever work out that well.

Aside from that one thing he didn't find so funny, though, Tommy had a keen sense of humor. He loved a good joke, and – again, aside from the one thing – if the joke was on him, so much the better.

But his last good joke, as it turned out, was on me. Not long after the 2019 turkey season I visited Tommy in the hospital, only a month or so before he died. I told him I'd gone back to the Devil's Backbone that spring on a turkey hunt, and I'd passed by the spot where he'd broken his nose. I told him it was going to be my last trip, though, because the landscape was just too rough for old men.

A little smile flirted with the corners of his mouth. "Oh, you never know," he said. "You might go there again someday." I should have smelled a rat, but I didn't. Not right then.

Spreading Tommy's ashes

A few weeks later, when Tommy's daughter-in-law Elizabeth called to tell me his time was about used up, she also told me he had two requests for me and wanted to let me know what they were ahead of time, so I wouldn't be blindsided. Suddenly I caught a whiff of that rat.

One of the requests was that I do a eulogy at his memorial service. It was an honor to be asked, and I accepted gladly and, I think, did it fairly well when the time came. Parts of that eulogy have been included in this chapter.

The other request was Tommy's final joke. He wanted me to scatter his ashes. Guess where?

So, he was right and I was wrong. I did indeed make one more trip to the Devil's Backbone. Let me tell you exactly what that entails:

First, you somehow get yourself to West Plains, in southern Missouri. Then you take a narrow farm-to-market road about 20 miles west and turn on a bumpy gravel road that hasn't seen much maintenance since the Reagan administration. Take that road to its end, about 5 or 6 miles, and park at the sign at the wilderness boundary that says "No vehicles beyond this point." Then lace up your most comfortable hiking boots, and don't forget your water bottle because you're going to need it. (Check to make sure it's water, ha ha.)

Then you start walking. And you walk. And you walk some more. And then you climb some, and go down in holes some, and climb back out of them. Then, to finally get out on the Backbone itself (a narrow spine of granite and rotten limestone surrounded by thin air and soaring buzzards,) you have to go down a steep 300-foot slope covered with baseball-sized rocks that like to roll under your feet and try to break your ankles. Finally, four rough miles from the truck, you're there. You're on the Devil's Backbone. Then you have to do all that in reverse to get back to your ride.

I gotta hand it to you, Tommy, that was a good one. "Oh, you never know. You might go there again someday." No wonder you were grinning; I bet it took considerable effort to keep from laughing out loud. At least you didn't saddle me with a chore like Gus McCrae hung on Woodrow Call in Lonesome Dove. I didn't have to lug you from Montana to Texas in a buckboard wagon and bury you in a grove of pecan trees. That's something to be thankful for, I guess.

On a warm September day in 2020, Jill and I parked the truck at the old campsite and trekked into the Devil's Backbone Wilderness Area, following the familiar path I'd walked hundreds of times. I wore my tattered old hunting vest, in the blood-stiffened game pouch of which were the following items:

- Three one-liter water bottles
- A turkey hunter's lunch for two (sardines, crackers, Beanee Weenies, fruit cups)
- A copy of Tom Kelly's *Tenth Legion* (Tommy's favorite book)
- A ½-cup metal measuring cup with a handle
- And the heaviest yet lightest item of all – a plastic bag containing about a half-gallon of gritty whitish ashes

Finally we walked out onto the Backbone, and it was as pretty as I've ever seen it. We sat on that rotten limestone spine beside what Tommy and I used to call our "listening rock," and ate a redneck king's feast. Then I scattered the ashes, a half-cup at a time. Then I opened Tenth Legion and read a few pages out loud. Then we put the book in the bag that had held the ashes and sealed it as best we could. I pried the listening rock out of the ground and we put the book under it, and I stomped the rock back into place. Then we hiked back out of there, got in the truck and drove home.

Difficult as that trip was (in more ways than one,) it was one of the highest honors of our lives.

Tommy Aycock died on a hot, beautiful summer Sunday in 2019, just shy of his 82nd birthday. Jill and I were leaving a convention in Springfield, Missouri when the news came. We were just south of town, headed for Russellville, Arkansas to tell Tommy goodbye, when my phone chirped. It was a text message from Elizabeth telling us we were too late. My amigo had chased his last gobbler.

It's an established fact that big ol' rough he-man turkey hunters don't cry. A couple minutes later I was driving along, being a big ol' rough he-man turkey hunter, swiping at the dust or grit or whatever it was in the truck that was making my peepers water, when out of the corner of my eye I glimpsed a black blob in a field.

This next is God's truth. You can't make this stuff up.

When I saw the black blob it looked familiar, and hunter's instinct took over. I jerked my head to the right and focused on a mature gobbler in full strut, 50 yards off the highway. Just as I made him out as a turkey he ran his neck out and double-gobbled, and just that quick we were past him.

I couldn't hear it, of course. We were driving fast, the windows were up and the air conditioner was blowing a hurricane. But I didn't need to hear it. I knew what it sounded like.

I bet Tommy heard it, though, and when I saw that big gobbler send his double-barreled salute to my old friend, I knew things were all right. Things were as they should be. Tommy wasn't uncomfortable or in pain any more, and he had his strength and his youth back after several years of failing health. He was on his way to a place where the turkeys gobble every day, and the fish are always biting.

Additionally, I knew one day soon I'd be making one more trip to our favorite hunting place with my old friend.

Thank you for that, Tommy. I'll see you on the Backbone.

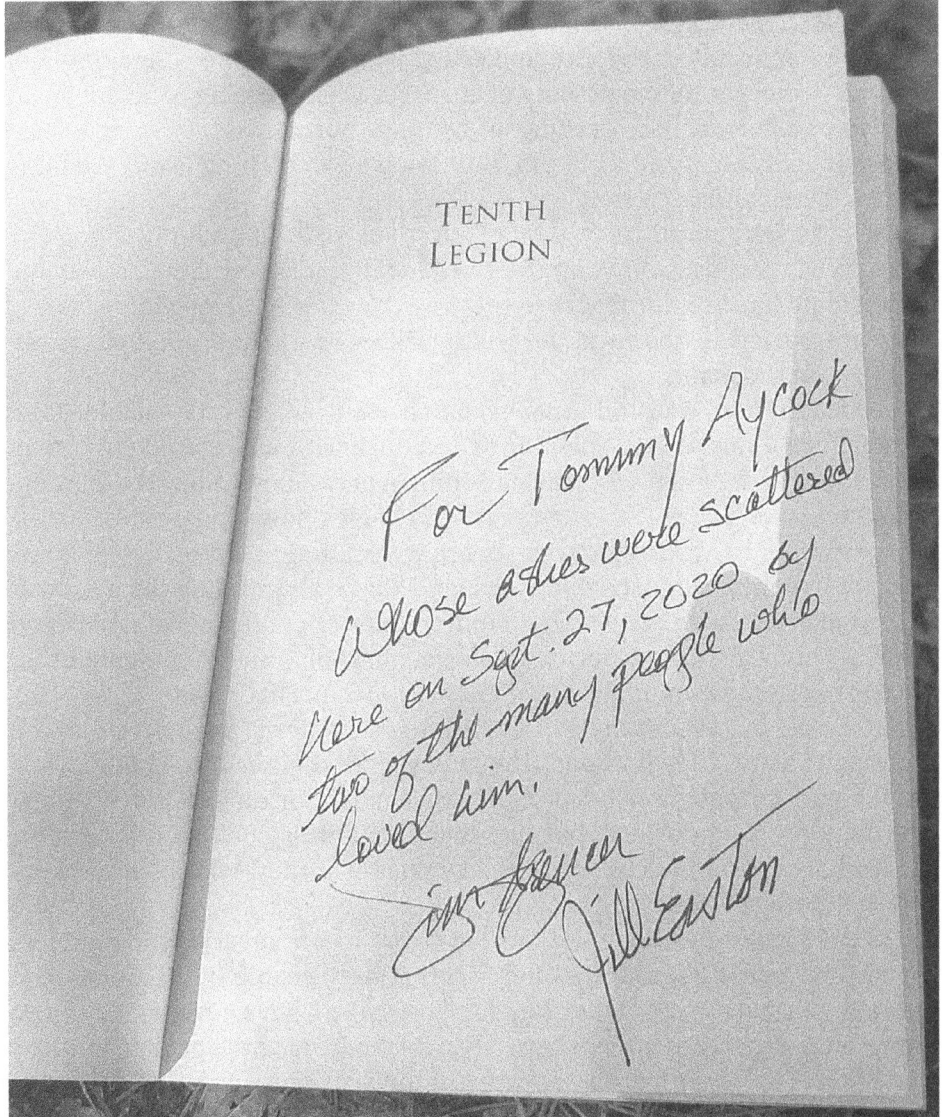

Chapter 60

Just Another Passing

By Larry Dabemont

The New Year is close...at precisely midnight a great uproar will be raised in the city and there will be great noise-making and celebrating the passing of an old year, the coming of a new one.

Deep in the woods, nothing is coming, nothing is going, it is just continuing, as it has and as it will. Nothing is new, nothing is old. And it is still and quiet, and perfect.

At precisely midnight, a pair of raccoons will be ambling along the small creek that leads down to the river, looking for food that is becoming increasingly hard to find because the crawdads are in deep water and the frogs are buried in the mud, just as it has been for hundreds of years... maybe even thousands.

A great horned owl will leave his perch at the edge of the meadow and sweep down upon an unsuspecting deer mouse without a sound other than the rustling in the grass when he nails him. A great horned owl's wings still make no noise, just as it has been for who knows how long. Unfortunately for the mouse, he won't live to see the new year, but he doesn't even know that. He has lived almost 10 months, and that's a long time for a mouse. In the meadow, there are several hundred deer mice, and several hundred voles, a group of shrews not much bigger than the mice, and some other species of ground mammals which are in semi-hibernation.

In the big oak where the owl sat, there are a pair of fox squirrels asleep in a small cavity. They will miss the new year festivities too. In fact, when the temperature gets really cold, they may sleep for days. Squirrels don't hibernate for long periods, but like many creatures such as the raccoon, and the dozens of species of ground mammals, they will go into semi-hibernation when times get tough.

In the sycamores along the bluff over the creek, several wild gobblers spend New Year's Eve asleep, their forms plainly visible in the moonlight. Three are big old toms, but there are five jakes which have never experienced a new year's party before. They sleep through it, with locking tendons tightly securing their feet to the limbs of the sycamore, and it is much like it was with their ancestors, who weathered the passing of hundreds of new

years past in much the same way.

Beneath a cedar, buried in the grasses, a covey of bobwhites form a ring, eight of them in all. There were nearly twice as many in November.

The new year brings little to celebrate. With their bodies huddled together, they preserve heat, and when there are too few and the temperature plunges, there is less chance of survival. As the new year begins, they will join with birds of another covey and in number, find greater strength to resist the cold. Huddled beneath the cedar, they are unaware of the grey fox which passes as the new year approaches. His is an eternal quest for food, and if he only knew they were there, what a party he would have. But like the owl, he will settle for small mammals on this night of nights as a new year begins.

A half dozen mallards spring to flight as a bobcat streaks across the river gravel bar where they rest, and takes one of their member for a new year's meal. The young hen is a substantial meal for the bobcat. The rest of the flock circles in the bright moonlight and settles into another hole upstream.

The last protests of the quacking hen breaks the stillness, but the sounds of nature at midnight are subtle. A buck snorts from a cedar thicket above the creek. A dying rabbit shrieks from the field across the river, as a mink ferrets him from a brush pile. Smaller than the rabbit, the mink wraps his body around the cottontail's neck and hangs on, his teeth buried in the soft fur as the life and death struggle which marks the beginning of a new year is just as it has always been.

Here where the creek joins the river, where the woodland breaks into meadow, where thickets of briar and cedar stand as they have since men first came to change and scar the land...life goes on. There is no old year. There is no new year. It is only the passing of another night, the coming of another day.

And I know that for some it is necessary to group together and make much of the ticking of a clock, where alcohol flows and the noise grows to a deafening crescendo. But I'll walk that quiet wooded ridge above the creek at midnight, and listen for the distant yodel of a coyote. I'll survey the river bottoms in the moonlight and be thankful for the stability of unchanging nature...wild creatures living as they always have, evidence of God's unchanging laws which every man will eventually answer to.

There is perfection here...thank God we haven't ruined it all. We will, in time. These mushrooming numbers of human beings will destroy it all eventually. But not in the new year. For now, there is evidence of nature's strength to be found far from the masses who herd into New York's Times Square like cattle. Here on this little Ozark ridgetop, there is the security of life continuing as it always has. Nothing special here at midnight, no observance of anything different or new. And I will not celebrate the coming of a new year while I linger there. I will mourn the passing of the old one. It was a good year, one to give thanks for. And on a quiet wooded ridge overlooking the moonlit river, it will be a good place to ask that the coming year be a good one as well...a year wherein wild things and wild places continue to exist, where good is good and right is right, and men haven't yet come to make it otherwise.

OTHER BOOKS BY JIM SPENCER

TURKEY HUNTING DIGEST
334 pages, 47 chapters, more than 300 photos, with a foreword by Tom Kelly, author of Tenth Legion. Covers turkey hunting from A to Z in an easy-to-read, entertaining format. Also has a bonus 16-page color section with 60 additional photos. $25.

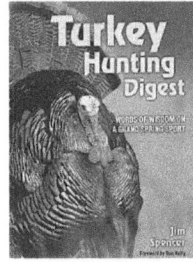

BAD BIRDS
224 pages, 43 chapters, 70 photos, with a foreword by Brian Lovett, longtime editor of Turkey & Turkey Hunting magazine and author of The Turkey Hunters. This book is a collection of the first 40 installments of Spencer's long-running Bad Birds column in Turkey & Turkey Hunting, with several other articles added – including a special contribution by Larry Dablemont. $16.

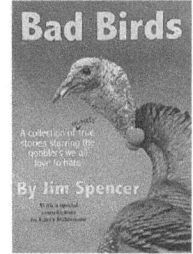

BAD BIRDS 2
300 pages, 41 chapters, 70 photos, with a foreword by Ron and Tes Jolly, authors of *Memories of Spring*. This one is a collection of the second set of Spencer's Bad Birds columns (33 of them,) plus eight additional chapters about turkeys and turkey hunting. $22.

GUIDE TO TRAPPING
200 pages, 19 chapters, 120 photos, with a foreword by Keith "Catfish" Sutton, author of *Hardcore Catfishing*. This book covers trapping from A to Z: basic trapping techniques for harvesting popular furbearer species like raccoon, muskrat, mink, otter, beaver, coyote, red and gray fox, bobcat and others; trap modification and preparation, fur handling and marketing; and much more. $22.

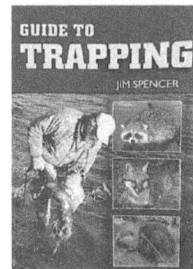

Special offer: Buy a Bad Birds 2 and get a huge discount on any or all three other books – $12 each. For For Bad Birds 2 alone, $22. For BB2 and one other title, $39. For BB2 and two other titles, $46. For BB2 and all three other titles, $58, a discount of more than 42%. There's a $5 shipping charge. There's a no-questions-asked, money-back guarantee if you're not satisfied. Send check or money order to Treble Hook Unlimited, P.O. Box 758, Calico Rock, AR 72519. Or buy through PayPal to modernmountainman@gmail. com.